About the Author

BARBARA LOUNSBERRY is an associate professor of English at the University of Northern Iowa and a member of the Iowa Humanities Board. She is currently co-editing with Gay Talese an anthology of literary nonfiction for Harper & Row, as well as editing her own college reader titled *The Writer in You: A Writing Process Reader/Rhetoric*. Her essays have appeared in the *Philological Quarterly, Georgia Review, Hemingway Review, Modern Drama, Black American Literature Forum,* and other publications.

The Art of Fact

Recent Titles In
Contributions to the Study of World Literature

THE ART OF FACT
Contemporary Artists of Nonfiction

Barbara Lounsberry

CONTRIBUTIONS TO THE STUDY OF WORLD
LITERATURE, NUMBER 35

GREENWOOD PRESS
NEW YORK · WESTPORT, CONNECTICUT · LONDON

Library of Congress Cataloging-in-Publication Data

Lounsberry, Barbara.
      The art of fact : contemporary artists of nonfiction / Barbara
Lounsberry.
      p. cm.—(Contributions to the study of world literature,
  ISSN 0738-9345 ; no. 35)
   Includes bibliographical references.
   ISBN 0-313-26893-2 (lib. bdg. : alk. paper)
    1. American prose literature—20th century—History and criticism.
  2. Reportage literature, American—History and criticism.
  3. Journalism—United States—History—20th century. 4. Nonfiction
novel. I. Title. II. Series.
  PS369.L68 1990
  818′.540809—dc20

British Library Cataloguing in Publication Data is available.

Library of Congress Catalog Card Number: 89-17222
ISBN: 0-313-26893-2
ISSN: 0738-9345

First published in 1990

Greenwood Press, Inc.
88 Post Road West, Westport, Connecticut 06881

Printed in the United States of America

The paper used in this book complies with the
Permanent Paper Standard issued by the National
Information Standards Organization (Z39.48-1984).

10 9 8 7 6 5 4 3 2 1

To nonfiction artists, past and present

Contents

Acknowledgments

No acknowledgment can adequately express my debt to Gay Talese for his generosity in allowing me personal interviews at various intervals from 1983 to 1989. Similarly, I am grateful to John McPhee for his kind and eloquent phone conversations and correcting correspondence, and to physicist Theodore Taylor for his willingness to talk with me by phone about his travels with John McPhee. I also wish to thank Norman Mailer for his prompt and precise letters.

This book was begun with the support of Dr. John Downey and a University of Northern Iowa Summer Research Fellowship. I also wish to express my great thanks to poet and novelist Nancy Price, who read and responded to the first draft of the manuscript; to editor and Mailer scholar J. Michael Lennon for his helpful comments on the Mailer chapter; to Greenwood editors Marilyn Brownstein and William Neenan; and to my mother, Jane Palen Severin, for careful reading of the final page proofs of the volume.

Introduction

The Realtors

The artistry of nonfiction is the great unexplored territory of contemporary criticism. This is ironic, for the second half of the twentieth century has been an age of nonfiction. American book clubs, which began in the 1920s offering primarily fiction, now emphasize nonfiction. Today's *New York Times Book Review* reviews nonfiction over fiction almost three to one. In truth, our age has stopped subscribing to the belief that the novel is the highest form of the literary imagination. It is beginning to think of fiction as only one of many artful "prose narratives in print," to use Lennard Davis's accurate phrase (44). Other compelling prose narratives are certain artful memoirs, autobiographies, biographies, histories, travelogues, essays, works of journalism, forms of nature and science writing, and ingenious combinations of these forms.

If we live in an age of nonfiction, then why is critical appreciation of this work so rare? This is explained, in part, by the inevitable lag of the critic behind the artist, but also by the lack of a satisfactory name for this work. How do we distinguish what I will call artful *literary nonfiction* from the often artless and droning expository prose that floods the category "nonfiction"?[1] The very term "nonfiction" discloses the former Romantic bias toward fiction: everything not fiction is nonfiction. Pity the nonfiction artists! Caught in this catchall category, their works are ignored. Scholars skilled at tracing artistic and rhetorical strategies in fiction, poetry, and drama seem to halt at the border of nonfiction; they have made few forays toward even a simple taxonomy of the form.[2] As a result, critical appreciation of such a highly esteemed writer as John McPhee exists primarily in the form of brief book reviews.[3] The same is true of Gay Talese, whose prodigious research and continuing efforts to explore the boundaries of "fact writing" have earned him the

wide respect of his peers. Even the controversial writings of bad boy
Tom Wolfe have generated only a handful of extended studies in the
nearly thirty years of his career.[4]

Perhaps Wolfe has recently turned to fiction to gain some critical
attention for his work. Of the five major artists of nonfiction treated in
this study, Norman Mailer and Joan Didion have received the greatest
critical scrutiny, but that is perhaps because Mailer and Didion are also
novelists, and critics have come to their nonfiction through their fiction.
Writers like McPhee and Talese, who are committed to nonfiction, as
well as other elegant artists of nonfiction such as Lillian Ross, Anne
Morrow Lindbergh, Lewis Thomas, Edward Hoagland, Tracy Kidder,
Annie Dillard, Maxine Hong Kingston, and many others, currently appear to be doomed to neglect.

What label might be applied to these writers' enterprises? Terms like
the French *reportage*, "journalit," or the "new" or "high" journalism seem
too narrow, given the reach of much work beyond reporting or journalism. Other names, like Dwight Macdonald's "parajournalism," are
merely pejorative. Phrases highlighting the "hybrid" nature of the form,
its application of narrative techniques often associated with fiction to
nonfictional subject matter, seem somewhat better. However, Truman
Capote's "nonfiction novel" or Norman Mailer's "true life novel," tip
the scales toward the fictive side of the equation. "Faction," Alex Hal-
ey's term, avoids this problem, but it has not caught on. Neither has
the even more attractive term "realtor" proffered by the late artful historian Barbara Tuchman. Citing historian George Macaulay Treve-
lyan's assertion that history *ideally* should be the presentation of the
facts about the past "in their full emotional and intellectual value to a
wide public by the difficult art of literature," Tuchman continues:

I see no reason why the word [artist] should always be confined to writers of
fiction and poetry while the rest of us are lumped under that despicable term
"Nonfiction." . . . I cannot very well call us "Realtors" because that has been
pre-empted—although as a matter of fact I would like to. "Real Estate," when
you come to think of it, is a very fine phrase and it is exactly the sphere that
writers of nonfiction deal in: the real estate of man, of human conduct. I wish
we could get it back from the dealers in land. Then the categories could be
poets, novelists, and realtors. (46)

Our current semantic quandary would amuse Daniel Defoe, Samuel
Richardson, and Henry Fielding. In the first half of the eighteenth century, they were struggling to name their own new narrative prose form—
a form we have no difficulty today calling the novel. In desperation
Fielding finally called *Tom Jones* a "comic epic-poem in prose"! Historical perspective in fact is what has been missing in many of the "new
journalism," fact/fiction debates of the 1960s, 1970s, and 1980s. In some

respects we are seeing the turn of the wheel back to the time, only 200 years ago, when serious writers chose nonfiction over fiction for expressing their views and crafting their art. The novel was considered frivolous.

Similarly, we seem to have forgotten that the great prose writers of the past have been by and large authors of literary nonfiction: Montaigne, Robert Burton, Sir Thomas Browne, Samuel Johnson, Thomas Macaulay, Ralph Waldo Emerson, Henry David Thoreau, John Ruskin. Annie Dillard, the artful twentieth-century essayist, has noted that "fine writing" in fictional prose has come to the fore only in the past 140 years with Flaubert and the Modernists—with Henry James, Marcel Proust, Virginia Woolf, William Faulkner, Samuel Beckett, Franz Kafka, and "the lavish Joyce of the novels" (104). Taking the long view, the novel's reign has been short indeed. Germaine Bree has even suggested that the term "novel" is being used rather consistently now in critical studies to apply only to the realistic fiction that dominated the nineteenth century (88).

I am not suggesting the death of the novel, or of fiction as a form for serious writing. I am saying that our current historical awareness of the origins of the novel and its complex relation to other prose narratives places us in an ideal position for studying the many strands of literary nonfiction now in abundance and meriting serious attention.[5] Although it may be uncomfortable, we can proceed to study these works without a term for this discourse. I am asserting, however, that there is an identifiable discourse—recognizable in its solid central particulars, though blurring (as all genres do) at the edges—that might be called literary or artistic nonfiction. Its four constitutive features are these:

   *1. Documentable subject matter chosen from the real world as
   opposed to "invented" from the writer's mind.*

Such subject matter includes natural phenomena, such as John McPhee's *Oranges* or *The Pine Barrens*. It includes human phenomena, portraits of: individual human beings such as McPhee's "A Room Full of Hovings"; human institutions, such as Gay Talese's *New York Times* volume *The Kingdom and the Power*; or cultural sub-groups, such as Tom Wolfe's *Right Stuff* pilots. It embraces human places, such as Joan Didion's *Salvador*, or human events, such as Norman Mailer's *The Armies of the Night*. In short, anything in the natural world is game for the nonfiction artist's attention.

   2. Exhaustive research.

Thorough research not only enables writers to uncover "new" and "novel" perspectives on their subjects, it also permits them to establish the credibility of their narratives through verifiable references in their texts. Gay Talese's volumes are weighty in names and miniature histo-ries not only because he wishes to preserve the unnoticed in history, but also to make his narratives so factually solid and verifiable that we do not doubt his broader and more subjective conclusions about his subjects. This is precisely the importance of Tom Wolfe's "status de-tail," his brilliant catalogs of dress and style—from his Flak Catcher's $4.99 brown Hush Puppies to his aviators' cheap Robert Hall suits and expensive watches. Because Wolfe assumes the satirist's liberty with comic exaggeration, to increase his credibility he works hard to ground his work in as many concrete, verifiable particulars as he can.

The Realtor's research and its presentation in a verifiable manner in the text thus are crucial to establishing reader confidence (so far as is possible today) in the "truth" of the account. Many artists of nonfiction go a step farther and create frames for their works in which they de-scribe the writer-reader contract—just as the early novelists did. Such frames vary from Truman Capote's subtitle for *In Cold Blood*, "A True Account Of A Multiple Murder And Its Consequences," to Norman Mailer's Afterword to *The Executioner's Song* in which he explains and justifies his artistic decisions.[6] Frames today may even piquantly insist, as does Annie Dillard in her Author's Note to *Teaching A Stone To Talk*, that the volume is not just another miscellany of an author's occasional pieces, but her "real work."

I would argue that when the factual accuracy of a work is questioned, or when authorial promises are violated, a work of literary nonfiction is either discredited or transferred out of the category. Tom Wolfe's vision of *The New Yorker* magazine, and particularly of its former editor, William Shawn, in his controversial articles "Tiny Mummies" and "Lost in the Whichy Thicket," was seriously undercut in many readers' eyes by the plethora of large and small factual errors in the work that were immediately exposed.[7] The large and small errors and inventions in Capote's *In Cold Blood* constitute a violation of contract for many read-ers; any claims to greatness that book now tenders must be predicated on the "truths" of fiction rather than fact.[8] In short, verifiability is fun-damental to successful literary nonfiction. The invented quotation is anathema to serious artists of nonfiction, most of whom scorn compos-ite characters as well, believing they court the twin dangers of inaccu-racy and oversimplification.

3. The Scene.

Tom Wolfe was right to list the scene as the first characteristic of his "New Journalism." Along with its nonfiction subject matter, the scene is the trait by which literary nonfiction is most readily recognized. In-stead of merely "reporting" or "discussing" an object or event, the artist of nonfiction recasts it in narrative form. The remarkable effect of such transformation is that the moment is reprised; it lives again, yet with the subtle lights and shadings of the author's vision. The facts gain life, depth, and subtle reverberation. Often the scene (or scenes) will be only part of the artful form a work of literary nonfiction may take. Nevertheless, the scene is frequently a sign that the form of the work is consciously artful.

Tom Wolfe lists dialogue as the second trait of his "New Journalism"; however, dialogue is not as essential to the scene for other artists of nonfiction as it is for Wolfe, with his interest in presenting conflicting points of view. Little direct quotation, for example, can be found in John Hersey's artful *Hiroshima*. This is probably because the scrupulous Hersey did not trust words recollected six months after the atomic explosion—without a second or third confirmation. Gay Talese scorns the direct quotation for an entirely different reason. Talese considers most spoken language to represent "first draft" thinking; therefore, he believes he can usually present his subjects' views in both a more aesthetically pleasing and comprehensive manner than they can.[9] John McPhee also infrequently resorts to quotation and dialogue, usually for humorous revelation of character, while Joan Didion uses only those quotations that underscore her vision of her subjects. In fact, she famously allows her subjects to damn themselves with their own words. Even the multiple voices in Wolfe have been challenged by Wilfrid Sheed—for sounding suspiciously like the same Wolfe voice (2). Dialogue, then, can come and go, but the narrated scene is the constant. It is, furthermore, what limits this discourse I am calling literary or artistic nonfiction to a small portion of the huge "nonfiction" category.

4. Fine Writing: A Literary Prose Style.

Verifiable subject matter and exhaustive research guarantee the nonfiction side of literary nonfiction; the narrative form and structure disclose the writer's artistry; and finally, its polished language reveals that the goal all along has been literature. Annie Dillard calls it "fine writing," while Gay Talese calls it "writing with style." Such writing may splurge on assonance and alliteration (as does Talese's), or on parallel structures and repetitions (as does Didion's). Fine writers may launch metaphors as probes (like Norman Mailer), dazzle us with verbal and typographical pyrotechnics (like Tom Wolfe), or employ plain prose for clarity and for purity of form matched to subject (like John McPhee). Call it what you will, care for language can be used as a strainer to separate *literary* nonfiction from the glut of nonfiction written in pedestrian prose. If the subject of a nonfiction work is compelling, its research exhaustive and verifiably elaborated, and its form artful and narrative, it may still fail the standards of literary nonfiction if its language is dull or diffuse.

If, then, these four features delimit an important art form of our time, a discourse grounded in fact but artful in execution that might be called *literary nonfiction*, what is needed is serious critical attention of all kinds to this work: formal criticism (both Russian Formalist and New Critical), historical, biographical, cultural, structuralist and deconstructionist, reader-response, and feminist. Because so little has been attempted, the chapters that follow, largely formalist in cast, seek to offer strong readings of the works of Talese, Wolfe, McPhee, Didion, and Mailer—perhaps the five most prominent contemporary artists of nonfiction. Besides their prominence, another criterion for their selection is that each has produced a considerable body of literary nonfiction. Critics to date, however, have tended to focus on only one or two of each writer's works, to illustrate particular critical points. I have tried instead to be comprehensive. My goal has been to describe themes and rhetorical strategies which unfold across the writer's whole body of nonfiction to date, and even to project likely future directions for their work, given current artistic trajectories. I have tried to describe the specific artistry of each writer and to demonstrate that the artistry of literary nonfiction can be equal to that of fiction, poetry, and drama. Ultimately I have tried to make my criticism "demonstrably right" in F. W. Bateson's terms—that is, "accurate, just, helpful, relevant, comprehensive" (122).

If we, with Bateson, regard literature as "life frozen into immobility at its points of highest consciousness and integration" (131), then it is also important to explore contemporary literary nonfiction for its cultural content and criticism. William Zinsser, the former editor of the Book of the Month Club, has called nonfiction "the new American literature" (53). Besides demonstrating the artistry of such work, I have tried to indicate the importance of this genre in addressing many of the persistent themes of the American imagination. These include conflicts between the individual and society, as well as the continued efficacy of the "American Dream." As the postmodern fiction writers of the 1960s and 1970s pursued the intellectual and aesthetic challenges of metafiction and surfiction, it has seemed, indeed, that it has been artists of nonfiction who have been most attentive to the American tradition.

Their response has been both preservative and expansionary. Gay Talese is obsessed with generational legacies. Whether writing of *The New York Times*, the Mafia, or sexual pioneers, he expands the specific dilemma of how to honor one's father in a changing age to the larger question of how to honor the national spirit, the American Dream of our *forefathers*, in a similarly changing and diminished era. The past is always a character in Talese's works, and the individual psychodramas of his subjects become the national psychodramas of us all.

My chapter on Tom Wolfe suggests that this rebel dandy has been, all along, an American Jeremiah, cloaking his Calvinism and evangelicalism in the sophisticated guise of a Menippean satirist. Wolfe finds much to criticize in contemporary American society, yet far from being either "pop" or "hip," he is carrying on the tradition of Jonathan Edwards and his "new light" revivalism.

In contrast, John McPhee preserves and extends the ideals of the nineteenth-century transcendentalists. He is a nature writer in the Thoreauvian mold, one who celebrates self-reliance and rugged individualism in the twentieth century. McPhee is both a link to nineteenth century America and a charming temperer of Emerson's and Thoreau's relentless idealism.

Far from transcendental, Joan Didion has a fiercely conservative vision, one that is correctively constricting rather than expanding or expansive. Didion's gaze is always backward to the fall. She insists on human sin and punctures all illusion of individual or national melioration.

Norman Mailer takes the opposite stance. In his literary nonfiction through *The Fight* (1975) he seeks to demonstrate that individual growth and change can be a model for social growth. His artful metaphors not only expand our sense of his subjects, but also are designed to animate us, to literally stimulate us to social action. Mailer is acutely aware of the American literary tradition and relies on such great predecessors as Walt Whitman, Henry Miller, and Ernest Hemingway to provide inspiriting visions and challenging literary models for him to refashion. Through his literary acts Mailer regenerates not only himself, but his predecessors as well; he preserves while he expands the American literary tradition.

This preservative/expansionary tension in contemporary literary nonfiction is true to the essential doubleness Davis has demonstrated in the "news/novels discourse" of the seventeenth and eighteenth centuries, from which the English novel emerged. Davis asserts that the novel came into being as a result of both political and technological pressures during those centuries. He argues that England's severe libel laws forced writers to all sorts of literary sleights-of-hand, and finally to fiction, in order to write about their times. Simultaneously the printing press made their words readily available to the lower classes, encouraged political and social action, and enforced the idea of immortality through print.

Each of the five writers in this study exemplifies a strand of nonfiction narrative that both predated and contributed to the news/novels discourse: history (Talese), the sermon (Wolfe), travel writing (McPhee), autobiography (Didion), and epic narrative (Mailer). We might query what cultural forces in the twentieth century have returned narrative to the genetic pool and have fostered a bubbling forth of new artful versions of the early nonfictional narrative strands. The impact of science on contemporary culture—as my metaphor of the genetic pool suggests—has increased public interest in every aspect of the natural world. At the same time, growing recognition of the subjectivity of all perspective, that all visions are in a sense "fictions," has undercut fiction's claim to sole proprietorship of the territory of the imagination. Fiction no longer is perceived as special.

In addition, technological advances have furthered the possibilities of global literacy begun by the printing press, thereby creating an even larger audience for literature of all kinds than in the eighteenth century. This hospitable climate has been enhanced in the United States by liberal censorship rulings in the 1960s which have permitted greater freedom of expression (as opposed to the restrictive pressures of the eighteenth-century English libel statutes). All these factors may be encouraging both a wider exploration of artistic form and subject matter and a sense that ideas can be offered through literary nonfiction rather than through the once-removed realm of fiction. In a sense, the political need for fiction is not as strongly felt in England and the United States today as it was at the time of the emergence of fiction, although this is not true in Central and South America, South Africa, and the European Soviet satellites, where the novel today is flourishing.

Through literary nonfiction, writers may believe they are finally able to have the best of both worlds. They can gain the reader credence novelists have forever sought by insisting that their fictions were true, and, through the arts of literature, they can make their visions of the world memorable, influential, even immortal. We may be witnessing, in addition, a drawing apart of the strands of narrative in order for a new synthesis to be formed.

The Art of Fact

1

Gay Talese's Fathers and Sons

Gay Talese files his research in shoe boxes. He outlines his books on shirt cardboard. He fastens minuscule swatchlike character cards with tailor's hat pins to a styrofoam board never far from his typewriter. As he shapes his nonfiction, he seeks to join his scenes into a seamless whole.

Later, when his finished pages are typed and pinned across his study wall, he takes out binoculars and reads his work from across the room—to achieve "distance."

The above may be taken as a true portrait of a nonfiction artist. Research is prodigious and objectivity conscientiously sought, but the swatches, the hat pins, the shirt cardboard reveal both the artistry and the inescapable subjectivity of the son of a master tailor, one whose carefully crafted garments are books.

Talese worked as a reporter for *The New York Times* from 1953 to 1965 before quitting to write three consecutive best-sellers. He was never, however, a traditional journalist. Even as a college sports columnist at the University of Alabama, from 1950 to 1953, he was experimenting with three of the four techniques Tom Wolfe would later identify as characteristic of the 1960s New Journalism: the scene, dialogue, and unusual points of view. Talese admired the stylish writing of Red Smith and *Times*man Gilbert Millstein, but his real literary heroes were fiction writers like John O'Hara, Irwin Shaw, and Ernest Hemingway who were writing about the lives of ordinary Americans. Talese wanted to do what O'Hara and company were doing, but only in nonfiction rather than in fiction; he thought of his feature writing as "stories with real names."

Talese's distinctive gifts as a nonfiction artist are for exhaustive research, for the unnoticed but intimate (often behind-the-scenes) angle, and for formality of style suited to the respect he feels for his ordinary subjects. Thorough research, he maintains, is what gives the nonfiction writer the freedom to be an artist. In order to describe a climactic meeting at *The New York Times* for his volume *The Kingdom and the Power*, Talese interviewed individually all ten persons at the meeting. Not only could he double-check facts and impressions by this method, and thereby increase the accuracy of his report, but ultimately he had the choice of narrating this dramatic episode from any one of the ten editors' perspectives. Had he been less thorough, he would have limited his artistic choices, as well as missed vivid details. Talese's skills as a researcher include a genuine earnestness in questioning, tenacity in returning to a specific moment again and again with his subjects, and patience for what he calls "the art of hanging out."[1] Together these traits are formidable and have enabled Talese to write of the private lives of the Mafia and of the sexual lives of Americans in ways many writers have thought impossible.

Talese's research techniques have grown from his special artistic sensibility. He has never been interested in what is called "the big story"; instead, he gravitates to the unnoticed story, the story that is there but ignored by everyone because they are following the big story. While all the other New York sports writers were writing about the fight at Madison Square Garden, Talese was watching and writing about the man who rang the bell between rounds. When *The Times* sent him to the United Nations, he wrote about the barber who cut the delegates' hair. When his editors sent him to Albany to cover New York politics, Talese wrote about the gold spittoons in the general assembly. All these subjects were present yet unremarked upon and thought unremarkable until Talese turned his research and vision and respectful language upon them. At times his detailed, dignifying language seems almost a prose poem, such as the opening to his paean to the unnoticed life of New York City, *New York: A Serendipiter's Journey*:

New York is a city of things unnoticed. It is a city with cats sleeping under parked cars, two stone armadillos crawling up St. Patrick's Cathedral, and thousands of ants creeping on top of the Empire State Building. The ants probably were carried up there by wind or birds, but nobody is sure; nobody in New York knows any more about the ants than they do about the panhandler who takes taxis to the Bowery; or the dapper man who picks trash out of Sixth Avenue trash cans; or the medium in the West Seventies who claims, "I am clairvoyant, clairaudient and clairsensuous." (FO 277)

Talese's penchant for writing about the ordinary rather than the extraordinary event, and the unnoticed rather than the noticed derives from his early life as the unnoticed son of an immigrant Italian tailor. Talese identifies strongly with the unnoticed, and writes of obscure *Times*men and Mafia wives and children from an urgent sense that they not be overlooked by society—or history. Of the artists of nonfiction in this study, he comes closest to being a *histor*. By making his histories read like novels, he makes them more accessible and memorable than traditional histories, and thus helps to ensure that his unnoticed figures will not be lost in time.

Like writers of fiction, Talese follows his artistic sensibility where it takes him. As a result, repeated themes can be found across his work despite the varied nature of his subject matter, just as a novelist explores repeated themes in varied plots. One of the strongest themes in Talese's work is his focus on generational legacies. Whether writing of bridge builders, celebrities, the Mafia, sexual pioneers, or *The New York Times*, Talese tends to be drawn obsessively toward the parent-child relation. In his works he expands the specific dilemma of how to honor one's father in a changing age to the larger question of how to honor the national spirit, the American dream of our *forefathers*, in a similarly changing and diminished era. Cultural critic Raymond Williams has observed that "a father is more than a person, he's in fact a society, the thing you grow up into" (Green 218). Thus the individual psychodramas of Talese's subjects become the national psychodramas of us all.

EARLY WRITING AND *THE BRIDGE*

During his years as a writer for *The Times*, Talese was also free-lancing articles to the *Saturday Evening Post*, to *Reader's Digest*, and, most important, to Harold Hayes's *Esquire* magazine. "The Soft Psyche of Joshua Logan," a 1963 *Esquire* article, offers the most straightforward illustration of the theme that will compel Talese's imagination throughout his career. The "news peg," or journalistic excuse, for this article was the 1963 opening of Joshua Logan's new play, *Tiger Tiger Burning Bright*, and Logan's attempt to make a Broadway comeback after such past glories as *Mr. Roberts* and *South Pacific*. Talese is quick to note the similarity of the play's plot to Logan's own parental conflict: *Tiger Tiger Burning Bright* is about "a mother who dominates her children in a dream world she has created in Louisiana—a play that gradually, as rehearsals progressed, churned up more and more memories for Logan, haunting memories of his days in Mansfield, Louisiana" (FO 62).

In his author's note to *Fame and Obscurity* Talese writes that one of his ambitions is to remain with his subjects long enough "to see their lives change in some way." Most of his works gradually mount to some dramatic crisis that reveals the son's success or failure in living up to his father's (or mother's) spiritual tradition or expectations. In "The

Soft Psyche" Logan shares the personal psychodrama behind his current theatrical effort:

No, he is by no means modest, he said, even though his mother is a bit disappointed in him, and once, after he had reminded her that he was a Pulitzer Prize winner (for *South Pacific*) she reminded him that *that* was for a collaboration—letting him know she knew the difference between a man who could win such a prize, and a man who could ride the horse *alone*. . . .

"But," he continued, now more slowly, thinking more deeply, "I think if I were free of whatever it is—if I were free-r—I think I could write . . . and write more than Marcel Proust . . . couldn't *stop* writing. But it is as though it were all damned up to here," he said, gripping his throat with his left hand, "and I have a theory—*just* a theory—that if I wrote, it would please my mother *too much*. It would be what she wanted. And maybe . . . maybe *then* I'd become like my father. And I would die." (FO 73)

Here boldly stated is Talese's archetypal situation: a son failing to live up to parental ideals, failing to become like the father, and the personal agony and introspection which that failure entails. Talese ends this article with the fate of Logan's venture. *Tiger Tiger Burning Bright* opens to praise, but Logan, ill, is unable to attend opening night:

one television announcer summed them up [the reviews] as "respectful." This is all Logan had hoped for. Something respectful. He did not need the big, box-office smash; he'd had plenty of those. And what he *did* want, he suspected he might never get. . . . And after thirty-three performances, the play closed. (FO 76)

The "play" closes as well on many of the sons in *The Bridge*, Talese's fascinating 1964 account of the building of the Verrazano-Narrows Bridge from Brooklyn to Staten Island. Here, in a more extended work, Talese is able to move beyond the simple individual parental obsession of a famous figure like Joshua Logan to suggest the broader, indeed national, implications of the theme. Bridge builders *literally* "span" the nation and regard themselves, Talese tells us, as "the last of America's unhenpecked heroes" (TB 3). Across the ten chapters that make up this work Talese stresses family relationships again and again, particularly emphasizing the difficulties sons experience trying to escape the dangerous family tradition of bridge building:

The boomer's child might live in forty states and attend a dozen high schools before he graduates, *if* he graduates, and though the father swears he wants no boomer for a son, he usually gets one. He gets one, possibly, because he really wanted one, and maybe that is why boomers brag so much at home on weekends, creating a wondrous world with whiskey words, a world no son can resist because this world seems to have everything: adventure, big cars, big money—sometimes $350 to $450 a week—and gambling on rainy days when the bridge is slippery, and booming around the country with Indians who are sure-footed as spiders, with Newfoundlanders as shifty as the sea they come from, with roaming Rebel riveters escaping the poverty of their small Southern towns, all of them building something big and permanent, something that can be revisited years later and pointed to and said of: "See that bridge over there, son—well, one day, when I was younger, I drove twelve hundred rivets into that goddamned thing."

They tell their sons the good parts, forgetting the bad. . . . (TB 2–3)

Chapter 6 of *The Bridge* is titled "Death on the Bridge," and here Gerard McKee, a handsome, popular youth from a "boomer" family, falls to his death from the Verrazano span. Gerard has two brothers who are also boomers, and his father—"a man whom Gerard strongly resembled—had been hit by a collapsing crane a few years before, had had his leg permanently twisted, had a steel plate inserted in his head, and was disabled for life" (TB 84). Of all the mourners at Gerard's funeral this father suffers most: " 'After what I've been through,' he said, shaking his head, tears in his eyes, 'I should know enough to keep my kids off the bridge' " (TB 92).

But McKee doesn't, and *The Bridge* ends with another son's death on the next bridge in Portugal. Talese's title explicitly links his vision of the nation with Hart Crane's in his famous poem of the same name. Both works proffer the bridge as a symbol of hope for a permanent spanning to some national ideal, and yet both show the negations that in the present somehow keep us from achieving the affirmations of Whitman's American prophecy. Failure, death, or, at best, a short-lived success like Joshua Logan's are the fates of the sons of bridge builders. A further irony of the title is that a bridge is created to take one someplace, yet, as Talese suggests through the boomer song he quotes for the final line of his volume, the bridge builders are "*linking everything but their lives.*"

That Talese was never a typical newspaper reporter is shown in a remarkable series of thirty-eight articles on boxer Floyd Patterson that he wrote from 1957 to 1966. It is rare for a newspaper or magazine writer to write more than one feature on a given celebrity; three or four stories over a span of years might seem excessive to most journalists. That Talese returned again and again to Patterson, indeed thirty-eight times, suggests not only his interest in reporting change (in individuals and institutions) over time, but also his (perhaps unconscious) attraction to a father-son conflict.

The Floyd Patterson story, in Talese's telling, has as many resonances of the failed American Dream as *The Bridge*, but it is, in some ways, more complex. It is the story of not one son, but two; the story of a bad son and a good. Furthermore, for the first time the father is not the literal (biological) father, but a surrogate father, Patterson's Italian manager, Cus D'Amato. As the son of a strong Italian father himself, Talese may have found Patterson's painfully intricate relationship with D'Amato ringing a very personal bell.

Talese begins to limn this father-son story in his seventh Patterson article, a feature following Patterson's knockout in 1959 by the Swedish fighter Ingemar Johansson.[2] Talese asks Patterson if D'Amato has "mismanaged" him, and Patterson replies: "No. Cus is the greatest, most honest person I know. He's like a father to me." Patterson reminds the reporters that D'Amato had no starving fighters and that none of his fighters went broke like Joe Louis. "Cus trained us to save," he says, implying that D'Amato's influence extended well beyond the boxing ring. We also learn that this loyal twenty-four-year-old shares a phobia with D'Amato: a fear of flying.

Four stories, thirteen months, and a victorious rematch later, Talese reports a change in Patterson's filial posture:

The angry words yesterday were from the "new" Patterson. He no longer is the shy, quiet man who looked to D'Amato for verbal guidance. . . .
"I'm doing the talking. My eyes were opened after my defeat by Johansson. . . . I decided if I ever won the title back, I'd make the decisions. I'd see that it doesn't happen again."[3]

This article ends with the news that Patterson has decided to fly to Sweden for a five-week European boxing exhibition, and that he will be met there by D'Amato, who had departed earlier—by ship.

Talese's articles in 1961 and 1962 reveal signs of Patterson's continued growth in self-reliance, as well as growing criticism by boxing promoters and writers of D'Amato's overprotection of the heavyweight champion. This tension comes to a dramatic climax in Patterson's decision to fight Sonny Liston in September 1962—against the wishes of D'Amato. The week of this widely publicized fight *The New York Times Magazine* printed a Talese article that defined with amazing prescience the dimensions of the contest:

For the first time in the fighter's relationship with D'Amato, he has publicly defied the will of the Father Image in the choice of an opponent.
D'Amato will not say exactly why he opposed the Liston fight. He likes to give the impression that he did so because of Liston's police record and because the challenger's Philadelphia backers are allegedly not Main Line. But maybe, in his heart, D'Amato fears something he will never openly admit. And that is,

for the first time in his career as a manager, he has gone ahead and helped make the arrangements for a battle that he thinks his own fighter will lose.[4]

Patterson does lose this battle, and it is a loss of more than personal dimension, for this fight is treated in the press (and in four Talese articles) as an American melodrama with Patterson representing "good" and Liston, "evil." Two days before the fight Talese writes: "being nurtured on the American ethic that good must prevail—that Wheaties-eaters must win—many seem to feel that if Patterson loses, it somehow will be a slam at the American ideal, a defeat for Our Way of Life."[5] Patterson himself seems to have sensed the symbolic role he filled, for in describing his pre-fight emotions for an *Esquire* article Talese would title "The Loser," Patterson explained: "You have no idea how it is in the first round. You're out there with all those people around you, and those cameras, and the whole world looking in, and all that movement, that excitement, and *The Star-Spangled Banner*, and the whole nation hoping you'll win, including the President" (FO 43).

Despite this national support, the son loses. He fails to live up to national expectations. His defeat, however, causes a poignant reconciliation scene with D'Amato—which does not go unnoticed by Talese:

There had been a touching scene between D'Amato and Patterson last night in the ring following the knockout. Patterson lay his head on D'Amato's shoulder and the 54-year-old manager put his arm around the fighter.

"It was like the old days," D'Amato said afterward. He was referring to the days when the fighter was almost totally reliant on D'Amato's wisdom. . . .

In defeat, there seemed to be a warmth and compatibility between them that had been lacking in victory.[6]

But this reunion is only crisis-bred, for immediately after the fight Patterson begins to take flying lessons, and the abridgment of D'Amato's paternal influence continues, from that of trainer and manager to merely manager, to final exit of D'Amato in 1964 from any role in Patterson's career. "The Loser," Talese's lengthiest treatment of this American father-son story, hints at many ironies. The father, D'Amato, appears to have been right. The defiant son was, perhaps, wrong. Yet, in Talese's telling, the son's defiance (and perhaps his failure) has been necessary, even admirable. And Talese's title is deliberately ironic. In his growth into a sensitive human being, a man who has conquered his fears and realized that fighting "isn't a nice thing" (FO 45), Floyd Patterson is a winner in life, though a loser in the ring.

I mentioned a second son. This son was Jose Torres, and during the years Talese was returning thirty-eight times to Floyd Patterson, he wrote five articles on Torres. In the first, written in October 1958, Talese included this revealing exchange presented in a scene and dialogue unusual for newspaper sports writing:

"Cus, he is like a second father to me," said the young prizefighter yesterday in a small room on Eighth Avenue.
    D'Amato, a square-shouldered man in a dark blue suit, smiled, and asked, "Have you ever disapproved of anything I've done for you?"
    "No," said the fighter.
    "Haven't I always welcomed suggestions from you?"
    "Yes," said the fighter.[7]

Surely it is revealing that Talese is more strongly drawn to the defiant son, the failed son, the bad son than to the good.
    The denouement to this father-son drama comes in Talese's thirty-sixth Patterson story, a feature filed in April 1965, shortly before Talese's resignation from *The Times*. In it Talese describes Patterson, in disguise and unrecognized, at a Torres victory at Madison Square Garden:

[Patterson] had come to watch Jose Torres try to take the light-heavyweight title away from Willie Pastrano. Once, Patterson and Torres were very close. They used to train together, and visit each other's homes. Both were managed by Cus D'Amato, a dominating but dedicated father figure who tutored them both in the peek-a-boo boxing style, who soothed their psyches, who dreamed of the day when both would be champions.
    In recent years, however, the Patterson-Torres relationship became at times cool and complex, with hurt feelings on both sides. As Patterson became more his own man, listened less to D'Amato, he was more or less replaced in D'Amato's affections by Torres. When Patterson, over D'Amato's objections, took on Sonny Liston and lost the heavyweight title, D'Amato slowly ceased to be his manager.
    Yesterday Torres, the new light-heavyweight champion, flushed in triumph and posing for photographers, announced that he would now like to take on heavyweights. Among those he challenged was Patterson—not realizing that in the Garden on Tuesday night, Patterson was watching every move he made in the ring.
    Why was Patterson in disguise? One person who knows him quite well speculated that Patterson did not want to see D'Amato. There were never any harsh words between the two men, but there is a deep and complex hurt: the older son rebelling against the father; the father incapable of understanding the son's need for complete independence.[8]

THE KINGDOM AND THE POWER

An even more complex American father-son story is that told in *The Kingdom and the Power*, Talese's suggestively titled "human history" of *The New York Times* published in 1969. This work represents the best and most complex unfolding of Talese's artistic vision; furthermore, many readers have not yet appreciated the searing indictment of *The Times* contained in this artfully woven document. Those who read *The Kingdom and the Power* carefully will find more than just the "human history of an institution in transition" that Talese claims; they will find a powerful arraignment of that institution, many of its top executives, and the U.S. Establishment as well.

Talese creates this arraignment through subtle equating and interweaving of three father figures. He begins by defining the central subject of his book as the transmission of *The Times* tradition from Adolph Ochs to each generation of his successors. This *Times* tradition is also depicted (through Talese's religious rhetoric) as a veritable *patriarchal religion* to Ochs and his fellow *Times*men. Finally, Talese equates *The Times*'s tradition/religion with the secular vision of the U.S. Establishment. To the extent that Talese also continuously undercuts this Establishment, particularly for its indifference to the lower classes, his book indicts *The Times* as an example of the American Dream gone wrong, of American idealism gone elitist.

Talese begins by describing Adolph Ochs's intention of founding a grand and lasting newspaper tradition in *The New York Times*:

Ochs's desire [was] to have *The Times* run as he wished not only until his death, but long after it. . . . in his final years, Ochs became almost obsessed by his last will and testament, consulting endlessly with his lawyer lest there be confusion about his ultimate dream: *The New York Times* must, upon his death, be controlled only by his immediate family, and in turn by their families, and it would be the responsibility of them all to govern during their lifetime with the same dedication that he had during his. (K&P 12)

As the book unfolds, Talese depicts this patriarchal obsession as a ghost haunting the *Times* building.

Adhering to tradition becomes, through Talese's rhetoric, a matter of being true to the "father spirit," of keeping the "faith," and this religious diction elevates *The Times*'s history to one of wider social implication. Talese presents Adolph Ochs as a quintessential Horatio Alger figure: "He truly believed that honesty was the best policy, and he honored his father and mother and was never blasphemous, and he was convinced that hard work would reap rewards" (K&P 85). With this American idealism Ochs is able to resist business "temptations" and run *The Times* "not merely for profit but somewhat along the business lines of a great church, gilding the wealth with virtue," committing his family "to an orthodoxy stronger than their religion—and establishing Adolph Ochs as their benefactor, a little father-figure even to his own father" (K&P 13, 81).

Indeed, Talese presents *The Time*'s third-floor newsroom as a vast humming rectory. The reporters seat themselves behind rows of desks "like parishioners at church" (212), the foreign deskmen are "supplicants at the altar of the wire god" (106), and the copyreaders are "Ochsian disciples" upholding "traditional standards" (296). And if all "remained faithful to the principles of Ochs, a sense of responsibility and caution, the old morality, they need not worry" (6); "Ochs, after death, could live long in the liturgy" (13).

Such was the hope, the dream. Such indeed, Talese argues, is the reality. Adolph Ochs was the father of "*Times*ism," a secular religion, and Talese's institutional history becomes a story of an American patriarch, his theocracy, and the "shrinekeepers" selected to carry on his tradition. Yet, through Talese's skillful rhetoric, the story also becomes the story of the United States's patriarchy, its theocracy, and the struggle of its citizens who toil, like the *Times*men, under the burden of tending the national shrine. For if Ochs is our Horatio Alger patriarch, his paper, Talese tells us, becomes "the bible of the American establishment" (60), and here begins the final turn of the screw, the linking of the "religion" of *The New York Times* with that of the U.S. power Establishment.

From its inception, when Adolph Ochs solicits a letter of recommendation from President Grover Cleveland, *The Times* is intimately involved with the political Establishment. In 1908, when a *Times* reporter interviews Kaiser Wilhelm II and quotes him as predicting that Germany would someday go to war against Britain, Adolph Ochs, "after consulting with President Theodore Roosevelt," decides not to publish the interview. "It would undoubtedly inflame American opinion," Talese writes, "and Ochs and Roosevelt both agreed that the impulsive Kaiser did not really mean all that he had said in the interview" (K&P 168).

After Ochs's death in 1935 the relationship with presidents continues. Talese describes the cooperation among *Times* Washington Bureau Chief Arthur Krock, Joseph Kennedy, and Henry Luce in publishing and promoting John F. Kennedy's book *Why England Slept*. Lyndon Johnson, three months after becoming president, drops in for lunch at *The Times* building, and in Talese's account this luncheon becomes a symbolic tableau of the symbiotic relationship between *The Times* and the government. Johnson sits at the table cozily between the two generations of Ochs's successors, "Arthur Hays Sulzberger and Arthur Ochs Sulzberger, father and son" (123), and eats from gold-rimmed dishes and silverware embossed with *The New York Times* emblem, the American eagle. In the final scene of the volume, at Arthur Hays Sulzberger's funeral in 1968, President-Elect Richard Nixon is now among the statesmen and business leaders at the service, and Talese notes that "it was obvious that the next President of the United States did not wish to continue his dispute with *The Times*, which had, after Nixon's election, immediately begun to build its bridges back to the White House" (K&P 525).

Throughout his volume, then, Talese describes in mounting detail the connection between *The Times* tradition and that of the U.S. Establishment. It is because of this long tradition as part of the Establishment's "little club" that *Times* executives are particularly horrified at the accusations made against the paper during the congressional anti-American hearings in 1955 and 1956. What was *The New York Times* if not the paper of U.S. patriotism? But these accusations are symptomatic of the crisis in "faith" that emerges in the nation during the 1950s and 1960s, and that is reflected in *The Times*. The printers' strike in 1962 reveals that some *Times*men "now looked to the labor leaders for guidance, not to the spirit of Ochs" (K&P 223), and the founder's daughter, Iphigene Sulzberger, wonders if *The Times* had "lost some of its sense of mission" (K&P 517).

Indeed, from his first chapter Talese presages his ultimate conflict (between New York and Washington and between different styles of *Times* leadership) through the figures of managing editor Clifton Daniel and former Washington Bureau Chief James Reston. *The Kingdom and the Power* begins with Daniel and ends with Reston. In between, the two men—of similar backgrounds but antithetical styles—engage in a struggle for control of *The Times*'s future, and in the end Adolph Ochs's grandson must decide between them. His crisis and his decision will reveal his faithfulness to his patriarchal heritage and the future direction of the "*Times*ian" liturgy.

The Daniel/Reston conflict is posed, however, in a most sophisticated manner. Although Talese sees in Daniel and Reston distinctly different aspects of the *Times*'s corporate personality and uses them in this symbolic way, in no sense does he present the two in any simple or diametric opposition. They are both, after all, faithful sons of *The Times*. My feeling is that Talese chooses to begin his story with Clifton Daniel because Daniel epitomized to him the "public image" of *The Times*—the image that Talese wishes to debunk. As he writes near the end of the volume: "People are very curious about *The Times*, and many of them get from hearing and seeing Daniel a confirmation of their own ideas about the paper, its calm posture and pride in appearance, the respect for its tradition and the certainty of its virtue. They get from Daniel the image the institution has of itself, which is not necessarily all the reality beneath the surface" (K&P 410–11).

Clifton Daniel thus represents *The Times* as a whole—its public facade and its private struggle with tradition—as he conducts his daily four o'clock conference with the eyes of Turner Catledge, his predecessor, staring at this back (and Adolph Ochs's eyes presumably behind his).

Yet Daniel also represents a new style for *The Times* with his interests
in the women's and society pages, in columns on culture and the arts.
James Reston, however, represents another and more fundamental element in the newspaper. With the grand patriarch now thirty years gone,
Reston is the living *Times* executive who, in Talese's eyes, most embod-
ies the past, *The Times* "tradition," and particularly the distinctive Ochsian philosophy of religious idealism and business pragmatism. Talese,
indeed, goes to great length to link Reston with the holy *Times* trium-
virate of tradition, religion, and the U.S. power Establishment. Unlike
Daniel (but like Adolph Ochs), Reston is a legacy builder. He becomes,
Talese tells us, "the *paterfamilias*" of his Washington bureau (K&P 289),
establishing a line of succession passing from himself to Tom Wicker
and Max Frankel, and standing up and protecting his "sons" from New
York attack.

Reston is not only a tradition builder, however; he is also, like Ochs,
a man committed to *The Times* as "a religion, a cult" (K&P 346). Ochs's
successor, Arthur Hays Sulzberger, knew that in Reston "he had a
preacher on the payroll who could pack the church" (K&P 17). And
what is Reston's favorite sermon in his columns? The religion of the
power Establishment, of course: "His writing expressed faith in the nation's future, was gentle with the Establishment—he did not rock the
boat" (K&P 16). Such was the situation in the 1960s during one of the
first big crises of that decade: "And so it was not surprising then, when
the Bay of Pigs story demanded a big decision . . . that Orvil Dryfoos,
newly in command, would turn to Reston for advice—and Reston, so
sensitive to the national interest and to *The Times*' stake in that interest,
would advise that the story be toned down; and it was" (K&P 23).

This was the critical decision and its critical implication in the "reign"
of the third heir to Adolph Ochs's succession: Orvil Dryfoos. The crisis
for the fourth successor, Adolph Ochs's grandson Punch Sulzberger,
comes over the appointment by Daniel of James Greenfield to replace
Tom Wicker as Washington bureau chief in 1968, and over Reston's
subsequent opposition. This is the final moment of conflict toward which
the entire volume builds. Talese increases the suspense of this moment
by describing Punch Sulzberger in ambiguous terms. To Talese, he is
one of the "older young men . . . caught between the prismatic vision
of the generation above and the one below" (K&P 512). Sulzberger is
thus, like so many sons in Talese's work, a son caught between the past
and the future. We are also told that he has been a failure to his father
in the past, that there was in him "a hint of deep hurt at the dark
memory of his father's displeasure" (K&P 323).

Even his office suite reveals his uncertain and ambiguous posture. In
Talese's symbolic sweep of the fourteenth-floor offices in the book's
final chapter he suggests merely through decor the stakes of the final

conflict. At center, when the elevator doors open, is the bronze bust of Adolph Ochs "star[ing] across the wide corridor" and the ticking of his grandfather clock (K&P 498). In the eastern wing is the "rarely occupied office" of Arthur Hays Sulzberger, Punch's ailing father (K&P 499). The founding vision is thus hauntingly present, but the immediate fathers have somehow weakened, or abdicated. Punch's own office, in the opposite "modern" wing, continues the suspenseful ambiguity:

an elegant suite that is filled with antiques and rather resembles the parlor of the elder Sulzbergers' home—although, when Punch Sulzberger is present, he seems to dominate the large office with his informality. . . . The bookshelves around him are stocked with leather-bound volumes of enduring interest, but the books that he keeps close at hand concern the latest techniques of running a large corporation—books with such titles as *Management Grid* and *Management and Machiavelli*. (K&P 499)

Punch Sulzberger, the latest son, has failed his father in the distant past, and, by folding *The Times*'s overseas edition, has shown himself not sentimentally bound to his father's wisdom in the recent past. Will he choose the past (Reston) over the present (Daniel) at this moment? This passage by Talese perhaps most clearly reveals Punch Sulzberger's (and the United States's) dilemma: "Sulzberger now more than ever wanted to experiment with modern systems and to learn more about them; his newspaper could not merely follow the formulas of his father or grandfather. *The Times* would have to preserve what was inviolable in its tradition, yet adjust to changing trends and new tools" (K&P 336).

"*Preserve what was inviolable in its tradition.*" That is the key phrase, for what is inviolable in Adolph Ochs's *Times* tradition is its place as righteous spokesman for the U.S. Establishment. And so when the chips are down, Punch Sulzberger proves himself a faithful son and grandson, a faithful heir and steward of the Ochsian theocracy; he chooses, of course, Washington and Reston over New York and Daniel.

In Talese's language (as well as in my own), there is something distressingly sinister about this gesture of "honoring thy father." Punch Sulzberger's decision to preserve and elevate the past, the "tradition" as embodied in James Reston, is distressing to the degree that Talese has also suggested the elitism, and thus limitation, of that tradition. Here we have the anti-Establishment, anti-*Times* motif that Talese also weaves through his volume. In Talese's view, American society is divided into the "haves" and "have-nots," and the elitist circles of the rich and powerful hardly even recognize, much less support, the disestablished. At repeated points in the volume Talese ironically juxtaposes the nearsighted elitist world of the Establishment with the real problems and suffering of the poor:

The ads recorded the average man's tragedies, too, but only in the smallest print in the back of the newspaper, back between the stock-market listings and the bland photographs of executives on the rise—here, buried near the bottom, one could read in tiny type the names of those who had gone bankrupt, those who had been abandoned, *those who had lost something including dreams and sought recovery*. (K&P 76, emphasis added)

James Reston is particularly associated with Establishment elitism. And this is the man and the spirit triumphing at the end of *The Kingdom and the Power*. Reston sees the future dominated by a "new class of public servant," which is nothing less than an Establishment clique "operating within the 'triangle' of the university-foundation life, the communications media, and the government" (K&P 472). His method of reporting what the young people of the nation are thinking and saying is to print the remarks of college valedictorians—the elite of the youth—in *The Times*. Surely this limited, elitist view is criticized in *The Kingdom and the Power*, and surely, to this degree, James Reston is the villain of the work.

In 1977 Iphigene Sulzberger, the grande dame of *The New York Times*, said of Talese and *The Kingdom and the Power*: "That young man didn't know what he was talking about. . . . Evidently he liked *The Times*, but not the people who created it."[9] I suggest that, at heart, Talese does not even like *The Times*. *The Kingdom and the Power* is a most subtle work of literary nonfiction in the way it undercuts *The Times* at the same time it is carefully presenting its history. *The Times* may be *the* U.S. newspaper, but to the extent (as Talese repeatedly suggests) it was from its beginning and continues to be an organ firmly linked to the elitist U.S. Establishment, its history and tradition represent a limitation and even a falsification of the original vision of our forefathers. And to the extent (as Talese's rhetoric also implies) that its history is a microcosm of U.S. history, its falsification of the original Jeffersonian dream of equality and justice, under the pressures of money and power, illustrates the fate of the nation in the late twentieth century.

HONOR THY FATHER

The title, *The Kingdom and the Power*, with its evocation of the Lord's Prayer (and its ironic equation of "Our Father, who art in heaven" with the deceased Adolph Ochs), reveals the association in Talese's mind of powerful paternal influences with patriarchal religions.[10] The title of his next best-seller, the 1971 *Honor Thy Father*, makes this point even more explicitly. As is by now clear, the fate of America's sons is poignantly ambiguous to Talese. Most of his sons are failures in one way or another. Floyd Patterson is a moral success, though a filial and professional failure. Punch Sulzberger is a moral failure in his filial and professional success. With Bill Bonanno, the mafioso's son in *Honor Thy Father*, Talese presents a filial loyalty that is ruinous to the son, an American failure story redeemed only by Talese's sense that Bill could not have behaved otherwise.

The personal dimension of Talese's interest in Bill Bonanno has received little attention. When Talese first saw the young Bonanno, standing in a federal courthouse corridor with his lawyer in 1965, he was, in some ways, looking across the Establishment divide at his double. Talese did not know at that moment of the remarkable similarities of their histories. He did not know that they had been born in the same year, both of fathers named Joseph with roots in southern Italy; that both of their immigrant grandfathers had died young; that both he and Bill were eldest sons with younger sisters; that both were outsiders in different ways in high school and went to colleges in the South where they joined R.O.T.C. He did not know then that their family albums would look remarkably similar, but he saw enough across that divide to be curious. He saw enough to wait until all the other reporters had given up their attempts to penetrate Bill's silence, and to go up to Bonanno's lawyer and say in front of Bonanno, "Some day, not now, not tomorrow, but someday I would like to know from this young man what it is like to be this young man. Some day."[11]

A Mafia son's story was "forbidden" in both professional and personal ways for Talese—and therefore perhaps especially attractive. Journalistic consensus at that time was that the Mafia's "code of silence" was like the Chinese wall, inpenetrable and enduring. In trying and succeeding in penetrating this "omerta" Talese was defying his editors' wisdom as well as entering a world his own father wished to deny. Talese has acknowledged that as he was growing up in Ocean City, New Jersey, his immigrant father (a very moralistic, law-abiding man who wished nothing more than to prove himself a good American) was "horrified and embarrassed beyond explanation" by the presence of Italo-Americans in the Mafia and, worse than that, by the publicity given them. "I think it was more out of responding to my father's embarrassment that I went into that world and wanted to find out truly what these men were like," Talese has said.[12]

Talese's father did not want him to write this book. So he wrote it, and like his other father-son stories, it is a story of a son failing to live up to his father's expectations, failing to become like the father, and the agonizing introspection this entails. At this point I need hardly rehearse this refrain, but I would like to highlight how Bill's father, Don Joseph Bonanno, is depicted in *Honor Thy Father* as an absent "god/father," and how this volume, more than any other Talese work, communicates the poignance of lost communication.

Honor Thy Father is an ironic Christian typology. Joseph Bonanno's position as head of the Bonanno crime family is a secular role affording him extensive power and reverential treatment. Indeed, Stefano Magaddino, a rival chieftain, believes that Joseph wishes to make himself "boss of bosses" (HTF 210). Talese makes it clear that from his earliest days, Bill Bonanno's attitude toward his father is one of fear, awe, and worship (6). Don Joseph can read the heavens and predict the weather (220). He speaks in "oracles," and offers "ancient remedies for contemporary ailments" (41). He orders young Bill to sit with his left ear cocked to the sun—and it heals. He heals his daughter's wound with lemon juice and a special laying on of hands (41). Bill sits to the right of his father at the dinner table, and his wedding to Mafia daughter Rosalie Profaci becomes, in Talese's telling, a kind of "Last Supper" for the disintegrating Mafia, complete with the Judas figure, Magaddino, present (345, 11).[13]

In Talese, immediate fathers are either ailing (like Arthur Hays Sulzberger in *The Kingdom and the Power* and James McKee in *The Bridge*) or absent but strongly felt (like the fathers of Joshua Logan, Floyd Patterson, and, in the course of *Honor Thy Father*, Bill Bonanno). Part I of *Honor Thy Father* is titled "The Disappearance," and in his twenty-month absence that hangs over the volume Joseph Bonanno becomes an emblem of the lost or departed God. By disappearing, Joseph Bonanno "left everybody in trouble," explains Sam De Cavalcante, who plays the role of priest/confessor in Talese's account, listening for hours to those "whose words were really intended for someone else, someone who was never there—Joseph Bonanno" (HTF 358, 348).

Bill Bonanno, Joseph's anointed son, is most challenged and jeopardized by this abandonment, and if Joseph Bonanno can be seen as the lost father spirit, Bill Bonanno's poignant efforts to reach him, to hear his voice, to understand him, assume larger national and spiritual resonance. *Honor Thy Father* is a study in failed communication. Even before his disappearance Joseph Bonanno rarely explains himself to his son. After Bill has dropped out of college in order to join his organization, Joseph keeps Bill waiting for twelve hours in front of a drugstore; when he finally emerges, he neither apologizes nor explains the extensive delay (55).

As Mafia tensions increase in the early 1960s, Don Joseph's response is to absent himself more and more from the changing scene, leaving Bill in the confusing and dangerous role of uninformed spokesman. In the summer and fall of 1964 Bill receives several messages from the national Mafia Commission, which also wishes to reach his father. These communications fail to achieve their objectives and culminate in Magaddino's kidnapping of Don Joseph in October 1964.

From October to December an isolated phone booth glowing in the dark is presented by Talese as an ironic modern-day equivalent of the confessional:

The trip was taking on a strange, almost mystical, meaning for Bonanno and Labruzzo—it was becoming an act of faith, a test of fidelity, and the booth, a solitary glowing structure in the vacant darkness, was approached almost reverentially. . . . If his father was alive, he would make the call, Bill said. If he did not make it this Thursday, then he would make it next Thursday, or the Thursday after that, and Bill said he would be there every time, just in case, until he was convinced that his father was dead. (52, 50)

The call does finally come, but it is not the father's voice; it is that of an intermediary—and the son misapplies the message. The glowing hope of the telephone booth is then transformed by Talese into a glowing television screen, another symbol of modern communication that the distraught Bill, significantly, destroys: "a remarkable little fireworks show of self-destruction was playing itself out within the 21-inch screen, and Bonanno and Labruzzo watched with fascination until the interior of the set had nearly evaporated into a smoldering hole of jagged edges and fizzling filament" (63).

Don Joseph's telephone message had told Bill not to "make waves." Whether Bill's defiance of these orders, though well intended, created publicity that made Don Joseph's return impossible is hard to say. What is known is that the father could have reappeared any time after December 1964, but chose to remain absent for seventeen more months—despite the difficulties this created for his son.[14] Bill's life from this moment on becomes a litany of ironic failed communications. Because he honors his father, and therefore refuses to communicate even his scant knowledge to the grand jury, Bill is jailed for contempt of court. After three months in prison he finally tells the grand jury about the phone call and his subsequent call to his father's lawyer largely because he had "received no sign indicating that his secrecy and imprisonment was acknowledged or appreciated by anyone" (127). Seven months later, his father still absent, Bill makes another dangerous misjudgment, this time regarding a "peace meeting" where he is nearly gunned down in the street. Nine months after that, in October 1966, Bill serves another jail sentence for failing to testify about the "peace meeting" shootings.

When Don Joseph finally stages his second coming it is not to offer explanations to his son. Talese writes that Bill

could not help but wonder where [his father] had been all those months, but he doubted that his father would ever discuss it with him. After all, a trial would be coming up sooner or later, although it might take years because of various delays; in any event Bill would surely be summoned to testify, and the less he knew the easier it would be. Still, Bill was intensely curious. . . . (166)

A trial does come in several years, but it is Bill's, and he is found guilty and faces a four-year prison term. Bill's final visits to his father, before his trial and before he turns himself over to prison authorities, are among the most moving (and ironic) in *Honor Thy Father*. Talese writes that among the reasons Bill journeys to the desert of Tucson before his trial is that "his father had been so vague and incomprehensible on the telephone the other night that Bill had no idea what he was talking about, and he therefore decided that a personal visit was in order" (334–35). Father and son discuss many things during this visit, none of which Talese reports, and none of which serve to save Bill from his fate. When Bill returns for his final visit, after his conviction, Don Joseph embraces him and, through tears, utters the richly ironic *"Dio ti binidici*, God should bless you" (471).

But blessings do not fall on any sons of Talese. One of the strengths of Talese's work is that he shows filial agony in many dimensions. Talese has acknowledged that from the outset, he knew he was writing a "family story." During his first meeting with Bill Bonanno at Johnny Johnson's Steak House in New York Talese invited Bill to bring his wife, Rosalie, to a dinner with his own family. In *Honor Thy Father* Rosalie Bonanno's difficult struggle with her father-in-law is presented by Talese as a revealing echo of Bill's own. Rosalie, like her husband, regards Don Joseph as a "distant, almost occult, figure" (214). To her, "his mind seemed always in motion, he was always talking to the men in a strange oracular manner that confused her, he missed nothing that was going on" (234). When he speaks to her she feels "tested," just as Bill does, and words he employs to fortify her fail to achieve their effect:

Her father-in-law . . . seemed to be reading her mind when he said *pazienza*, patience, *coraggio*, courage. He spoke these words almost in the form of an exhortation, spoke them as a high priest might at benediction; but she could not respond to her father-in-law. At night, in bed, she quietly cried. (232)

Rosalie cries, and she ultimately tries to escape. In this Christian typology Rosalie is the Mary figure, first the Virgin Mary "remain[ing] awake pondering the . . . unexplained origin of her first son," the son who will be "her salvation for a while" (115, 121). Later, when she tries to free herself and her children from "the pressure of being a Bonanno," she becomes like the fallen Mary Magdalen, and Bill must "properly prepare his father for her return" (216, 245). Although she tries, Rosalie is no more successful than Bill in freeing herself from the dangerous paternal legacy.

And just as Talese portrays filial struggle in its many forms within Bill's and Rosalie's generation, he hints at its cross-generational repetition as well. In the following passage we learn that even Don Joseph has *his* absent "father image":

Joseph Bonanno, an orphan at fifteen, had been independent and self-reliant and had never had a father to answer to except in a mystical sense—his father, dead at thirty-seven, became an idealized figure preserved in a dozen sepia photographs and religious cards and in the exalted, reverential collections of Joseph Bonanno, recollections that were all part of his dated, idealized world rife with ritual and rigidity. Bill Bonanno had been lured into that world through the magnetism of his father, realizing too late that his father was a rare natural inhabitant of that demanding state of mind. (455–56)

Bill Bonanno fails to reach that exalted state, and even though he plans to explain himself to his children (as his father had never done to him), he ultimately fails even in this effort at communication, and the generational miscommunication continues:

It was a bizarre period, a time when the nation seemed pulled between its twin forces of violence and puritanism, balanced by hypocrisy, and perhaps that was one reason why Bill was unable to explain during the summer to his children, and to himself, why he was going to be spending four years in jail . . . he had done the expedient thing and not the wise thing in using Torillo's credit card; but that did not fully explain why he would be going away for four years or why he had already been in and out of jails: there were other important, complex factors that had shaped him, had influenced what he had done and what had been done to him, and in order to explain these to his children he would want to explain his whole life, beginning with his birth in 1932 and the beat of the different drum to which he had marched during most of his maturity. He would want to explain his father's life, the spirit of that loving and destructive father-son relationship. (454)

Clearly what Bill fails to explain is precisely what Talese succeeds in communicating in *Honor Thy Father*. He explains Bill's whole life, and his father's life, and "the spirit of that loving and destructive father-son relationship" set in America. That Talese saw himself as supplying this communication bridge is evident from the final words of his "Author's Note" to the volume:

[Bill] was feeling a tremendous need to communicate when I first met him. While my initial proposal to write about him might have been flattering, particularly since he then felt so misunderstood and had gone through life being his father's son, I do believe that later I served as an instrument through which he could communicate to those closest to him. He could reveal through me, who respected and understood him, thoughts and attitudes that he did not wish to personally express to his family, to his father.
    I sensed, later, that Rosalie also confided to me thoughts that she wished to

convey to Bill or to her father-in-law; and Catherine, too, [Bill's sister] and other members of the family as well had told me what they wished others to know—I had become a source of communication within a family that had long been repressed by a tradition of silence. (479–80)

It is ironic, yet sadly of a piece, that Talese's efforts as father-son interpreter, as generational go-between, backfired so bitterly for Bill Bonanno. Don Joseph, on reading *Honor Thy Father*, stopped speaking to his son for a year—a year that Bill was locked away in prison and, presumably, might most be in need of paternal support.

In this ironic Christian typology Bill Bonanno is the sacrificed son. And although it is true that *Honor Thy Father* represents Talese's fullest acknowledgment of the weaknesses and errors of a son, the volume also implies that the son's failure perhaps is in loving too much—while the father loves too little:

[Bill] doubted, for example, that he could have joined the training program of a large American corporation and risen within the structure unless he had changed his name or disowned his father. And, if he had done that, he would not have been Bill Bonanno, a son who deeply loved his father although recognizing that the relationship had been destructive; curiously, more destructive to him than it had been to his father, who had not spent time in jail, who had fewer legal problems than Bill, and was no doubt more cunning, more careful, stronger, more selfish perhaps, and less loving. (455)

Talese sets the final scene of *Honor Thy Father* in a federal marshal's office. Bill sees two signs there, one marked "civil," the other "criminal." Bill's movement, of course, is toward the "criminal" and the volume's last line is "Salvatore Bonanno has surrendered," yet Talese's two signs remind us that, taken together, his first two best-sellers represent the "civil" and "criminal" sides of America's filial odyssey. From 1965 to 1969, all the while Talese was giving his major attention to the success story of Punch Sulzberger and *The Kingdom and the Power*, he was simultaneously keeping track of the dark side and the dark son of the American Establishment, Salvatore Bonanno. *The Kingdom and the Power* and *Honor Thy Father* should be read as companion pieces showing the upper and undersides of the American Dream. Talese leaves no doubt regarding his belief that Joseph Bonanno's empire-building is as quintessentially capitalistic as Adolph Ochs's, although a hypocritical American public fails to make this acknowledgment. And who is to say which is the better son? And which failure is of greater moment?

THY NEIGHBOR'S WIFE

Each of Talese's major books is foreshadowed in works that come before. In *Honor Thy Father* Bill Bonanno's first real rebellion after he joins his father is to have an extramarital affair with a German waitress, an action that was considered as "scandalous" in the underworld (HTF 77) as in the proper middle-class American society Talese chronicles in his most recent bestseller, the controversial 1980 *Thy Neighbor's Wife*.

In one sense, Talese was simply following his curiosity the evening in 1971 when, returning home from P. J. Clarke's tavern with his wife, he investigated a neon sign flashing "Live Nude Models" on the third floor of a building within the shadows of Bloomingdale's. Eighteen years before, for his first story for *The New York Times*, he had climbed a similar staircase to find what lay behind the pulsing, circling neon headlines on the Times Square building.[15] In another sense, however, something more personal lay behind Talese's exploration of the world of sexual license. Just as the Mafia represented a denied and forbidden subject to Talese as a boy, sexuality was, if possible, an even more repressed and whispered reality to a proper immigrant's son brought up in a Catholic grade school in a small town founded by sober Methodist ministers. By associating for the next five years with "the obscene people of America," as Talese has wittily characterized his research, he was defying the sexual repressions of his youth, of his hometown, of his parents.[16] That he should suffer mightily, both in his hometown press and in reviews at large, for this act of defiance seems, perhaps, inevitable.

How can sex and adultery relate to fathers and sons? This was the question I pondered as the 1970s rolled by and word kept appearing that Talese's now notorious book about "sex in America" was yet to appear. Talese was having trouble with the generational aspect of his story, and this *is* what caused his delay. The fact that Talese was forced to abandon his first idea for his book is one of the reasons *Thy Neighbor's Wife* seems to lack the dramatic tension and resolution of his previous works.

Talese believed that the story of changing sexual mores in America was the biggest story of his time, and he has acknowledged that he wanted to approach it as a generational story. He told David Susskind in 1980 that his original idea was to find a young, college-age masseuse who would trust him enough to tell him her story and allow him to use her name.[17] He would ask her to take him to her home to meet her parents, and report on the conflicting generational values. His book would then follow her back to the massage parlor and deal with the men whom she met. Here, he admits, he was looking for a man forty to forty-five, a man who felt "passed over." He hoped, then, to tell a kind of father-daughter story, the story of a young, liberated masseuse who befriends and helps liberate an older man. Writing about himself in third person toward the end of *Thy Neighbor's Wife*, he explains that

> it was Talese's intention, though he had yet to organize the scenes and story line, to write about a relationship between two real-life characters in a massage parlor—a middle-aged conservative businessman and a hippie co-ed who services his erotic needs, capitalizes on his inhibitions, and eventually befriends him and helps to extricate much of the shame and guilt that he usually brought with him into the massage parlor. From meeting and chatting with hundreds of male customers . . . the author knew he had little difficulty in identifying with them—he *was* them in many ways. . . . (432)

For more than a year Talese was successful in this effort. While managing the Secret Life Massage Parlor on Lexington Avenue in New York he interviewed for employment a former teacher from Baton Rouge who had gone to Tulane University and was then working for *Look* magazine. She arrived for the interview with a copy of a Walker Percy novel under her arm, and Talese found her to be bright and articulate.[18] She not only got the job, but in time Talese paid her more than $100 extra a week to keep a diary of her experiences as a masseuse. After each session she would describe her client and write down what he requested and what they talked about, as well as her own thoughts and feelings at the time.

Diaries are valuable sources for those seeking to write literary nonfiction, and in time the older man Talese sought began to emerge in the diary. He was a middle-aged Harvard-trained psychologist, and as the weeks went on the young woman recorded going out to dinner with this "client"—something that would have been taboo to most masseuses. Then she was ill for three weeks, and when she returned she wanted to quit the business. The unexpected had happened. She had fallen in love. The masseuse and the psychologist married and did not wish any longer to be in Talese's book. They had no objection to his telling their story, but only if he used fictitious names. This he refused to do.

Talese had invested more than a year and considerable cash in this couple, and in 1973 he was forced to start over. He has described the book that emerged from this setback, the book we know as *Thy Neighbor's Wife*, as a "breakthrough" book for him that includes some of his best writing.[19] Much of the language (particularly alliterative passages and delicate descriptions of erotic acts) *is* exceptional, and the volume does represent a breakthrough for Talese in a number of ways. *Thy Neighbor's Wife* embraces both a larger subject and a larger historical period than either *The Kingdom and the Power* (which centers on a specific newspaper from its founding in 1851 through 1968) or *Honor Thy Father* (which focuses on a specific family from approximately 1890 to 1971). *Thy Neighbor's Wife* treats the vastly wider subject of sex and censorship in America from the Puritans to the present.

In addition, with the loss of the masseuse and the psychologist, Talese abandoned the central stage he had originally chosen for his story: the massage parlor. Each of Talese's previous works had a setting that supplied a convenient structure for the book. New York City itself is the stage for *New York—A Serendipiter's Journey*, while the Verrazano span provides a fascinating expanding stage for the action in *The Bridge*. The *New York Times* building is used by Talese as a way to move conveniently through the many departments and people in *The Kingdom and the Power*, while the Bonanno family represents a less concrete but still reliable (family) structure for *Honor Thy Father*.

Thy Neighbor's Wife is a breakthrough book for Talese in the sense that he offers not one but three interrelated stages for the book's action: Chicago, California's utopian Sandstone Community, and Ocean City, New Jersey. As in Henry James, each setting represents an important psychological state. It is no accident that Talese elects Chicago for the opening of *Thy Neighbor's Wife*. That city represents for him not only the heart of middle America, but a city of religious and political rigidity and repression that is the formative experience of so many of the sons in this work. These include Harold Rubin, Hugh Hefner, Barney Rosset, William Hamling, Marvin Miller, Raymond Gauer, Ed Lange, David S. Alberts, and John Bullaro. Talese writes that

the great Irish immigration of the mid-1800s had imported into Chicago a fierce brand of Catholicism founded on sexual regulation and orthodoxy, and the city gradually reflected these values politically and socially, becoming less tolerant of unorthodox thought and behavior. . . .

[The late Mayor Richard] Daley's neighborhood was not so different from other ethnic white areas largely populated by the Polish, or Czechoslovakians, or Italians, or Russian Jews; nearly all were inhabited by socially conservative Chicagoans tightly tied to their families and trade unions, and they were more enduringly insular and immutable than the ethnic Americans living in more liberal cities. . . . (TNW 52, 53)

The movement of all the sons, save Rubin, away from Chicago and primarily to Los Angeles and Sandstone suggests a defiant movement away from this repression toward greater freedom. Indeed, Talese describes Los Angeles as "unconnected to Old World ties and traditions" (108), and Sandstone in the early 1970s as "undoubtedly the most liberated fifteen acres of land in America's not-always-democratic Republic" (442). The fact that Talese's opening character, Harold Rubin, never escapes Chicago and that the Sandstone "utopia" does not survive suggest the power of formative, restrictive forces. This point is underscored by the book's concluding stage, Ocean City, New Jersey—Talese's personal "Chicago." Here, at the volume's end, is an additional artistic "breakthrough": Talese's first effort to depict himself as a character in his work. Talese's answer to Thomas Wolfe's *You Can't Go Home Again* is that, in fact, we can never get away.

The most important breakthrough in this manifoldly ambitious *Thy Neighbor's Wife*, however, is the change in the filial stance of the sons. Whereas in his previous works Talese creates poignant and ambiguous tragedies of sons failing to live up to the expectations and ideals of their fathers—causing them painful introspection—*Thy Neighbor's Wife* offers repeated portraits of sons *not* seeking to honor their fathers, but to defy them. *Thy Neighbor's Wife* in fact might be subtitled "Cameos of Defiance." At least twenty "sons" are depicted in the volume, and all in the posture of unrepentant rebellion.

The eight publishers of "pornographic" literature—ranging from the now quite admired Barney Rosset and Samuel Roth to the more discomforting William Hamling—are defiant sons in their efforts to publish what many wish to suppress. Talese notes that Samuel Roth, the first American publisher to challenge the censors of James Joyce's *Ulysses*, was banished from home by his father at the age of fifteen. This father, a pants maker, "had little sympathy for a son who challenged authority" (75).[20] Samuel Roth recognizes himself as a "rebel" (75), and defends his principles arrogantly and comes out of prison "unrehabilitated and certainly unrepentant" (78). Barney Rosset, the founder of Grove Press, "shared Roth's passion for independence," Talese writes (95). When he was in private school he coedited a newspaper titled *Anti-Everything* (96).

Many of the publishers of erotic literature are brought before the Supreme Court, and in tracing the swinging pendulum of American obscenity law Talese is symbolically tracing confrontations of rebellious sons with national authority. The famous 1965 *Memoirs v. Massachusetts* case, which allowed the publication of *Fanny Hill*, represented a victory for the sons and for "free-r" expression. The Redup decision in 1967 represented another victory for the sons, and Talese writes that "in Redup, the Supreme Court [i.e., the father] finally seemed to be relinquishing its role as the nation's literary arbitrator" (326). However, this lasts for only six years, when, in the Marvin Miller case, "Chief Justice Burger, together with the other Court conservatives, finally had an opportunity to express their outrage about sexual openness in America, and to exorcise the spirit of permissiveness that had been created by their judicial predecessors during the 1960s" (335).

Caught in the time warp of these opposing decisions is erotic book publisher William Hamling, one of the most interesting of the defiant sons in *Thy Neighbor's Wife* because he seems to represent the poor man, the average man on the street, rather than the rich. Through Hamling, Talese makes the point that the "frontiers of free expression in America" were often extended *not* by the literary establishment in New York, but rather by

déclassé California publishers like [Hamling] and Milton Luros and Sanford Aday—men who spent fortunes in court each year fighting the convictions of city vice squads, federal agents, and southern sheriffs in the Bible Belt, and in so doing they opened up the territory that would later be explored more easily and no less profitably by the reputable publishers of a Philip Roth or Norman Mailer, a William Styron or John Updike. (326)

Talese notes that Hamling had "in conscience, not quite escaped" the Chicago parish into which he was born, "even in the sybaritic atmosphere of Southern California," where he lived (314). His books' titles—*Sin Whisper, Sin Warden, Sin Servant, Passion Priestess, Shame Agent*—both acknowledge and rebel against this restrictive religious past.

Hamling's ultimate defiant act, however, is his publication of an illustrated *Report of the Presidential Commission on Obscenity and Pornography* after its 1969 unillustrated release. "This was the most brazen act of Hamling's career," Talese stresses (327). Hamling's subsequent indictment by Attorney General John Mitchell and his conviction bring him before the Supreme Court. This episode has the feel of the dramatic moments of climax in Talese's other works that reveal the son's failure or success. Hamling is defended by Stanley Fleishman, himself an immigrant's son who has defied not only physical handicap, but his mother's "dominating support" in becoming a successful trial lawyer (346). "Fleishman seemed unintimidated [by the Supreme Court]," Talese writes, "exuding a manner that would have bordered on cockiness were it not for his attitude of respect and formality" (353). Fleishman's ally on the bench is Justice William O. Douglas, and Talese is quick to supply the title of Douglas's book: *Points of Rebellion*.

Will these three defiant sons succeed? Talese increases the suspense by depicting the dramatic courtroom scene in religious terms evoking Hamling's Chicago boyhood:

Awaiting the arrival of the justices, William Hamling sat with his wife and daughter on a mahogany pew in the sixth row of the ornate and crowded sanctuary of the Supreme Court . . . and he felt, as he had decades ago during the High Masses of his Chicago boyhood, a mingling of anxiety and awe, a trembling sense of grandeur. On this morning Hamling's appeal would be heard, his destiny debated. But whether he won or lost, his name and his case, *Ham-*

ling v. *United States of America*, would everlastingly be listed in legal texts, the doomsday books of American jurisprudence. (339)

Like the other sons of Talese, Hamling loses, yet Talese's history of the vacillation of Supreme Court obscenity law serves to undercut this loss. Indeed, Hamling loses in part because he published his illustrated *Report* under the Redup climate but reaches the Supreme Court after the harsher Miller ruling. Furthermore, in his loss Hamling achieves a moral victory in the sense that, in Talese's view, his defiance is to be true to the vision of the *founding fathers* in the Bill of Rights, rather than to their diminished successors.

In some respects we might regret that Talese does not simply end with this typically ambiguous win/loss, but his goal in this volume seems to be to portray many profiles of defiance rather than one. He does this with cameos of sixteen women, as well as of more than twenty men. As in *Honor Thy Father*, daughters also struggle with parents and with patriarchal traditions, and their conflicts provide echoing reverberations of the fraternal archetype. Sally Binford's defiance is particularly noteworthy, not only because she represents defiant daughters of the upper class, but because, as with the Patterson-Torres story of the bad son and good, Sally is the bad daughter, the shrew to her conforming Bianca-like sister. Talese writes:

The social and sexual mores that influenced the behavior of most female members of [Sally's] generation were largely ignored by her from the time of her adolescence in suburban Long Island, where she was reared by wealthy parents in a home with servants, but where—unlike her favored older sister, a conformist whom she deeply resented—Sally Binford had been a rebel, a tomboy, a kind of changeling that her mother tolerated but could never understand.

Sally was no more understanding of her mother. (289)

When Mrs. Binford insists that Sally enroll in Vassar College, Sally responds by cutting classes so often she is expelled (290). Intriguingly, Sally defies her mother to become more like her freewheeling father.

This father has mistresses, and in this sense Sally Binford is like Christie Hefner, who brings a man home from college and sleeps with him in defiance of her mother but greatly pleasing her father (407). The Christie Hefner cameo offers not only another version of filial failure and success (Christie's brother failing to become like his famous father while Christie succeeds), but actually the tacitly incestuous father-daughter story Talese originally intended. In the late 1970s the liberated coed Christie Hefner helps revive the middle-aged (and somewhat slumping) Hefner empire. And Talese notes that "by her own admission, they shared a mutual attraction that was far more romantic than familial" (407).

The thirty-plus cameos of filial defiance I have quickly noted are only minor persona in the American gallery of defiance that is *Thy Neighbor's Wife*. Five rebelling sons are given major portraits, and provide the major action in the volume. Three are rebellious sons who become fatherly theocrats themselves; two are psychological surrogates of Gay Talese.

In John Humphrey Noyes, the founder of the Oneida Community; John Williamson, the founder of the Sandstone Community; and Hugh Hefner, the author of the Playboy philosophy, Talese depicts rebellious sons who become theocrats. Noyes, who came from a loving and distinguished New England family, was a diligent and unrebellious son who, "like his father, graduated with honors from Dartmouth College" (244). Things changed, however, when Noyes came under the influence of certain New England revivalist ministers who were "challenging the traditional interpretation of the Bible and . . . confronting in particular the Calvinistic doctrine on human unworthiness and the prevalence of sin" (244–45). Talese notes that Noyes's "mother and the rest of his family and relatives openly disapproved" of Noyes's actions (251). Nevertheless he formed his Oneida community to pursue Perfectionism, a system in which "harmonious groups of men and women lived and worked together and made love to one another regularly, though never exclusively, and were the collective parents of all children born among them" (241).

While Talese, no doubt, was drawn to the rebellious attitude and utopian features of Noyes's vision, he also does not fail to notice that a son rebelling against a dominating patriarchal system can, in turn, become an authoritative patriarch himself. "Noyes was not . . . [an] advocate of individual freedoms"; Talese writes, "he was a committed communist, an absolutist, a theocrat" (248). In fact, women wishing to join the Oneida community had to sign an application form that stated: "we do not belong to ourselves in any respect, but that we belong first to God, and second to Mr. Noyes as God's true representative" (259).

The gradual demise of the Oneida community is, in Talese's telling, remarkably similar to the Bonanno Mafia decline. If John Humphrey Noyes has a weakness, it is regarding his son, Theodore, who, although even more prodigal than Bill Bonanno, Noyes appoints as his successor. Noyes then becomes the disappearing father spirit: "On the night of June 23, 1879, without a word to most of his confidants, including Theodore, John Humphrey Noyes and an elderly colleague climbed aboard a horse-drawn carriage and passed through the Oneida gates, through which he would never return alive" (263). Although Noyes (like Adolph Ochs) appoints a committee of "caretakers" (including Theodore) and seeks to continue to influence the spiritual and business life of the community through "spirited letters of instruction and ad-

vice to be read aloud in the mansion auditorium, where a majority of
the residents still believed in his wisdom and supremacy," his absence
slowly takes its toll (263). The new sons become rebellious; Theodore
is a complete failure, and another, more successful son is only able to
preserve Oneida as a business empire. As a spiritually meaningful theocracy, Oneida (like the Mafia theocracy) declines.

John Williamson's less ambitious Sandstone community shares a similar but even shorter history. Perhaps Williamson's central flaw is that
he has no real interest in either his son (who dies partly from this neglect) or his daughter, and when he absents himself from Sandstone,
the commune (like Noyes's and Bonanno's) slowly deteriorates (143).

The rebellious hedonistic theocracy of Hugh Hefner, articulated in
his Playboy philosophy and practiced in his Chicago and Los Angeles
mansions, proves more enduring than Williamson's Sandstone.[21] Hefner names his first non-model Playmate "Janet Pilgrim" as a "subtle
thrust at the Pilgrim Fathers who had arrived on the *Mayflower* and
brought puritanism to America" (70). Indeed, Talese notes, "with each
passing year [Hefner] seemed to be undermining more defiantly the
Judeo-Christian tradition that associated excessive pleasure with punishment" (383).

However, as with Noyes and Williamson, Hefner is not a theocrat
without flaw. Talese locates contradiction in the double standard Hefner never escapes and a kind of hubris in his efforts to control his life,
his environment, and even time. When, in the 1970s, Hefner absents
himself more and more from the business side of his empire to pursue
even more vigorously his own hedonistic pleasures, revenue falls, associates are sought for prosecution, and the empire is threatened.

Hugh Hefner is a pivotal figure among the five major rebelling sons.
He is a defiant American son whose vision achieves some degree of
success. Though Talese does not see Hefner as totally without flaw, he
also finds him a man whom he, in many ways, admires—indeed even
resembles. As with Bill Bonanno, little attention has been paid to the
similarities between Hefner and Talese. Both were raised by parents
who were "extraordinary examples of restraint and repression" (35),
and both rebel against Methodist and Catholic influences in their formative years. Both, furthermore, were sexually frustrated young men who
became nocturnal wanderers of their respective cities, Chicago and New
York, where they dreamed the American dreams of their favorite writer,
F. Scott Fitzgerald (29, 64).[22] Talese observed in his 1980 *Playboy* interview:

I'm one of the few people who read [*The Playboy*] *Philosophy* three times. I *know*
that *Philosophy*. So much of what he wrote in that important series did find its
way into [*Thy Neighbor's Wife*], but the book does not always quote *The Playboy*

Philosophy, because some of Hefner's attitudes and research were similar to my own. (106)

Finally, while both rebellious sons have attained success beyond their fathers' (and their own) grandest expectations, both live with the fact that their fathers have refused to read their work.

Thus Hugh Hefner receives prominent treatment in *Thy Neighbor's Wife*, not only because he was a significant figure in the changing sexual scene after World War II, but also because he is one of Talese's first experiments with a son who might succeed. The important place *Thy Neighbor's Wife* holds in Talese's canon is as the first *major* work in which he allows sons to move from submission to defiance—and even toys with the possibility of filial success.

That Talese was (and remains) uncomfortable with that possibility is shown in the ambiguous portrait he paints of Hefner's success, and in the fact that Talese gives even more chapters to John Bullaro, a more ordinary and less successful Chicago son than Hefner. My belief is that Harold Rubin, who opens the book, and John Bullaro, whose story dominates the book's center section, are Talese surrogates until he finally dares to step forward in person at book's end.

Through the story of Harold Rubin, Talese is able to depict male masturbation, but he is also able to portray the teenage sexual and paternal defiance that he himself was unable to achieve.[23] John Bullaro follows, representing Rubin/Talese after college and near midlife. Talese tells a revealing story about another incident that delayed his progress on *Thy Neighbor's Wife* for more than six months: he did not know how to introduce John Bullaro. His opening seven chapters pleased him with their movement back and forth between male fantasy and male reality. Chapter One begins with male fantasy (with Harold Rubin's masturbation) and then moves to the reality behind the fantasy with Chapter Two on model Diane Webber. With Chapter Three Talese turns to the marketer of male fantasy, Hugh Hefner, and into the reality of his life. Chapters Four through Seven depict the censors of male fantasy and the rebellious sons who historically fought against them, ending with the greater freedom in 1959 and 1960 that made possible the activities of Hugh Hefner and Harold Rubin. But how to introduce Bullaro? Talese takes years to complete his books because he labors, like a tailor, to make the many pieces of his story come together so smoothly that the work appears seamless.

In seeking a thread that would join John Bullaro to these first chapters, Talese confesses that he considered briefly the notion of making one composite character of Harold Rubin and John Bullaro because "their backgrounds had been so similar."[24] Because Talese is as philosophically opposed to composite characters as to fictitious names, he

ultimately rejected this solution. However, the equation of these two
defiant sons in his mind is revealing, for Bullaro's life also reveals remarkable parallels with Talese's own. John Bullaro is the son of a conservative Italo-American tradesman. He abandons the Catholicism of
his father and seeks escape from the insular world of his upbringing.
After moving to Los Angeles from Chicago Bullaro "felt less self-con-
scious and ethnic in the sprawling open atmosphere of Southern California, where there were no insular neighborhoods dominated by the
Irish or Italians or Slovaks or Germans" (107–108).

No doubt Talese also saw reflections of his own early efforts to climb
the establishment ladder at *The New York Times* in Bullaro's efforts to
be a corporate success in insurance. Indeed, when he describes Bullaro's experience at New York Life Insurance Company, Talese could
just as easily be telling his own history with New York City life:

While he believed that he was sufficiently diligent and self-effacing to eventually qualify for the hierarchy of New York Life, he was never unaware of that
deepest part of him that rebelled against corporate conformity, that was lured
by fantasies of freedom, although, while in New York, he firmly repressed any
expression of this. (123)

Both Bullaro and Talese throw-over establishment success to pursue
their fantasies of professional and sexual freedom. Bullaro's story, which
is the most prominent in *Thy Neighbor's Wife*, is a typical Talese story of
a son who loses. Bullaro's drive for freedom leads to the loss of his job,
his wife, and his children. Although Talese's very last words on Bullaro
in the final chapter are that he and his wife are "partners in an open
marriage" (444), when he ends Bullaro's story-proper (five chapters
earlier) it is with Bullaro in a "state of dejection . . . alone, jobless,
without a sense of hope" (280). That Talese identifies intensely with
Bullaro, despite the fact that he himself has been extraordinarily more
successful than Bullaro—both professionally and in maintaining his relationship with his wife and children—is shown in the defensiveness
with which he responded to questions regarding Bullaro in his 1980
Playboy interview:

Playboy: You say that [Bullaro is] a happy man *now*, leading a much freer life
    as a result of his experiments in sexual openness, so why did you end his
    story at a period of his life when he was "without a sense of hope"?

Talese: I don't believe that's right.

Playboy: We're quoting from the manuscript.

Talese: Well, look, you can quote one line out of a book and say "Without a
    sense of hope," and that does not say a damned thing to me about that
    character. I don't think that character comes off without a sense of hope.

And I know for a fact that he has been very revived by his new experiences. I saw it myself. . . .

   Bullaro is about 47 now, my age, and when I picked up his story in the
mid-Sixties, when he was in his early 30s, he was a corporation man out of
the Eisenhower years. . . . I think Bullaro is going to touch a lot of men.
He was a Fifties man who put himself through some dramatic changes and
who feels at the beginning of the Eighties that time hasn't left him behind.
(105–6)

I believe Talese thought John Bullaro would "touch a lot of men" because he touched Talese himself so personally. Talese's difficulty in depicting more "success" in Bullaro—even when he felt it—suggests the
difficulty he experiences envisioning victory or success for American
sons. Happiness would seem to be out of the question for a Talese son;
being "less worried" is as close as Talese in 1980 could come.

   Another reason Talese may not have continued on to a more affirmative Bullaro conclusion is that he was planning to take over from
Bullaro and end the book with himself. In respect to Talese's evolving
vision of the American father-son story, it is significant that he chooses
to end his book with himself, not as a failure, not as a success, but as a
son returning home to the insular island of Ocean City (his Chicago),
standing naked, defiantly eye to eye with the town fathers. "They were
unabashed voyeurs looking at him"; runs the final line, "and Talese
looked back."

Thy Neighbor's Wife was an extraordinary financial success for Talese,
marred only by the intensity of the critical thrashing the book also received.[25] *Thy Neighbor's Wife* was criticized for failing to include all aspects of sexuality, such as homosexuality, incest, and contraception, and
for giving women secondary status.[26] Many reviewers were also outraged at Talese's opening the doors of sexual privacy, at his hinting at
the social benefits of the massage parlor, at his widely publicized parti-
cipatory research methods—in fact that he had dared to do what he
had dared to do.[27] More to the point were those reviewers noting the
"joylessness" in a book that seemed to be about sexual freedom.[28]
Knowing the difficulty Talese experiences envisioning success (much
less happiness) for his sons, readers should no longer find this surprising.

   What has not been said about the critical reaction to *Thy Neighbor's
Wife* is that perhaps one reason the response was often so angry is because *Thy Neighbor's Wife* itself is a book of unrelenting defiance. The
tone of the book invites confrontation. Rarely, as in his earlier works,
does Talese present the pain and introspection of his aspiring sons (and
daughters) that heretofore had created reader sympathy. Instead, the

children, and especially Talese, come eye to eye with their fathers. They dare equality, and even supremacy.

In describing the "news/novels discourse" of the seventeenth and eighteenth centuries from which the novel emerged, Davis has noted that the movement from ballad-reading and printing to the novel involved an increasing eroticism of the text. It saw a decreasing distance between what was considered public and private, and between the reader and narrator and the event. Through his behind-the-scenes news/novels Talese continues to foreshorten this distance without giving readers the escape clause of the label "fiction"; this very intimacy makes certain readers uncomfortable, while it attracts others. Talese's formal, respectfully distant prose style at times may be at odds with the intimacy of his narrative stance, yet its very formality places that intimacy in higher relief.

This is the current status of Talese's artistic vision, his ongoing American father-son story. He was hurt and angered by the reaction to *Thy Neighbor's Wife*, particularly by a critical editorial that appeared in the *Ocean City Sentinel*, the newspaper that gave him his start as a high school reporter, and by the repercussions felt by his parents, wife, and children. His response was defiance—on both professional and personal levels. Shown the Ocean City editorial and told of the slighting remarks addressed to his father on the Ocean City golf course, Talese offered to sell his home in Ocean City and spare his family further embarrassment by never returning. Professionally, his response to suggestions that he do a "respectable" book was his desire to do a sequel to *Thy Neighbor's Wife*.[29]

The movement of Talese's artistic vision, as I hope the preceding pages have made clear, has been to make the personal more and more explicit in his nonfiction. He went behind the scenes of his job in *The Kingdom and the Power*, and to his family taboos in *Honor Thy Father* and *Thy Neighbor's Wife*, the book in which he allows himself to appear for the very first time. His work since 1980 continues this direction.

After the controversy of *Thy Neighbor's Wife* in 1980 many of Talese's friends urged him to write a small book to give himself a vacation from the exhausting research that had gone into his three previous long bestsellers. For awhile he followed this advice, deciding to write about one of the loves of his boyhood, the New York Yankees. The book Talese determined to write was to be called *The Stadium*, a small book (like *The Bridge*) that would not be about the famous Yankee baseball players, but about Yankee Stadium itself through the changing seasons and about the ordinary people who work there, "the businessmen who sell peanuts and popcorn," as Talese respectfully describes them.[30]

It was while researching this book in 1981 that Talese met Lee Iacocca. Both were sitting in George Steinbrenner's box during the World

Series, and both, they discovered, were sons of Italian immigrants. In October 1981, furthermore, the newspapers were full of predictions of Chrysler Corporation's imminent failure. What also captured Talese's attention was Iacocca's revelation that he had been keeping a diary since the time of his firing by Henry Ford II. Iacocca invited Talese to come to Detroit and to stay in his home. He asked Talese to write the Chrysler story, and Talese spent the next four months living and traveling with Iacocca. As the days went on this story got bigger and bigger; Talese would be telling the story of the son of an Italian immigrant who turned failure into one of the greatest of American success stories. It was thus beginning to run against his artistic grain.

On December 21, 1984, I received a telephone call from Gay Talese. He had been sent an article I had written bearing the title of this chapter but only discussing his treatment of fathers and sons in the Joshua Logan article, *The Bridge*, and *The Kingdom and the Power*. He called to tell me that I was closer to the truth than I actually knew. He said he had dropped the biggest story of his career, the Iacocca story, in order to write what, for him, was an even bigger story, his own father-son story. "Iacocca was an Italo-American success story, but it was not my story," he told me, revealing more than *he* probably knew. "My father was going to be eighty and he might die without my having told his story."

Talese's forthcoming book, on which he has been working since February 1982, is the story of Italian immigration to America as told through his own family history. This book will not be the small book Talese's friends urged him to write. Its historical and geographical scope is even larger than that of *Thy Neighbor's Wife*, for he has traced his family name back to the fourteenth century and his father's southern Italian village back to the ancient Greeks. Indeed, Talese currently conceives of the work as two volumes, with himself as a major character.

How does Talese's father feel about this new volume, and what are Talese's chances for success, confronting head on, as he is, the major mythos of his work? Joseph Talese talks of this volume as "the Tenth Symphony," a characterization that throws down quite a gauntlet.[31] My own intuition is that Joseph Talese will get more than he anticipates, for I doubt that he is aware of the painful complexities of his son's feelings for him, feelings as intricate as any Talese has limned before.

On the one hand, there is the unmistakable love Talese bears for this proud father. "I know my own father has not let me down personally," he told me during our first interview in 1984. "The relationship even now is very strong with a feeling of both love and obligation on both sides." Although both his parents were strong-willed, complementing each other in their work in the family dress shop, it was his father to whom Talese turned when he was in need—"even for something to eat, like toast." Talese recounts an incident during his college days when his car broke down in Elkton, Maryland, almost 100 miles from home. He called his father, who said, "Stay there," and drove to help him.

But Talese also tells other stories, stories of an authoritative father, a father who marched his family up and down the Atlantic City boardwalk every Sunday and then took them to a movie, out of which he would invariably (and embarrassingly) march them after the film had barely begun, but begun enough to fail to reach his standards. In a draft of the "Prelude" to his new work Talese presents this portrait of a son in perpetual wonderment at the sources of confidence in his father, sources that the son could neither see nor tap:

I was olive-skinned in a freckled-faced town, and I felt unrelated even to my parents, especially my father, who was indeed a foreigner—an unusual man in dress and manner to whom I bore no physical resemblance and with whom I could never identify. . . .

My father . . . seemed during the war years to share none of my confused sense of patriotism. He joined a citizen's committee of shore patrolmen who kept watch along the waterfront at night, standing with binoculars on the boardwalk. . . . He made headlines in the local newspaper following his popular speech to the Rotary Club in which he reaffirmed his loyalty to the Allied cause, declaring that were he not too old for the draft (he was thirty-nine) he would proudly join the American troops at the front, wearing uniforms dedicatively cut and stitched with his own hands.

Trained as an apprentice tailor in his native village, and later an assistant cutter in a prominent shop owned in Paris by an older Italian cousin, my father arrived in Ocean City rather circuitously and impulsively in the spring of 1922 at the age of twenty with very little money, an extensive wardrobe, and the appearance of one who knew exactly where he was going, when in fact nothing was further from the truth. He knew no one in town, barely knew the language, and yet, with a self-assurance founded upon elements that have always mystified me—and nonetheless disturbed me—he adjusted to this unusual island as readily as he could cut cloth to fit any size and shape.[32]

Talese follows this passage with an outline of what will come:

1) further explanation of father/son conflict . . . The resoluteness of the father, the clarity of his vision, the optimism in spite of setbacks, the unending commitment to my welfare and betterment—all these things, instead of inspiring within me admiration and contentment, separated us further. I wore *his* style in my clothes, listened to *his* music, demonstrated obedience and respect in ways that were outwardly convincing to him, if not to the quiet rebel I was soon becoming. . . . I did accept his many favors—and were it not for him, I would never have escaped the island, gained entrance to a university, etc. But all these favors, I knew, came at a cost. There would come a day when the

debts would be repaid; he would hardly have to ask, so aware was I of what was expected. And, of course, the day came when I did what was expected.

Whether Talese will resolve the father-son conflict in his forthcoming Italian family history is the central critical question. Will he be able to rise above his current defiant, eye-to-eye posture to be able to write of his family as Eugene O'Neill wrote of his own *Long Day's Journey Into Night*: "with deep pity and understanding and forgiveness for *all* the . . . haunted Tyrones"?[33]

And will the odyssey he recounts be of American success, failure, or some bittersweet vintage in between? Talese, who made his career by writing of the unnoticed, misunderstood, and forgotten people of society with whom he profoundly identifies, has by so doing left their ranks and become, by practically any measure, a success. Can he accept this and write of filial victory? "I'm not at all concerned with the mythology of fame and success but with the real *soul* of success and the bitterness of attaining and the heartbreak of not attaining it," he told *Playboy* in 1980 (116). To this degree, Gay Talese is an American histor, crafting "stories with real names" in the tradition of William Dean Howells, Theodore Dreiser, Sinclair Lewis, and his beloved F. Scott Fitzgerald.

2

Tom Wolfe's American Jeremiad

> There's such a yearning in everybody—there always has been—for
> blind faith. . . . And people always want it, one way or another,
> me included, although I hide it from myself, as do most people
> who think they are really sophisticated and learned.[1]
>
> Tom Wolfe

To chart the artistic vision of Tom Wolfe is to chart quicksilver. He is
wary, and he is slippery. In 1966, when queried regarding his views on
the Vietnam War for an anthology presenting thoughts of the international writing community, Wolfe adroitly sidestepped personal commitment:

Dear Mr. Woolf and Mr. Baggeley,
   I predict your book will be marvelous stuff. Moralism is a foxhole for incom-
petents. I think everybody will be delighted to see all the writers screaming
Yes! or No! or Arrrgggggh! and jumping in there.   Best Wishes[2],

Wolfe was not about to jump into any foxhole himself. This personal
and professional diffidence is camouflaged in Wolfe's writing—one might
even say *compensated for*—by a sophisticated narrative technique: a
speaking in tongues, a cacophony of multiple points of view. Wolfe has
acknowledged that he tries to create his scenes from a triple perspective: the subject's point of view, that of other people watching, and his
own (Dundy 153). His daring technical virtuosity in shifting among these
conflicting perspectives, often from sentence to sentence, is what gives
the post-modernist zest to his "Rocket Scholarship" (Dundy 153).

Wolfe's personal diffidence and resultant interest in viewing and re-creating the world through others' eyes has led him to the role of Men-ippean satirist. Instead of declaring outright his own moral or intellec-tual position, he exposes the follies of others through a colloquy of their own outrageous voices. This removed stance has confused readers seeking to isolate Wolfe's views of his subjects. Is he praising or damn-ing Ken Kesey and the Merry Pranksters in *The Electric Kool-Aid Acid Test*, or John Glenn and the Mercury astronauts in *The Right Stuff*? As Dwight Macdonald wrote in his famous attack on Wolfe's "parajournal-ism": "Every boost [is] a knock. . . . With Wolfe for the defense you don't need a D.A." (4). Some have even wondered if Wolfe has a per-sonal or social vision at all.

My own view is that Wolfe has a strong social vision, one he is ad-dressing, like Gay Talese, more directly as his career progresses. It is the vision of an American Jeremiah. If Talese is a *histor*, Wolfe is a *rhetor*; his work illustrates the rhetorical strain in American literary nonfiction.

While pursuing his doctoral degree in American Studies at Yale, Wolfe discovered Max Weber, the German sociologist. Weber's writings pro-vided Wolfe with the framework for perceiving cultural movements in religious terms that he would apply with great effect in *The Electric Kool-Aid Acid Test, The Painted Word, The Right[eous] Stuff, From Bauhaus to Our House*, and in most of his shorter articles as well. Undoubtedly Weber's work would have appealed to Wolfe. His command of the con-crete details of cultural life was unsurpassed, and he sought to under-stand human motive from a "subjective" point of view, that is, "the investigator attempting to put himself in the actor's place" (Parsons xxiii). In addition, there was much in Weber's approach that was congenial to Wolfe's own American evangelicalism. Weber, in a sense, provided in-tellectual respectability for Wolfe's jeremian temperament. Wolfe found in Weber's *The Sociology of Religion* and *The Protestant Ethic and the Spirit of Capitalism* a derogation of socialism, an assertion of the seminal role of the middle (rather than lower) classes, and an evolutionary perspec-tive—all of which were congenial with his own Protestant (Presbyterian) orientation.[3] Even more compatible was Weber's stress on charismatic leadership and the power of Calvinistic aestheticism.

Sacvan Bercovitch has best described both the characteristics and im-pressive influence of *The American Jeremiad*. It is as part of this remark-able rhetorical legacy that the seemingly contradictory facets of Wolfe's writing can be understood. As Bercovitch explains, the American jere-miad was

a mode of public exhortation that originated in the European pulpit, was trans-formed in both form and content by the New England Puritans, persisted through the eighteenth century, and helped sustain a national dream through two hundred years of turbulence and change. The American jeremiad was a ritual designed to join social criticism with spiritual renewal. . . . (xi)

No prophet stressed repentance as much as Jeremiah. In 1679, according to Perry Miller, who has best described the dark, denunciatory side of the American jeremiad, a synod of leading Puritan clerics listed the colonies' errors under twelve general headings. Thereafter, Miller writes, preachers

would take up some verse of Isaiah or Jeremiah, set up the doctrine that God avenges the iniquities of a chosen people, and then run down the twelve heads, merely bringing the list up to date by inserting the new and still more depraved practices an ingenious people kept on devising. I suppose that in the whole literature of the world, including the satirists of imperial Rome, there is hardly such another uninhibited and unrelenting documentation of a people's descent into corruption. (15)

Miller has called the jeremiad America's first distinctive literary genre, and in this sense Wolfe is carrying forward America's earliest literary tradition.

The paradoxical other side of the American jeremiad, only recently given full appreciation by Bercovitch, is the optimistic sense of spiritual renewal that was always the context for the damnations. America's Jeremiahs could castigate unmercifully because they believed the people already "chosen" and the promise previously assured. Thus the paradoxical exultation that accompanied the lament, and that we feel when reading Wolfe's exhilarating twentieth-century excoriations. As an American Jeremiah, Wolfe has set himself to record the failings of both the status quo and most new-wave phenomena; yet, by seeking and chronicling each new social wave, he is simultaneously affirming that "there is no limit to the American trip" (EKAT 113). Like the other American Jeremiahs, he is pessimistic for the present but optimistic for the future. Tocqueville might have been describing Wolfe when he wrote of the "innumerable enthusiasts roaming the [American] land."

Wolfe's transformation of the Puritan sermon into Menippean satire—into a pandemonium of human voices—provides him a way of presenting the complexities and conflicting idolatries of his time. It also reveals his sense of "belatedness," to use Harold Bloom's term. Fortunately for Wolfe the American jeremiad itself has evolved from the specific religious narrative of our Puritan foreparents to the story of America itself (Bercovitch 69); thus such sticky elements of the original American covenant as Election and ultimate promise have been, for most citizens, quite literally lost. Wolfe is in a similar belated position.

As the epigraph to this chapter suggests, Wolfe wants to believe but is too "sophisticated and learned" to articulate his belief in an overtly religious form or forum. He is wary. He believes that "moralism is a foxhole for incompetents," a foxhole, moreover, that many of his readers wish to avoid. In 1966 he told an interviewer: "You can't approach a subject with a moral commitment and come up with something *new*. As soon as any approach has reached the stage that it takes on a moral tone it is already out of date—it's frozen" (Dundy 153). It can be satirized, he might have added. In writing his own manifesto for *The New Journalism* in 1973—an act he would later regret—Wolfe stressed that this form's innocence was its strength:

There were no manifestos, clubs, salons, cliques; not even a saloon where the faithful gathered, since there was no faith and no creed. [. . .] In this new journalism there are no sacerdotal rules; not yet in any case. [. . .] With any luck at all the new genre will never be sanctified, never be exalted, never given a theology.[4] (TNJ 23, 33, 35)

Wolfe is wary of codified belief and yet, I would say, he believes. The rhetorical form and diction of his work belie what he is shy to acknowledge. Wolfe's earliest articles are satires of hypocrisy and false idolatries, and I will devote a whole section to his most extensive harangue—that against "Culture" as false religion. The movement of Wolfe's vision has not only been toward more open and explicit use of the form and diction of the American jeremiad, but also from a more optimistic vision of the American future in *The Electric Kool-Aid Acid Test* (1968) to greater lamentation in *The Right Stuff* (1979) and after.

EARLY JEREMIADS

In June 1965, the same month *The Kandy-Kolored Tangerine-Flake Streamline Baby*, Wolfe's first collection of articles, appeared, his first jeremiad was unleashed in the pages of *The Saturday Evening Post*. "Down With Sin!" the article was forthrightly called, and in this wry satire of the "Sin Cult," the co-opting of sin by the middle class in order to escape the label *bourgeois*, Wolfe is able to clothe his condemnation in mock sophistication. "The need for a denunciation of sin occurred to me the other day," he begins, as if he were a Puritan divine:

I don't imagine there are more than two or three people in New York today—a couple of old Presbyterian preachers, maybe, but none of the younger ones—not more than two or three people in the whole town would take a public stand against Adultery. [. . .]
   Santa Barranza! I want to help all these people! [. . .] I want to tell all the

TV panelists and Presbyterian preachers they can come out against Adultery or any other sin when the spirit moves them, and nobody is going to look down on them. That isn't true, of course, but I think it would be reassuring to tell them that. [. . .] Mainly, though, I am just trying to encourage all these people to stop beating me over the head with their Wickedness like a pig bladder. [. . .] Relax! I want to say. It's not even Sin anymore. It's a cliché. It's a bourgeois convention. It's a _____.

Well, anyway, what is needed is some kind of suicidal Castro to raise the banner and come out against the Sin Fad. [. . .] It is a shocking position, but I will come out now, flatly, against Sin. Right now!

I am against Pride, Sloth, Greed, Envy, Lust, Gluttony and Anger! *La historia me absolva!* (12, 14)

Though suggesting here that the Sin *Fad* is passé, Wolfe is able to assert the ongoing seriousness of sin.

Within two weeks *The Kandy-Kolored Tangerine-Flake Streamline Baby* appeared, with its opening sentence asserting through denial an evangelistic metaphor. "I don't mean for this to sound like 'I had a vision' or anything," Wolfe begins, and proceeds to describe how his new writing style came to him during an all-night vigil.

"Las Vegas (What?) Las Vegas (Can't Hear You! Too Noisy) Las Vegas!!!!," the volume's opening article, begins on Sunday morning with Raymond, whose "total effect is that of an Episcopal divinity student" (5), mocking the Las Vegas crap shooters. However, Las Vegas has corrupted Raymond, as it has Clara, Abby, Earl, and Ernest, slightly tipsy senior citizens whom Wofe encounters reeling out of the Mint Casino at church time. Among the "baggage" they brought from Marshalltown, Iowa, Wolfe notes, was "the entire cupboard of Protestant taboos against drinking, lusting, gambling, staying out late, getting up late, loafing, idling, lollygagging around the streets and wearing Capri pants— all designed to deny a person short-term pleasures so he will center his energies on bigger, long-term goals" (20). The witty rhetorical sinking in this passage—"and wearing Capri pants"—should not keep readers from seeing that Wolfe is here tolling the headings of sin. Las Vegas is where these middle-class middle Americans seek in vain liberation from their Protestant heritage, Wolfe implies, and in his depiction it becomes an apocalyptic city inflaming the senses:

On the streets of Las Vegas, not only the show girls [. . .] but girls of every sort, including, especially, Las Vegas' little high-school buds, who adorn what locals seeking roots in the sand call "our city of churches and schools," have taken up the chic of wearing buttocks décolletage step-ins under flesh-tight slacks, with the outline of the undergarment showing through fashionably. (10)

The show girls in the latest nude extravaganza, the Casino de Paris, represent "sex riding the crest of the future," and in his description of this show's finale Wolfe's own lament for better times can be found in his allusion to Frank Lloyd Wright amid the apocalypse: "with one vast Project Climax for our times, Sean Kenny, who used to work with this fellow Frank Lloyd Wright, presses the red button and the whole ya-hooing harem, shrieking ooh-la-la amid the din, exits in a mushroom cloud" (18). "Las Vegas" is the template for many Wolfian pandemonia to come; indeed, Wolfe's obsessive dwellings on the flesh throughout his work should be understood as part of his Puritan temperament. "Las Vegas" ends with another image of Revelation, with a new Dunes sign "flaming-lake red on burning-desert gold" topping the *control* tower at the airport (28).

If *The Kandy-Kolored Tangerine-Flake Streamline Baby* begins with a vision of hellfire and damnation, its closing section shifts to New York City and its Jeremiahs. In "Putting Daddy On," Wolfe and his friend Parker descend into the "lower depths" of the East Side to redeem Ben, Parker's hippie son. Bewak, as Ben's fellow beats call him, has leaflets from the Gospel Teachers, but he lives in a room in which "the gas jets burn" (281, 283). Parker's attitude mirrors Wolfe's in "Down With Sin!" He comprehends it all, yet, employing sophisticated irony, still calls for zeal:

[Parker] understands why pot-smoking is sort of a religion. He understands Oneness, lofts, visions, the Lower East Side. He understands why Ben has given up everything. [. . .]

"What do you want me to tell your mother?"

"What do you mean?" Ben says. [. . .]

"Well, she's been praying for you again."

"Are you being funny?"

"No, it's true," says Parker. "She has been praying for you again. I hear her in the bedroom. She has her eyes shut tight, like this, and she is on her knees. She says things like, 'Oh dear Lord, guide and protect my Ben wherever he may be tonight. Do you remember, O Lord, how my sweet Ben stood before me in the morning so that I might kiss him upon his forehead in the early brightness? Do you remember, O Lord, the golden promise of this child, my Ben?' Well, you know, Bewak, things like that, I don't want to embarrass you."

"That was extremely witty," Ben says.

"What do you want me to tell her?" says Parker.

"Why don't you just go?" Ben says.

"Well, we're all going to be on our knees praying tonight, Bewak," says Parker. "So long, Bewak."

Down in the hallway, in the muddy tableau, Parker begins chuckling.

"I know what I'm going to tell Regina," he says. "I'm going to tell her Ben has become a raving religious fanatic and was down on his knees in a catatonic trance when we got there."

"What is all this about kneeling in prayer?" [Wolfe inquires.]

"I don't know," Parker says. "I just want everybody who is japping me to get down on their knees, locked in a battle of harmless zeal." (276, 284)

Parker's behavior is highly meaningful in terms of the jeremiad tradition. Jonathan Edwards's eighteenth-century revivalism placed special emphasis on prayer. Bercovitch notes that

Whereas the Puritan covenant renewals called the children of New England to their filial obligations, the Edwardian concerts of prayer sought to awaken all prospective American saints, north and south, to the state of their souls, the shortcomings of their society, and the destiny of their New World Canaan. (106)

Parker's projected prayer more than 200 years later bears the traits of Edwards's New Light entreaties. Benjamin was the name of one of Jeremiah's peoples, and Parker's prayer seeks to recall Ben to the "early brightness" of a former state of grace. It asks the Lord to recall the "golden promise of this child, my Ben," as well as to "guide and protect" him in the present and future. Parker's sense of being "chosen" is underscored by the instantaneous arrival of a taxi after his jeremiad, a New York City miracle he interprets as a "good augury," a "sign that you are on top of it in New York" (285). This is not an indication of mammon in Parker, as many contemporary readers might think. As Bercovitch again explains: "For Edwards as for the seventeenth-century clergy, personal salvation was linked to public success and both flowed into the process of the work of redemption" (103). Ben may be "Putting Daddy On" in this article, but Parker (and Wolfe) turn it into an occasion for a jeremiad.

The final article in *The Kandy-Kolored Tangerine-Flake Streamline Baby*, "The Big League Complex," returns once again to the "lower depths" and presents a literal Jeremiah. Although ignored, this American Jeremiah persists, and Wolfe's description, linking the Bible and the American flag, evokes the legacy:

A small and ancient man with a Bible, an American flag and a megaphone haunts the subways of Manhattan. He opens the Bible and quotes from it in a strong but old and monotonous voice. He uses the megaphone at express stops, where the noise is too great for his voice to be heard ordinarily, and calls for redemption. (334)

The Pump House Gang, Wolfe's second collection of articles published in 1968, also begins on a note of apocalypse and closes with a jeremiad. Los Angeles burning is the backdrop for Wolfe's Introduction, and he sounds the note of his stern Calvinistic forebears by warning that the "real apocalyptic future" was not Vietnam, as the intellectuals and politicians were insisting, but "ego extension, the politics of pleasure, the self-realization racket, the pharmacology of Overjoy" (14). In the opening, title article Los Angeles is still burning, yet the Pump House gang thinks it is "immune" from death and destruction, from "gods-own chronometer" (27, 39). In "King of the Status Dropouts" Hugh Hefner indicts himself with his repeated claims of living a "damned full life," while Wolfe notes the "sweet, modern, up-to-date *venery*" of Hefner's Chicago pleasure dome (69, 72, 77).

Wolfe closes *The Pump House Gang* with a direct jeremiad once again aimed at New York City: "O Rotten Gotham—Sliding Down into the Behavioral Sink." It is not only the title that recalls the rhetoric of Puritan divines. In his opening paragraph Wolfe seems to be tolling the twelve headings of sin as he describes the current state of American depravity: "And here [New Yorkers] are, turning bilious, nephritic, queer, autistic, sadistic, barren, hyped up, batty, sloppy, hot-in-the-pants, chancred-on-the-flankers, leering, puling, numb—the usual in New York, in other words, and God knows what else" (295). Wolfe's surrogate Jeremiah, anthropologist Edward T. Hall, admires the Church of the Epiphany next to a pile of rubble in Harlem. He tells Wolfe "the handwriting is already on the wall" (308). In his own voice Wolfe continues the imagery of doom: "Until people can actually see the smoke or smell the sulphur or feel the sting in their eyes, politicians will not get excited about it, . . . " (302). In the end he pictures himself sliding into the sink.

CULTURE AS RELIGION

Wolfe rails against numerous vanities and idolatries in his writings, but his most extensive jeremiads have been against the transformation of Culture (Art) into religion. Wolfe first noticed the phenomenon when watching Robert Frost at the 1960 Kennedy inauguration. He described it in a 1962 article titled "Those Improbable Pals, TV and Books." Noting that a poet had joined "the succession of Catholic, Protestant, Jewish and Greek Orthodox clergymen who took to the lectern to call down their deities' logo of approval upon the [inaugural] ceremonies," Wolfe continued:

With shrewd divination, the President had invited a representative of a religion that has picked up thousands of devotees, many of them highly educated, in the last 10 years alone, a body of true belief known popularly as Culture. For untallied numbers of Americans, Culture—the Hiroshige prints, the mid-morning fugues on the good-music stations, the roundtable discussions of the Irish Renaissance in fiction, the coffee houses, the L.S.D. novelists, the Danish pot throwers and so on—had become not merely like a religion, but the real article. (3)

Wolfe's method of undercutting this idolatry is to point to the unholy alliances and disturbing trends within this belief. Books, he notes, are the scriptures of the religion of Culture, and television has always been the enemy, the anti-Christ. Now, however, librarians have gone to the anti-Christ to promote their wares. Perhaps not surprisingly, this alliance has produced not quite what the librarians expected: "there is no assurance that these books are read at all. They may merely be looked at, felt, rubbed, kept near the breast; in short, used as totems between times when the natives' true corpus of divinity, Dennis the Menace or Matt Dillon, appears to his followers" (3).

Wolfe pursues this theme in "A Feast of Tempting Titles And That Supermarket Trance," a 1963 article on paperback book stores. Observing the rapt gazes of paperback browsers, Wolfe attributes the success of the new paperback stores to their re-creation of the atmosphere of a "good cathedral or wayside chapel":

What we are watching, [. . .] then, are true believers in a hypnotized attitude of communion, secure in a sanctuary [. . . .] The scriptures, by the thousands, are already on the shelves, the liturgical music plays, and the faithful are all around. Lacking only is a focal symbol: a sanctum, lined with blown-up Roualts from the Skira books and mystical devices by Salvador Dali, with the till disguised as a crypt and supported by caryatids of Wilkie Collins and Walter Savage Landor.

True, later on there will be schisms, but the stores that move in fastest with the mostest will endure. For one thing, they can always spot the heretics and apostates right off. (3)

They will catch them, Wolfe suggests, because heretics will have the self-assertion to blink.

Wolfe's most vehement and sophisticated early jeremiad against Culture as religion is found in a December 1966 *Saturday Evening Post* Speaking Out column titled "The Courts Must Curb Culture." By 1966 Wolfe is declaring that "Culture—the arts and letters—has become *the* major religion of the educated classes in this country" (10). Indeed, he asserts, the religion of Culture has debased the Puritan doctrine of the elect: "For 'saved' substitute 'cultured,' 'artistic' or 'intellectual' and you have thousands, perhaps millions, of people in American cities who seek solace on an isle of the mind" (10). Solace for Wolfe and the American Jeremiahs must be founded on sterner, more righteous stuff. Wittily basing his argument on the constitutional separation of church and state, Wolfe insists that since Culture is now a religion, tax funds should not be used for the construction of such "culture temples" as public museums, opera houses, and art centers.

Dissenting Protestants repeatedly sought to ground their faith in the

truths of their own experience, and part of Wolfe's criticism of Culture
as false religion is that it ignores the actual experience of Americans.
He closes his jeremiad with a modest proposal that reveals both the
preservative and expansionary facets of his rhetoric:

Would the keepers of Culture be willing to make a supreme sacrifice? Would
they be willing to give up their grand design for preserving the totems of 19th-
century Europe in the new culture temples and give entry to some of the culture forms Americans really care about? It is a scary idea—but one day they
might try opening the door and letting in the America of 1966. (12)

Wolfe's jeremiads were not only against Culture per se as a false religion; he began to single out specific cultural forms for individual attack. In "The Saturday Route," published in *The Kandy-Kolored Tangerine-Flake Streamline Baby*, he presents the Saturday society promenade
through Manhattan art galleries as a debased Sunday processional. "In
New York there is the new religion, Art," he writes. "In New York, on
the Saturday Route, they give each other New York's newest grace, the
Social Kiss" (KK 224–225). John Marion, the auctioneer at Parke-Ber-
net, "chants in his pulpit" and "Society, the bright young people, the
celebrities, Seventh Avenue, the vergers, the beadles, the heirophants
are bubbling up on all sides" (228, 229). Wolfe indicts both this idolatry
and the decline of the church in noting that "the Route through the
art galleries bears approximately the same relation to Art as churchgoing, currently, bears to the Church. Formerly, Saturday was the big
day for the collectors. Now they come around knowingly Tuesday
through Friday, avoiding 'the mob' " (227).

With his Calvinist's eye for status, Wolfe cannot fail to note the irony
of the new religion's hierarchy. In "The New Art Gallery Society," which
chronicled the reopening of the Museum of Modern Art in 1964, he
notes that while the Museum walls bear the enlarged signatures of the
"entire pantheon" of modern art deities—Picasso, Matisse, Cezanne,
Braque, Jackson Pollack, Robert Rauschenberg—outside, poor artists
are picketing (251). Inside, the 600 "leading artists" invited to the opening
are kept in the dark on the terrace, "like sacred monsters in a pen,"
while only twelve of their number are among the true illuminati, the
society leaders and politicians who are invited to the dinner (252).

Idolizing the Art elite and the elite's idolatry of Art are further un-
masked in "The Shockkkkkk of Recognition," a subtle satire deserving
more attention from readers and critics. Published in *The Pump House
Gang*, this artful article switches back and forth between a photographer fawning over his idol, actress Natalie Wood, and Wood's own
fawning over Courbets, Monets, Corots, and Toulouse-Lautrecs. While
the reader immediately deplores the photographer's primitive efforts

to capture Natalie Wood's image, "jerking into jungle-cat crouches, batting all over the sidewalk, emitting groans, gurgles, directions, supplications," Wolfe makes us see that her art collecting is merely a higher class version of the same impulse (282).

"The painting frame had replaced the cross as a religious symbol" Wolfe laments in *In Our Time* (48). *The Painted Word* (1975), a travesty of "the Word made flesh," is Wolfe's most extensive jeremiad against this substitution. During a 1980 interview Wolfe noted that "It is the fulfillment of a prophecy made by Max Weber, who said that in the twentieth century, *aesthetics* would replace *ethics* as the standard for moral conduct" (Flippo 37). *From Bauhaus To Our House* (1981) is Wolfe's jeremiad against the false jeremiad of socialist architecture. What appears to annoy Wolfe most about the International Style of architecture is that its bareness, severity, and emphasis on purity strike familiar Puritan chords, yet it arose from European socialism rather than from the American experience. In 1981 Wolfe sees no real apostates on the artistic horizon except himself, and the volume ends with Wolfe the lone voice crying in the wilderness over which shines the false European light rather than America's true Whitmanian sun: "The outside world remained as out of it as ever. The new masses still struggled in the middle-middle ooze. The bourgeoisie was still baffled. The light of the Silver Prince still shone here in the Radiant City. And the client still took it like a man."

EXPANDING THE LEGACY:
THE ELECTRIC KOOL-AID ACID TEST

Crucial to appreciating Wolfe as an American Jeremiah is recognition that "expansion" and "revolution" have been essential elements in the jeremian legacy. American history, in fact, often involved expansion *through* revolution. As Bercovitch vividly documents, at the end of the seventeenth century the descendants of the original Puritans, who were legally granted the status of the Elect by the Halfway Covenant of 1662,

were being forced by history to enlarge their ideal of New Israel into a vision that was so broad in its implications, and so specifically American in its application, that *it could survive the failure of theocracy*. . . . During the 18th century, the meaning of Protestant identity became increasingly vague; . . . what passed for the divine plan lost its strict grounding in Scripture; "providence" itself was shaken loose from its religious framework to become part of the belief in human progress. The Yankee Jeremiahs took advantage of this movement "from sacred to profane" to shift the focus of figural authority. In effect, they incorporated Bible history into the American experience. . . . (92, 93 emphasis added)

Jonathan Edwards was the most famous of these Yankee Jeremiahs, and he and his New Light revivalists occupy a position in the unfolding American story not unlike Wolfe's own. Edwards began his revivals at the time when the colonies were experiencing spectacular economic growth parallel to the economic boom Wolfe has observed in America after World War II. By 1740 the general living standard in the colonies seems to have equaled or surpassed that of any European nation (Bercovitch 115). This was the time of the emerging moneyed middle class, and Edwards, much like Wolfe today, "neither broke with the Puritans nor aligned himself with them, but molded their myth to fit the needs of his own times" (Bercovitch 105). Edwards's revivalist conversions had the effect of expanding the body of the Elect to include potentially "every White Protestant believer" (Bercovitch 106). The revivalism of the Second Great Awakening in the nineteenth century continued this expansion of the potential Elect, and, I suggest, the clearest reason for Wolfe's championing of custom car designers, stock car racers, demolition derby drivers, and other traditionally scorned American cultural subgroups is his wish to continue this expansion, to include them in the American mainstream.

"Revolution" has been part of this progress. As Bercovitch once again has noted, for the American Puritans "the church was advancing toward New Jerusalem through a series of revolutionary upheavals. Each upheaval constituted a revolution in itself, but all were linked in an ascending spiral" (133). Here we see the evolutionary perspective embedded in Christian, and particularly Protestant, thought. From the first, American ministers and politicians cast the Revolutionary War as a spiritual as well as political revolution and "acid test," and made a careful distinction between *revolution* and *rebellion*. Readers often think that Wolfe is championing social rebels in his books and articles. For him, I submit, they are generally *revolutionaries* in the most American sense of the word.

The Electric Kool-Aid Acid Test, published in 1968, represents one of Wolfe's most hopeful portraits of American revolutionaries, revolutionaries with the potential for expanding the American experience in the twentieth century. In many respects, however, the volume is a traditional jeremiad, for it revels in American failure as well as promise.

Wolfe's optimism can be seen in his equation of his story of Ken Kesey and the Merry Pranksters with the major movements in religious history. In Chapter III, after Kesey has accused Gleason of having "no faith," Wolfe writes in his own voice:

Faith! Further! And it is an exceedingly strange feeling to be sitting here in the Day-Glo, on poor abscessed Harriet Street, and realize suddenly that in this improbable crazy ex-pie factory Warehouse garage I am in the midst of Tsong-

Isha-pa and the sangha communion, Mani and the wan persecuted at The Gate, Zoroaster, Maidhyoimaongha and the five faithful before Vishtapu, Mohammed and Abu Bekr and the disciples amid the pharisaical Koreish of Mecca, Guatama and the brethren in the wilderness leaving the blood-and-kin families of their pasts for the one true family of the sangha inner circle—in short, true mystic brotherhood—only in poor old Formica polyethylene 1960s America without a grain of desert sand or a shred of palm leaf or a morsel of manna wilderness breadfruit overhead, picking up vibrations from Ampex tapes and a juggled Williams Lok-Hed sledge hammer, hooking down mathematical lab drugs, LSD-25, IT-290, DMT, instead of soma water. (31–32)

Many readers have noted this religious equation, but no one has yet documented how carefully millenarian possibilities are planted in the text. Indeed, like Talese's *Honor Thy Father*, the volume becomes a Christian typology with Kesey as Christ, Faye as Mary, Mountain Girl as Mary Magdalene, the Pranksters as the disciples, and Sandy as Judas.[5]

While Kesey is depicted variously throughout the volume as Esau, when he has sold his birthright and is living in Mexico (332); as Moses, when he leads his "people" out of the Cow Palace before the "snap" (214); and even as St. Paul, in his religious fit on the sands in Mexico (341), he is most frequently presented as a Christ figure. Wolfe increases Kesey's stature from the beginning by delaying his entrance until Chapter III, thus making him, like Christ, long awaited and greatly anticipated. Kesey looks "serene" on his arrival and explains to Wolfe, "I think my value has been to help create the next step" (8). Kesey then proceeds to speak in diction immediately suggestive of Christ's. "If you don't realize that I've been helping you with every fiber in my body," Kesey says, but "in a soft, far-off voice, with his eyes in the distance" (30). "If you don't realize that everything I've done, everything I've gone through . . . " he says, breaking off, as if he were Jesus trying to make his disciples understand his mission. As the story continues Wolfe explains that "Kesey took great pains not to make his role explicit. He wasn't the authority, somebody else was," and his teachings are all "cryptic, metaphorical; parables, aphorisms" (131). At La Honda the Pranksters take all dissension to him, "all of them forever waiting for Kesey, circling around him" (166), and at a moment of crisis "Kesey materializes at the critical moment" and "delivers a line—usually something cryptic, allegorical, or merely descriptive, never a pronouncement or a judgment, [. . .] and just as suddenly he's gone" (166). Indeed, like Jesus, Kesey is the leader, provider, and protector of his "flock."

As Wolfe unfolds the Kesey saga his diction continues the Christian typology. Kesey is taken as a prophet by the Unitarians and others (199, 402). He absents himself in the desert and returns with a new "gospel."

While he is absent Wolfe quotes Hesse to the effect that "from that time, certainty and unity no longer existed in our community, although the great idea still kept us together" (280). Wolfe asserts that "sooner or later Kesey would reunite with the Pranksters" (316), and when he does it is with the ultimate goal of presenting himself "in the flesh," delivering the "vision of the future," and then vanishing, ascending "into the California ozone" (385). In a climactic scene in the garage Kesey looks distraught when people can't get near him as they circle around him "through the darkness toward the cone of light lighting up [his] head and back" (419).

If Kesey is Christ, Wolfe offers Faye to us as Mary. She is "Faye the eternal" (141), "Faye, the eternal beatific pioneer wife" (58), "one of the prettiest, most beatific-looking women I ever saw [. . .] radiant, saintly" (26), "practically a madonna of the hill country" (37). Mountain Girl is Mary Magdalene. Wolfe avers that only Kesey "truly understood Mountain Girl [. . .] it never occurred to anybody that a whole side of her was hidden. Except Kesey" (173). The Pranksters, of course, become the disciples, with Babbs the favored disciple, but others, like Hassler, preaching and offering "vesper service lecture[s]" (21). The Kool-Aid LSD becomes the modern equivalent of the sacramental wine, and even the police are given a part in Wolfe's biblical "movie." It is the role of Pontius Pilate of the Acid Tests: "Christ, man! It's too much for us even! We wash our hands of this ::::: Atrocity" (297).

Kesey and the Pranksters have considerable success in their religious crusade. The Unitarian youths, representing the "student rebels in an age of mediocrity," are drawn around the bus, and several of their ministers, the "Young Turks," get "on the bus for good," that is, become true revolutionaries rather than rebels (195, 200). Indeed, at Paul Sawyer's Unitarian Church

hundreds were swept up in *an experience*, which builds up like a dream typhoon, peace on the smooth liquid centrifugal whirling edge. In short, everybody in The Movie, on the bus, and it was beautiful . . . They were like . . . *on!* the Pranksters—now primed to draw the hundreds, the thousands, the millions into *the new experience*, and in the days ahead they came rushing in :::::.(284)

The bus, "Further," is carefully elevated through Wolfe's diction from a literal 1939 International Harvester bus to the major metaphor for expanded revolutionary consciousness in 1960s America. Yet, as in all jeremiads, this vision of promise is only half the picture. Wary Jeremiah that he is, Wolfe seems to harbor doubts regarding the efficacy of this new drug-centered millennium. Rather than discussing outright his doubts or ambivalence, however, he plants in his text all sorts of reservations regarding his religious figures and symbols, with the result that, as in all jeremiads, he seems to be both damning and celebrating his subjects.

"Further," the bus, for example, has no brakes (74) and frequently breaks down (76, 323). Furthermore, conditions "on the bus" are not always euphoric. Jane Burton is nauseated practically the whole time, and she and Sandy have to get "off the bus" to get a square meal (84, 92). Sleep, too, is "almost impossible" on the bus (84), and as the receiver and transmitter of American culture, the bus (and thus America in the 1960s) is depicted as a "pressure cooker" and a "crucible" (92).

Perhaps as a result, Wolfe's twentieth-century neo-religious odyssey is tarnished by "bad trips" from start to finish. Some of the Hell's Angels, Wolfe tells us, "had terrible bummers—bummer was the Angels' term for a bad trip on a motorcycle and very quickly it became the hip world's term for a bad trip on LSD" (184). A young Unitarian freaks out on her first LSD capsule and "starts wailing away," but fortunately the Pranksters are able to redeem her (199). Her "wails," however, foreshadow those of the "Who Cares Girl," who is not restored (294). In fact, Clair's rather positive account of the Watts "trip" is substantially undercut by the episode involving the "Who Cares Girl," and also by the disturbing detail that seven persons were committed after this first big "test" (296). Even the manufacturers of LSD, the "Mad Chemist" and Owsley, undergo "bad trips" in the course of the volume—the Mad Chemist becoming "loose in the head, [. . .] his brains all run[ning] together like goo" (218), and Owsley (perhaps symbolically) ending up in a car wreck. Indeed, the accident and mortality rate is high in *The Electric Kool-Aid Acid Test* with injuries to Julius Karpin and Mike Hagen (330), paralysis for Norman Hartweg, death at age thirty-two for Ron Boise (331), and, most ominously, for the "Gestalt driver," Neal Cassady, whose body is found, again symbolically, beside a railroad track.

These accumulating "bum trips" function as ominous counterpoint balancing the promise implied in Wolfe's religious analogy. Wolfe's cautions regarding the LSD movement are also conveyed through his extensive development of Sandy Lehmann-Haupt's perspective. The most compelling conflict in the volume is that between Kesey and Sandy, the only Prankster "on the bus" who ever extensively doubts or challenges Kesey. To return to the Christian typology, Sandy represents Judas. He betrays Kesey by stealing the Ampex, "the guts of the Acid Test." Through religious diction Wolfe places this theft in religious context:

to the Pranksters there was not the slightest doubt in the world that the equipment was the Pranksters'. Not Prankster Sandy Lehmann-Haupt's but the Pranksters'. The Prankster family, the Prankster order superseded all straight-world ties, contracts and chattel laws and who is my mother or my brethren? And he looked round about on them which sat about him, and said, Behold

my mother and my brethren! For whosoever shall do the will of God, the same
is my brother, and my sister, and my mother. (359)

Sandy views the Ampex as the "Prankster salvation machine" (239),
and Kesey, like Christ, has a foreboding of his betrayal (336).

Wolfe gives considerable attention and sympathy to Sandy's perspective—his bad trip on the bus and his reservations regarding Kesey—
and this serves to create doubts in the reader's mind about Kesey's vision. Indeed, Wolfe's intensive identification with Sandy is relevant in
respect to the lack of development of his own narrative persona in *Acid
Test*. Wolfe seems to have elected Sandy to speak for him. Sandy's role
in *The Electric Kool-Aid Acid Test* is that of ambivalent straddler of the
"sheerly Diluvial divide." He is, by turns, "on the bus" and "off the
bus," just as Wolfe is as he switches through his substitutionary narration from pro-Kesey/LSD perspective to anti. As a wary American Jeremiah, Wolfe is never swept away by the New Age phenomena he is
chronicling. Dangerous excesses or failures of vision are mercilessly
rendered in his texts. At the end of the Kesey saga, for example, the
superhero falls victim to the same fate as those he had helped in his
childhood. He is run off the highway. In a work in which the road
represents the course of America, this tableau is significant. Though
Wolfe makes clear that Kesey is on the farthest "edge" of new consciousness—Hassler sitting on the edge of the highway on the edge of
the bay, while Kesey runs through the "last blasted edge of land you
can build houses on before they just sink into the ooze and compost"
(387, 388)—he also suggests that Kesey has been overcome by the co-
matose American mainstream he had sought to change. This is apparent through the diction of hypnotism used in this final sequence. Kesey
is caught in the Bayshore freeway during rush hour:

shiny black-shoe multitudes are out in their 300-horsepower fantasy cars head-
ing into the rush hour, out the freeway, toward the waiting breezeway slots.
It's actually peaceful, this rush hour.[. . .] It's relaxing, the rush hour is, and
hypnotic, it drones [. . .] and [Kesey] takes off his disguise.[. . .] The cops
keep floating abreast grimacing and flapping, and drifting back and pulling
even again.[. . .] The great swarms of cars with hard-candy tails keeps sailing
past, hypnotically. (386–387)

Ultimately Kesey and his new religious vision are not powerful enough
to overcome the droning hypnotism of the American status quo.

Wolfe records the failings of each new revolutionary wave, yet he is
even more negative about this status quo. As John Hellmann has per-
ceptively noted, "[Wolfe's] insistent choices of hyperbolic, kinetic, or
baroque words and phrases make his descriptions as much an assault

as a representation. . . . These stylistic traits work like those of the cubists to break up the reader's usual modes of perception" (106). Practically *any* new mode of perception, *any* sensory flourish, is preferable to the status quo to Wolfe. Thus in both style and subject matter he seeks to expand American modes of perception.

Wolfe's kinetic prose can also be linked to Samuel Richardson's eighteenth-century experiments with what he called "spontaneous writing." Davis has reminded us that Richardson's real innovation was in making his fictive letters seem to be written by the parties themselves "at the very time in which the events happened" (182). Lovelace, in *Clarissa*, describes this technique as a "lively present tense manner," and it seems clear that Wolfe's substitutionary narration and his verbal and visual pyrotechnics are efforts to press this frontier even farther, to decrease the cognitive space between language and reality—to simulate :::::::: the day-glo consciousness! As with Richardson, language in Wolfe replaces reality. The distance between the reader and the text is further foreshortened as well.

Wolfe's criticisms of Kesey and other new wave phenomena should be understood, then, in the context of his larger denunciation of the American status quo. That Wolfe feels the tragedy of Kesey's failed experiment is suggested in the emblematic story of "the kid with the boiling teeth":

A dead towhee and a rumpled road and lying in the dust, a *mistake* . . . a *mistake*, but it's not important . . . Making a mistake is not *important* . . . it's the context in which the mistake is made. . . . A rumpled road and a dead towhee [i.e., the psychedelic movement] and four gasoline stations, white and sterile, refueling tailfins in mid-air for fat men in sunglasses who do not see the rumpled road and the dead towhee. (417)

Wolfe's role as an American Jeremiah is to make us see the rumpled road and the dead towhee. Yet, true to the double-nature of his calling, he holds out promise at his volume's end, for the best way that ambivalent bus should be taken is as a symbol of potential. Kesey and the psychedelic world may indeed have "blown it," but the final vision Wolfe gives us is not of Kesey's defeat, or of Neal Cassady's ominous death—although they are close by—but of the spring, and the return of the faithful, and, most of all, of Further the bus parked beside the house, like Wolfe, ready to go once again.

LATER JEREMIADS AND *THE RIGHT STUFF*

"Through Kesey's life and the Pranksters, you could show the heart of the whole psychedelic experience, and the whole religious movement of the Sixties," Wolfe told an interviewer in 1981 (Gilder 42). During the 1970s and 1980s Wolfe continued his exhortations regarding religion in America; indeed, his movement has been toward more direct engagement of the form and diction of the jeremiad.

The structure of "Three Merry Obsessions: Crime, Sex, Salvation," which appeared in the Christmas 1973 issue of *Esquire*, underscores the theme of sin and renewal. The final section, "Salvation," begins with a scene of pandemonium. At a Saturday night head dance in San Francisco a girl rips off her shirt and dances bare-breasted. The other dancers are reaching "the point of madness" when handwriting (once again) flashes on the wall: "WILL GOD PLEASE COME UP ON STAGE?" (201). Wolfe's point, as usual, is double-edged. Although he deplores the fact that seventeen of "the most blissfully twisted men and women" respond to this call and that "salvation" has become an idolatrous obsession itself, the plea for a genuine jeremiad, for the real appearance of God on the stage, still holds.

This scene, Wolfe declares, was the beginning of the Third Great Awakening, and as Wolfe continues he expounds revealingly on Jonathan Edwards and his fellow enthusiasts:

The First Great Awakening, as it is known to historians, came in the 1740's and was led by preachers of "the New Light" such as Jonathan Edwards, Gilbert Tennant and the hottest of them all, George Whitefield. They and their followers were known as "enthusiasts" and "come-outers," terms of derision referring to the frenzied, holy-rolling, pentecostal shout tempo of their services and to their visions, trances, shrieks and agonies. (308)

This last phrase rather precisely describes Wolfe's own rhetorical style. The Second Great Awakening, he continues, "took the form of a still wilder hoedown camp-meeting revivalism, of ceremonies in which people barked, bayed, fell down in fits and swoons, talked in tongues and even added a touch of orgy" (308). Though he may seem here to be mocking this behavior, Wolfe actually finds such American revivalism essential to the nation's progress:

The Second Great Awakening's mixture of fervor and Christian asceticism played a major role in the settlement of the West and helped create the atmosphere (known as "bleak" east of Rahway, New Jersey) of much of rural America. And the Third Great Awakening? [. . .] We will be able to start toting up the score about 1980. (310)

By 1976 Prophet Wolfe seemed to feel that his Third Great Awakening was in danger of being subverted by false rather than true believers, as he suggests in his famous essay "The Me Decade and the

Third Great Awakening." "In the beginning was LSD," he had written in "Salvation" (308), and in "The Me Decade" he notes that

without knowing it, many heads were reliving the religious fervor of their grandparents or great-grandparents—the Bible-Belting lectern-pounding Amen ten-finger C-major-chord Sister-Martha-at-the-keyboard tent-meeting loblolly pineywoods share-it-brother believers of the nineteenth century. (MG 151)

This psychedelic culture is replaced in the 1970s by believers who appear to continue the fervor. In fact, they seem to toll the headings of sin themselves:

They . . . all marched right up to the microphone and "shared," as the trainer called it. What did they want to eliminate from their lives? Why, they took their fingers right off the old repress button and told the whole room. My husband! my wife! my homosexuality! my inability to communicate, my self-hatred, self-destructiveness, craven fears, puling weaknesses, primordial horrors, premature ejaculation, impotence, frigidity, rigidity, subservience, laziness, alcoholism, major vices, minor vices, grim habits, twisted psyches, tortured souls—(MG 127)

Such personal scoriations could put a Jeremiah out of business! Yet, through hyperbolic simulation and final rhetorical sinking, Wolfe casts doubt on the righteousness of the whole enterprise:

"AAAAAAAAARRRRRRRGGGGGGGGHHHHHHHH!"
—which is not simply *her* scream any longer . . . but the world's! Each soul is concentrated on its own burning item—[repeated tolling of vices]—and yet each unique item has been raised to a cosmic level and united with every other until there is but one piercing moment of release and liberation at last!—a whole world of anguish set free by—
My hemorrhoids. (MG 131–32)

Self-obsession, rather than righteous action as one of God's Elect, appears to be the source of this Awakening. Such revivalists are putting Me rather than God on stage (MG 147). The result, Wolfe notes, is hardly American expansion. "There is no ecumenical spirit within this Third Great Awakening," he complains. "If anything, there is a spirit of schism" (MG 164).

In "The Intelligent Coed's Guide to America," published the same year, Wolfe offers Aleksandr Solzhenitsyn as the true Jeremiah of the Seventies. According to Wolfe, Solzhenitsyn's *Gulag Achipelago* answered those New York socialist intellectuals famous for castigating "the booboisie, the Herd State, the United States of Puritanism, Philistinism, Boosterism, Greed, and the great Hog Wallow" (MG 119) with his testament that "not only Stalinism, not only Leninism, not only Communism—but socialism itself led to the concentration camps; and not only socialism, but Marxism; and not only Marxism but any ideology that sought to reorganize morality on an *a priori* basis" (123). Solzhenitsyn, however, is denigrated in the press as a "Christian zealot" (MG 123), and Wolfe notes that he suffers the fate of other Jeremiahs. He is ignored. Like the dissenting Protestants, however, Wolfe will insist morality be organized—not *a priori*—but on the basis of personal experience. He closes "The Intelligent Coed's Guide to America" with a poetic plea for more sermonizing, and for the "heresy" of personal experience:

> Will you sermonize
> On how perceiving
> Is believing
> The heresy of your own eyes?

According to Wolfe, it was Jimmy Carter's *lack* of sermonizing that led to the defeat of his presidency. Elected as an evangelical "born again" Baptist, Carter "never seemed to understand the power that flowed through his pineywood veins," Wolfe wrote in *In Our Time* (1980): "He dissipated the power and the glory and threw away all his trump cards. The people yearned for hallelujah, testifying, and the blood of the lamb, and he gave them position statements from the Teleprompter" (11).

Wolfe will never make this mistake, and in *The Right[eous] Stuff* (1979), he gives further portraits of true charismatic figures. The space race dominated the news in 1962, the year Wolfe arrived in New York City as a reporter, but he did not become truly absorbed in the subject until a decade later when reports surfaced indicating "trouble in paradise" among the astronauts, and that one of the astronauts had become—an evangelist (Flippo 33). *The Right Stuff* represents Wolfe's most direct celebration of "righteousness" and the Puritan doctrine of the Elect, yet, true to the jeremiad, it also conveys a sense of loss. Indeed, Wolfe's movement is from the greater optimism of *The Electric Kool-Aid Acid Test* to greater lamentation in *The Right Stuff*.

Wolfe equates his righteous pilots with the Puritan Elect. Like the original Elect, aviators

looked upon themselves as men who lived by higher standards of behavior than civilians, as men who were the bearers and protectors of the most important values of American life, who maintained a sense of discipline while civilians abandoned themselves to hedonism, who maintained a sense of honor while civilians lived by opportunism and greed. (39)

Although a righteous sense of superiority characterized the Puritan Elect, their election was fraught with continual trials—and always the fear that they were mistaken, that they were among God's damned rather than chosen. Such is also the case with Wolfe's aviator brethren, who, after demonstrating literal grace under pressure, had then to go up again "*the next day*, and the next day, and every next day, even if the series should prove infinite—and, ultimately, in its best expression, do so in a cause that means something to thousands, to a people, a nation, to humanity, to God" (24). Indeed, Wolfe may have been drawn to the fliers because they demonstrated *physically* the terms of the Calvinistic contract. Night landings on aircraft carriers, he writes,

were a routine part of carrier operations—and perhaps the best of all examples of how a man's accumulated good works did him no good whatsoever at each new step up the great pyramid, of how each new step was an absolute test, and of how each bright new day's absolutes—chosen or damned—were built into the routine. (389)

It is, therefore, not surprising that the young pilots try to test their condition. Wolfe writes that "They were like believing Presbyterians of a century before who used to probe their own experience to see if they were truly among *the elect*" (30).

Settings become symbolic in *The Right Stuff* as American action shifts from the sacred wilderness of Chuck Yeager's Muroc Field to the progressively more profane tableaus of Cocoa Beach and Houston. Wolfe depicts Muroc (later Edwards Air Force Base) as a New World landscape, and Yeager and his brethren as having, like the Puritans, a special errand in the wilderness:

Air Force and Navy airfields were usually on barren or marginal stretches of land and would have looked especially bleak and Low Rent to the ordinary individual in the chilly light of dawn. [. . .] The enterprise the Army had undertaken in this godforsaken place was the development of supersonic jet and rocket planes. [. . .] Muroc seemed like an outpost on the dome of the world, open only to a righteous few, closed off to the rest of humanity, including even the Army Air Force brass of command control. (37, 49, 50)

Wolfe maintains that his aviators came from "native" or "old settler" stock (421), and that "for a good five years" the "holy plateau" of Muroc "remained primitive and Low Rent, with nothing out there but the bleached prehistoric shrimp terrain and the rat shacks and the blazing sun and the thin blue sky and the rockets sitting there moaning and squealing before dawn" (65, 300).[6] The Russian rocket Sputnik in 1958, and the Mercury Space Program that swiftly follows, change this New Canaan. First-time readers are likely to believe that *The Right Stuff* celebrates Chuck Yeager and the original "righteous stuff" and lampoons the Mercury Space Program and astronauts, but Wolfe's vision is more complex. His optimism as an American Jeremiah is shown in his suggestion that an elite few of the new generation of astronauts can show themselves worthy of Yeager's mantle.

These Elect are John Glenn, Scott Carpenter, and Gordon Cooper. In two interviews after the publication of *The Right Stuff* Wolfe expressed dismay at reviewers' reactions to his portrait of Glenn. "I've been surprised by the number of reviews that found my picture of John Glenn negative," he gold *Rolling Stone*. "I wasn't trying to send him valentines, but in my mind he came off as an exceptional and rather courageous figure. He did a lot of unpopular things" (Flippo 33). Acknowledging to the *Saturday Review* that Glenn came off to reviewers as the worst of the seven astronauts, he countered:

In my mind, I was presenting a rare and strangely colorful figure of our time. It's very rare to see a man in our day—outside the Church—who is a moral zealot and who doesn't hide the fact; who constantly announces what he believes in and the moral standards he expects people to follow. To me that's much rarer and more colorful than the Joe Namath-rake figure who is much more standard these days. (Gilder 44)

In short, Wolfe likes Glenn because he is a moral zealot—like Wolfe.

Such a Jeremiah is necessary when the Calvinist battle leaves the original wilderness for the more sinful site of Cocoa Beach. As if retracing American history, Wolfe writes:

Before the missiles came to the Cape, Cocoa Beach was a hard-shelled Baptist stronghold with more churches than gasoline stations, and practically all of them were of the pietistic or Dissenting Protestant variety. But the new Cocoa Beach, the Project Mercury boom town, was part of the new face of the 1960's: the little town whose life was completely keyed to the automobile. (168–69)

As in *The Electric Kool-Aid Acid Test*, cars become symbolic extensions of individual character. The less-than-holy coordinates of Drinking & Driving had existed even at Muroc Field as ways for pilots to prove that "the right stuff, being indivisible, carried over into any enterprise whatsoever, under any conditions" (36–37). Alan Shepard drives a Corvette; Wally Schirra, a Triumph, and Gus Grissom longs for a similar "hot car" to accompany the "Drinking & Driving & the rest"—meaning adultery—which seem to increase at Cocoa Beach. John Glenn, who lives in Spartan quarters, works out regularly, and drives a beat-up Peugeot, notes that "some of his confreres were loosening up" (164).

Glenn proceeds to act the role of Jeremiah in *The Right Stuff*. In fact, his background and saga are demonstrations of the continued efficacy of Calvinist election. Glenn grew up in New Concord, Ohio, the sort of town, Wolfe notes,

once common in America, whose peculiar origins have tended to disappear in the collective amnesia as *tout le monde* strives to be urbane. Which is to say, it began as a religious community. A hundred years ago any man in New Concord with ambitions that reached as high as feedstore proprietor or better joined the Presbyterian Church, and some of the awesome voltage of live Presbyterianism still existed when Glenn was growing up in the 1920's and 1930's. His father was a fireman for the B&O Railroad and a good churchgoing man and his mother was a hardworking churchgoing woman and Glenn went to Sunday school and church and sat through hundreds of interminable Presbyterian prayers, and the church and the faith and the clean living served him well. There was no contradiction whatsoever between the Presbyterian faith and ambition, even soaring ambition, even ambition grand enough to suit the invisible ego of the fighter jock. A good Presbyterian demonstrated his *election* by the Lord and the heavenly hosts through his success in this life. (134–35)

Glenn's wife, Annie, is described by Wolfe as "a Presbyterian pioneer wife living in full vitality in the twentieth century. She could deal with any five [of Lyndon Johnson's people] with just a few amps from the wrath of God when she was angry" (312).

When the astronauts first meet the press, Glenn speaks of his election, and after this meeting he emerges as first among the astronauts; his "light shone brightest" (121, 142). But Glenn's status seems to fall when he acts the role of Jeremiah to his backsliding Cocoa Beach brethren. "Could you believe," Wolfe writes from the point of view of the other astronauts, "that the day would come when you would actually see a pilot, an equal among equals, give his comrades a little sermon about keeping their hands clean and their peckers stowed? Where did he get off setting himself above them this way . . . ?" (174). Glenn is challenged by Alan Shepard, who "gave off the *aura* of a hot pilot" but is described by Wolfe as "probably stone atheist" (217, 172). However, in the peer vote that follows, Glenn's zeal loses him the first flight:

In the peer vote he was the prig who had risen at the seance like John Calvin himself and told them all to keep their pants zipped and their wicks dry. [. . .] He was the Harry Hairshirt who lived like an Early Christian martyr in the BOQ. He was the Willie Workadaddy who drove around in a broken-down Peugeot, like a lonely beacon of restraint and self-sacrifice in a squall of car crazies. (217)

This confrontation sets up a division in the astronaut corps. "It was the other five against the pious fair-haired boy [Glenn] and his sidekick, Carpenter," Wolfe writes (175), and once again he uses setting to communicate spiritual states. As Glenn drives home to tell Annie of his failure, "Even the scenery was depressing. There was nothing to see but the snow blowing over the road and the stunted countryside rolling by in slow motion. Between Langley and Arlington even the woods look stunted" (212).

Glenn's faith, however, sustains him through this setback. In fact, he "worked at being backup astronaut and charade master as if these were the roles the Presbyterian God had elected him to play" even when it becomes apparent that Shepard is not going to "get run over or break a leg or be struck down by an angry God" (229, 246). And God does work in mysterious ways. Even though Shepard demonstrates suitable righteous stuff during his flight, Glenn's later orbit vaults him to first place once again.

Like so many of Wolfe's works, *The Right Stuff* begins with an evocation of hellfire and death. In the opening chapter he presents a series of grotesque descriptions of aviators blistered, fried, "burned beyond recognition" (5, 8, 11, 12, 13, 15). After each death a supplication to God is made in the form of an old Navy hymn into which a stanza had been inserted especially for aviators: "O hear us when we lift our prayer for those in peril in the air" (11). John Glenn encounters his own peril during his orbital flight when it appears that his heat shield may come off during re-entry, causing him to "fry" (338). In fact, Wolfe depicts him as "inside of a ball of fire" (340), but Glenn places his faith in God and is delivered from the flames.

He returns to address a joint session of Congress where he seems to take on the role of evangelical preacher:

He was the Presbyterian Pilot addressing the world. [. . .] A couple of [senators and representatives] said, "Amen!" They said it out loud; it just came popping out of their good hardtack cracker evangelical dissenting Protestant hearts as the Presbyterian Pilot lifted up his eyes and his hand. . . . (345–46)

And Alan Shepard and Gus Grissom, who had flown the first two flights, "didn't know what the hell was happening. [. . .] even before John got back to the Cape from Grand Bahama Island, there was a note of worshipful swooning in the air that indicated that Al had not made the first flight, after all" (343). Glenn's righteousness triumphs. He "ascended to a status that only a Biblical scholar could fully appreciate," Wolfe writes as he compares him with David, who succeeds to the throne of Saul (362, 399).

Glenn's triumph is followed by the transfer of NASA (the National Aeronautics and Space Administration) from Cocoa Beach to Houston, and this move seems to signal that the battle for election continues, with victories won and lost in the final three chapters and Epilogue of the volume. Houston is supposed to be the new "Olympus" of the right stuff (391), but in Wolfe's depiction it is another scene of pandemonium. The astronauts step out of the airplane at the Houston airport "and started gulping in the molten air" (353). Five thousand Houstonians greet the astronauts at the Houston Coliseum, "amid the burning cattle" (356), and in this re-creation of Sodom and Gomorrah, Wolfe (as usual) allows the speaker's own words to convey his damnation:

It was always someone such as Herb Snout from Kar Kastle, and he would come up and say: "Hi, there! Herb Snout! Kar Kastle! Listen! We're damned glad to have you folks here, just damned glad, goddamn it!" [. . .]
    After a while, there were Herb Snouts and Gurney Frinks all over the place and the huge Hereford joints were sliding down every leg and splashing in the puddles of whiskey on the floor, and five thousand spectators watched their struggling jaws, and the smoke and the babble filled the air and the children screamed for mercy and relief. [. . .] It was two o'clock in the afternoon on the Fourth of July, and the cows burned on, and the whiskey roared *goddamned glad to see you* and the Venus de Houston [Sally Rand] shook her fanny in an utterly baffling blessing over it all. (357–58)

    The space program and the seven Mercury astronauts were supposed to "make Boom Town respectable, legitimate, a part of America's soul" (354). Wolfe writes that the parade for the astronauts was to signal "the start of the redemption of Houston" (354). But who is redeemed and who is damned Wolfe leaves up to the reader. Glenn's sidekick, Scott Carpenter, proves his election, at least in Wolfe's eyes, by his flight in his revealingly named capsule: "*Aurora 7* . . . *Aurora* . . . the rosy dawn . . . the dawn of the intergalactic age . . . the unknowns, the mystery of the universe . . . the music of the spheres" (380). Carpenter not only euphorically completes a dazzling checklist of scientific experiments and escapes his own burning (373), but he acts as if he "believed that the *astronaut*, the passenger in the capsule, was the heart and soul of the space program" (375).
    For his zeal Carpenter is damned by the engineers of NASA, as well as by fellow astronauts Deke Slayton, Gus Grissom, and others who— in Wolfe's depiction at least—appear to have failed election. Deke Slayton's own body has damned him to non-flight status, while Wolfe leaves little doubt that *he* believes Gus Grissom panicked in his flight. Wolfe defends Carpenter against the charges that he panicked in his. In fact, he suggests the irrational basis for these charges by equating them with "magical" primitive thinking:

But logic had nothing to do with it. One was in the area of magical beliefs now. In his everyday life doughty little Gus *lived* the life of the right stuff. He was a staunch bearer of the Operational banner. Here Gus's fate and Deke's fate came together. [. . .] They were both committed to the holy word: *operational*. Schirra was with them on this particular commitment, and Shepard threw his weight toward them, too, as did Cooper. (377)

Thus it is two against five once again, and Wolfe leaves little doubt that "The Operational Stuff" has little to do with the right[eous] stuff. Wally Schirra's stripped down, operational flight in *Sigma* 7, a name Wolfe denigrates as "a purely engineering symbol," clearly shows little of the imagination and risk that fires Wolfe's enthusiasm (380).

Gordon Cooper's final flight, however, offers Wolfe more hope. I have placed Cooper with the Elect in the new generation of pilots— despite his frequent siding with those of lesser status—because of his confidence in his own Election and because his perfect landing when the automatic controls fail prove resoundingly the righteous status of the astronaut. Gordon Cooper, Wolfe reveals, "never had a moment's doubt about himself" (401). Employing biblical diction Wolfe observes that

It was as if wherever he landed, the light shone 'round about him, and that was the place to be. Cooper knew as well as anyone else that it was more pres- tigious to be in Fighter Ops than in engineering at Edwards. But once he was in engineering, the light shone 'round about him, and the picture of him in that place was good. [. . .]

When the tests for selection of astronauts began at Lovelace and Wright- Patterson . . . well, it was obvious, wasn't it? Everything was now going his way. He never had the slightest doubt that he would be chosen. (145, 146)

Cooper is so cool he falls asleep on the launching pad, and after his flight he becomes "the most celebrated of all the astronauts aside from John Glenn himself" (409).

Wolfe might have ended *The Right Stuff* with this victory for the new generation of Elect, but he does not. He chooses instead to return to Edwards Air Force Base (Muroc) and Yeager for his closing chapter, and this helps to instill the sense of lament for forgotten righteousness that tends to dominate this volume. Yeager, who once lived in Victor- ville (411), now merely teaches the new fliers "so they could get a ticket to Houston" (413). Despite the fact that the X-15 project on which he is working is at its finest hour, "there was nothing [. . .] that even Chuck Yeager himself could say or do—that would change the new order. The astronaut was now at the apex of the pyramid" (414, 279).

What Yeager can do, however, is demonstrate his righteous stuff, and this he does in a dramatic final battle with death and the inferno in which his election is once again affirmed. When Yeager goes out to test the F-104 in 1963 it has been ten years since he has tried to break a record at Edwards. In a revealing passage, Wolfe exalts that

now Yeager was back on the flight line again to go for broke [. . .] and the righteous energy was flowing again. And if the good lads of the prep school could sense through him . . . and through that wild unbroken beast . . . a few volts of that righteous old-time religion . . . well, that would be all right, too. (423)

This, of course, is the effect of Wolfe's whole volume.

The F-104 had "an evil tendency to pitch up and then snap into rolls and spins," Wolfe explains (415), thus casting this flight as a trial of good versus evil. And like the damned pilots depicted in the opening chapters, Yeager enters the "jaws of the Gulp" and reaches his Armageddon: "There's not a goddamned thing left in the manual or the bag of tricks or the righteousness of twenty years of military flying . . . Chosen or damned! . . . It blows at any seam" (426). Yeager proves once again that he is among the Chosen, yet even he senses a diminishment in his witness, "the Good Samaritan, A.A.D.," whose initial response is "You . . . look *awful!*" (430). This lack of comprehension is echoed by Secretary of Defense Robert McNamara, who cancels the program. Wolfe's final chapter ends with the assertion that "the boys in Houston had the only ticket; the top of the pyramid was theirs to extend to the stars, if they were able" and "Yeager never again sought to set a record in the sky over the high desert" (431).

Wolfe's tone of lament continues in his Epilogue, which begins with the warning "the Lord giveth, and the Lord taketh away" (432). Although he acknowledges that the astronauts, who had fought for a true pilot's role in Project Mercury, finally win the esteem of their peers, he notes that by 1965 even their election is no longer certain. The final paragraph of *The Right Stuff* consists of Wolfe as Jeremiah, warning,

The Lord giveth, and the Lord taketh away. The mantle of Cold Warrior of the Heavens had been placed on their shoulders one April day in 1959 without their asking for it or having anything to do with it or even knowing it. And now it would be taken away, without their knowing that, either, and because of nothing they ever did or desired. (436)

Chosen or damned. The Puritan doctrine of the Elect. Lamenting the public's abandonment of Glenn—as well as of Yeager—Wolfe closes *The Right Stuff* with Glenn's loss in the 1964 Ohio Senate race and the gloomy prophecy that "the day might come when Americans would hear [the astronauts'] names and say, 'Oh, yes—now, which one was he?'."

Wolfe's stance as an American Jeremiah seems to have shifted from greater optimism in *The Electric Kool-Aid Acid Test* and the 1960s to greater lamentation in the 1970s and 1980s. *In Our Time*, published in 1980, is nothing but an extended jeremiad, a pictoral tolling of the headings of American idolatry and debasement. "The Tinkerings of Robert Noyce: How the sun rose on the Silicon Valley," which appeared in the December 1983 issue of *Esquire*, offers a bit more hope, and suggests what will probably be the future direction of Wolfe's mythos: return, as in *The Right Stuff*, to the "moral capital of the nineteenth century" the "long-forgotten light of Dissenting Protestantism" transplanted from New England (373). "The Tinkerings of Robert Noyce" celebrates nineteenth-century Congregationalism as embodied in computer chip pioneer Noyce.

Since 1983 Wolfe has turned from nonfiction to fiction, but he has continued toward more direct revelation of his evangelistic sensibility. The title of his first novel, *The Bonfire of the Vanities*, comes from fifteenth-century Venetian religious reformer Girolama Savonarolais, who exhorted Venetians to bring all their vanities out of their houses, pile them in the street, and set them on fire. The setting of Wolfe's *Bonfire* is New York—O Rotten Gotham—and its time is the present. Although the popular success of this novel may encourage Wolfe to continue in fiction, as recently as October 1987 he told an interviewer that two nonfiction topics of interest to him are the role of schools and colleges in society, and "new religionism from EST to charismatic Christianity" (Donahue 2D).

The confusing and seemingly contradictory tensions in Tom Wolfe's art are no longer confusing once he is understood as a wary twentieth-century Jeremiah. Surrounded by unbelievers in a pluralistic culture, the only way he can assert his zeal is through mock sophistication and satire. Nevertheless, the rhetorical forms he employs in his art—tableaus of pandemonium, the tolling of vices, speaking in tongues, and social denunciation—reveal him to be an American Jeremiah in camouflage, both criticizing vice and encouraging American expansion and revolution toward grace.

3

John McPhee's Levels of the Earth

John McPhee is as beguiling as Thoreau, whose tradition, along with Ralph Waldo Emerson's, he advances. Of the nonfiction artists in this study McPhee is the one most interested in the natural world. He carries forward the traditions of nature and travel writing in the twentieth century. "My deepest goals are aesthetic," he has insisted, revealing his stance as an artist (Drabelle 62), yet his aestheticism is devoted to the form and design he perceives in the natural world.

McPhee as a youth was a celebrity of fact. As a Princeton undergraduate he journeyed weekly to New York City to identify animals, vegetables, and minerals on the radio program "Twenty Questions." Like Gay Talese, he has celebrated unnoticed or unlikely topics—*Oranges*, for example, or the New Jersey *Pine Barrens*. Indeed, one reviewer remarked that McPhee seems deliberately to choose unpromising subjects just to show what can be done with them (Horwich 30). Like Talese, McPhee scorns the tape recorder, takes notes with pencil and pad, and "hangs out" with his subjects, often for long periods of time, in order to gather material.

He differs from the more unobtrusive Talese in his gift for arranging ingenious travels or events to showcase his subjects. In order to write of wild food genius Euell Gibbons, for example, he arranged a one-week foraging expedition in Pennsylvania, with Gibbons adding a new wild ingredient at each meal. To write of Atlantic City, he followed the streets of the Monopoly board, wittily interweaving his "Search for Marvin Gardens" with a championship Monopoly game. To explore the *Levels of the Game* of tennis, he took turns reviewing a videotaped match with players Arthur Ashe and Clark Graebner, ascertaining point by point their recollected thoughts and their reactions to each other.

Besides conceptual ingenuity McPhee also possesses singular clarity of mind. Theodore Taylor, the former bomb designer turned nuclear safeguard advocate, observed McPhee's gifts for research during their travels for McPhee's 1974 volume *The Curve of Binding Energy*. "John would open his notebook at 5 a.m. and begin asking questions, and often wouldn't close it till 9 at night," Taylor states. "He would amaze physicists by listening to highly technical explanations, stopping them if he didn't understand something, and then restating it for verification in a form infinitely clearer than first told. 'Exactly,' they would say. 'I wish I had said it like that.' "[1] Because of this lucidity, McPhee has been able to explore confidently technical subjects from nuclear physics to geology.

During his undergraduate days at Princeton, McPhee studied with Frost biographer Lawrance Thompson, and recalls his emphatic reaction to a Thompson lecture on the multiple levels of symbolism. "All of that is fine," McPhee remembers thinking, "but level number one has to be clear."[2] For McPhee, rendering accurately the complexity of any natural and human setting—that is, level number one—is the consummate artistic challenge. He is fascinated by form, dislikes structures that are "obvious," and believes that form should emerge from the subject matter; it should not be imposed artificially from without.[3] In writing more than seventy *New Yorker* articles, which have been reprinted in twenty books, McPhee derives or "solves" the problem of structure first, so that all that remains is to "tell the story as well as possible" (Singular 50).

Geometric figures and abstract forms come into play both in McPhee's perception of the world and in his artistic presentation of it. He is aware that "level number one," the natural earth, is composed of numerous sublevels and dimensions. He tends, therefore, to a gradient way of seeing and he uses the circle as a way of framing his subject.[4] McPhee's artistic vision is complex; it is rooted in Emerson and Thoreau and composed of circles and levels, the one and the many, the representative man or woman and levels of achievement. His early portraits are of representative men and women, of templates or types, who embody or unify a field. His eye obsessively notes levels of human attainment as well as of the geological earth because for McPhee it is essential to have "a sense of where you are," to quote the title of his first book. Forever seeking the panoptic perspective, McPhee would have us be aware, simultaneously, of heights of representative achievement; the many levels—like Holmes's chambered nautilus—to reach that height; and our own locations on this grid. When a representative type is passing or endangered he will lament its plight in writing that is itself a preservative measure.[5]

CIRCLES

The eye is the first circle; the horizon which it forms is the second; and throughout nature this primary picture is repeated without end. It is the highest emblem in the cipher of the world. We are all our lifetime reading the copious sense of this first of forms.

The last sentence of this opening passage from Emerson's essay "Circles" is a perfect scan of the McPhee canon. Circles and spheres, the primary form, are in McPhee's writing from beginning to end. He has written on basketball ("Basketball and Beefeaters," *A Sense of Where You Are*), tennis (*Levels of the Game*, "Centre Court," "Twynam of Wimbledon"), and "The Pinball Philosophy." He has celebrated *Oranges*, *The Deltoid Pumpkin Seed*, cranberries in *The Pine Barrens* and tree rings in "Firewood." Would McPhee have worked as a greengrocer in the New York City open market if it had not allowed him to write, in "Giving Good Weight," of those additional luscious spheres of nature, the tomato, peach, apple, melon, and onion? McPhee's pursuit of this primary form may have led him to Ted Taylor, the atom, and *The Curve of Binding Energy*, and to Taylor's "globe of ice" in the more recent "Ice Pond." The private joy of "Mini-hydro" may have been the description of the waterwheel. McPhee, in fact, recalls telling a friend early in his career, "Everything I write about is round."[6]

In McPhee's first volume, *A Sense of Where You Are*, his artistic vision is most simply and purely revealed. The book is about both a representative man, Bill Bradley, who reaches the highest levels of achievement in college basketball, and about basketball itself. Thus it is about the one and the many, about Bradley and his Princeton team, and about this team and its numerous competitors.

Bill Bradley's game is college basketball in its purest form, and in McPhee's presentation it is an enlarging series of circles. Bradley invariably begins his pre-game warmup "by shooting set shots close to the basket, gradually moving back until he was shooting long sets from twenty feet out. . . . Then he began a series of expandingly difficult jump shots" (20). The tiny central "eyelet" welded under the rim of the basket becomes a circle within the hoop for Bradley: his target when shooting free throws. Most important, Bradley's whole way of seeing is suited to the sport he exemplifies. McPhee explains that

The metaphor of basketball is to be found in . . . compounding alternatives. Every time a basketball player takes a step, an entire new geometry of action is created around him. . . . and this multi-radial way of looking at things can carry over into his life. At least, it carries over into Bradley's life. The very word "alternatives" bobs in and out of his speech with noticeable frequency. (48–49)

Emerson wrote: "Our life is an apprenticeship to the truth that around every circle another can be drawn." In taking Bradley to a Princeton ophthalmologist, McPhee tests the empirical validity of this statement. He finds that Bradley's superior vision is literal: the circle depicting his visual range is completely outside of and surrounding, not only fields of vision of the ophthalmologist's other patients, but the circle of a *perfect* eye!

Little doubt, then, that Bradley is a representative man, one who represents not only the highest levels of achievement in his field, but unites the field within himself. Here is the link of the whole, the representative figure, the one, with the many. McPhee notes that "[Bradley's] play was integral. There was nothing missing. . . . He did all kinds of things he didn't have to do simply because those were the dimensions of the game" (7–8). When the sportswriters make their choices for the 1964 Eastern regional five-man all-tournament team, one writes: "Bradley, Bradley, Bradley, Bradley, and Bradley" (128).

Emerson insisted, in *Representative Men*, that

true genius will not impoverish, but will liberate, and add new senses. . . . We love to associate with heroic persons, since . . . with the great, our thoughts and manners easily become great. . . . This is the key to the power of the greatest men—their spirit diffuses itself. A new quality of mind travels by night and by day, in concentric circles from its origin, and publishes itself by unknown methods. (18, 25, 33)

Bill Bradley enacts this Emersonian vision in *A Sense of Where You Are*. In the Princeton-Michigan game in Madison Square Garden, McPhee writes that "Bradley, playing at the top of his game, drew his teammates up to the best performances they could give, too, and the Princeton team as a whole outplayed Michigan" (87). When Bradley fouls out with four minutes and thirty-seven seconds remaining the spirit falters and Michigan overtakes the team to win by a single point. The Princeton team goes on, however, to win the Ivy League crown, and in the game with Cornell that clinches the championship even benchdusting Shank, the crowd's "mock-hero . . . proved to be a real one" (109).

A Sense of Where You Are is structured around Princeton's rise through level after level of tournament play. Throughout the modern era no Ivy League team had ever gone beyond the second round of the regional NCAA (National Collegiate Athletic Association) playoffs. When Princeton reaches the unprecedented championship game in the 1964 Eastern regional tournament, a *Washington Star* article states "in effect, that Princeton would need five Bradleys and a good night to beat Providence" (124). These words triggered something in Bradley, McPhee reports, and he called a team meeting to remind his teammates that they had won previous games with a good offense or good defense, but they had never fully combined the two in one game. In the Providence game this union occurs: "Providence, playing smoothly itself, found that it was in a game with a basketball team as well as with a star. . . . They were all passing like Bradley. They were all shooting like Bradley, dribbling like Bradley, thinking like Bradley" (125). Afterward Bradley states: "I had been the dominant factor, at times, in other games, but in the Providence game I was a member of the greatest team I had ever played on. . . . It was the happiest I had ever been in my life" (125, 127).

With this victory in the Eastern regional championship unranked Princeton establishes itself as one of the four best teams in the nation, and advances in national championship pairings to a rematch with Michigan. Michigan triumphs once again and Bradley, the representative man, understands it as a personal failure: "I failed as captain of the team. We weren't ready for that game mentally. The real place I failed was at half time. I should have had something to say. I sat there. I said something, but it wasn't much" (132–133).

As can be seen, McPhee's representative men, like Emerson's, exert spiritual as well as physical or intellectual leadership. "The world is upheld by the veracity of good men," wrote Emerson in *Representative Men*; "they make the earth wholesome" (3). Resented as a book-reading freshman starter on his high school basketball team, Bradley becomes a role model by his junior year. "Everyone looked up to him," says Sam La Presta, one of his teammates in those years. "He was sort of inspirational. Basketball was one-millionth of what he had to offer" (79).

Bradley continues this role at Princeton. "You look at yourself and you decide to do better," one classmate says (42). According to McPhee, Bradley believes religion is the main source of his strength (39). After his year at Oxford University as a Rhodes scholar he plans to go to law school and later "set a Christian example by implementing my feelings within the structure of the society" (42). McPhee could be writing of Emerson when he observes: "If he seems ministerial, that is because he is." (40)

"I believe! I believe!" the crowd chants in the final game of Bradley's college career, the consolation game of the 1964 NCAA tournament (137). In this 118-to-82 victory over Wichita State the one and the many, Bradley and his team, unite and rise to new levels of achievement. Following the insistent urgings of his teammates and coach, Bradley, in the final minutes of his college career, sets aside his "usual standards" and shoots every time he gets the ball. "In the next four minutes and forty-six seconds," McPhee writes, "Bradley changed almost all of the important records of national championship basketball" (136). Even more significant in respect to the one and the many: "Where the names of three individuals and four universities once appeared in the records of the championships, only the names of Bradley and Princeton now appear, repeated and repeated again" (139).

This pinnacle is not the end for Bradley, however, or for McPhee's account of him. Bradley, who first used the phrase "a sense of where you are" (22), comes home to Princeton to apologize for failing to finish higher, and to seclude himself from all publicity to complete his senior thesis and graduate with honors. McPhee does not hesitate to note that beyond Princeton and college basketball looms a larger circle for Bill Bradley: the standard of Oscar Robertson, nicknamed, perhaps not coincidentally, the Big O: "Robertson, who is known in basketball as The O, stands out among all professionals for the same reason that Bradley stands out among all amateurs. Other players have certain individual skills that are sharper, but Bradley and Robertson are brilliant in every aspect of the game" (79). Walt Hazzard of the Los Angeles Lakers tells Bradley: "Where I come from, you are known as The White O" (81).

During the final unbounded minutes of his college career Bradley takes steps toward this higher circle. His fifty-eight points break Robertson's individual scoring record in an NCAA tournament, and his twenty-two shots from the floor break Robertson's field goal record. But Bradley, with ever a sense of where he is, retains the proper perspective. "There are so many things [The O] does that I could never do in a hundred years. . . . He's the best basketball player alive" (80).

The Curve of Binding Energy, published nearly a decade later, depicts a representative man whose celebrity is the inverse of Bill Bradley's. This man is Theodore Taylor, the supreme miniaturist of the atom bomb. Taylor's lifework parallels McPhee's more closely than any other figure in his canon, for it represents a virtuoso performance up and down the periodic table and across the levels of the atomic sphere.

As a youth growing up in Mexico City, Taylor played billiards nearly every day after school, becoming a polished player. "He knew nothing of particle physics," McPhee writes, " . . . but in a sense he was beginning to learn it, because he understood empirically the behavior of the interacting balls on the table, and the nature of their elastic collisions, all within the confining framework of the reflector cushions" (10). Later Taylor would confess: "I have thought of billiard balls as the examples in physics as long as I can remember—as examples of types of collisions from Newton's mechanics to atomic particles" (10).

Precocious like McPhee, Taylor's "imagination outgrew his chemistry lab in Mexico City" (31), and in the fall of 1941 he first saw McPhee's beloved New England ponds and rivers as a prep school student at

Exeter.[7] There his enlarging sphere is symbolized by his exchange of the billiard ball for the discus, a sport in which he would excel in college, for he was "attracted to the shape and the flight of the thing" (31).

But Taylor was never the honors student and Rhodes scholar Bill Bradley would be. Taylor is truer to the Emersonian mold in slighting institutional education to follow his personal vision. At Exeter he barely notices the "D" he receives in Modern Physics, for he "was getting a look for the first time . . . at what he would call 'submicroscopic solar systems,' and he found that they had for him enormous appeal" (29). Though he graduates from the California Institute of Technology at the age of nineteen and works on the cyclotron at Berkeley, he twice fails his preliminary orals for a Berkeley Ph.D., bringing his confidence "as low, probably, as it would ever be in his lifetime" (60).

Fortunately for Taylor he was working at Berkeley under Robert Serber, the man who had helped construct the mathematical framework of the first atom bombs, and the author of *The Los Alamos Primer*. Serber saw that Taylor "was not a scholar, not a profound and thorough analyst. . . . He was more a conceiver of things" (59); so Serber sent the failed doctoral candidate to Los Alamos. It was 1949. Taylor was twenty-four years old.

His entry into Los Alamos, "ringed" as it was with signs shouting "DANGER EXPLOSIVES KEEP OUT," represents, in McPhee's telling, an entry into the first of many circles in his spiraling career as a bomb designer—and then confiner. In one of many ironies in *The Curve of Binding Energy* the symbol of Project Y, the Los Alamos division of the Manhattan project, which created the first atom bomb, is the letter *Y* "framed in a circle—an inverted peace sign" (150). One of Taylor's first jobs involves Pentagon photographs of Soviet cities, industries, and military bases. On these photographs Pentagon target analysts would draw circles; Taylor's job was to estimate how many kilotons would be needed to remove items within the circles.

A bomb "was a sphere within a sphere within a sphere within a sphere," McPhee tells us, repeating the motif of concentric circles employed in *A Sense of Where You Are*:

The small sphere in the center was called the initiator. . . . Around the initiator was the ball of fissile material. . . . Around the tamper was ordinary high explosive, the bulk of the bomb. Basically TNT, its purpose was to squeeze the uranium or plutonium from a subcritical density to a supercritical density, squeezing the initiator at the same time and creating an instant fireball. The high explosive had to be set off with something like absolute symmetry all around the sphere. . . . Mathematics had shown that charges shaped as lenses were best at starting such a process, so lenses formed the outer part of the sphere. The lenses looked like breasts. . . . (81, 82)

Little is nurturing about these breasts, however. A clockwise tour of the National Atomic Museum in Albuquerque is McPhee's way of re-creating the rising, then falling, curve of fissile bomb history, including Taylor's unique contributions. Taylor is "quite surprised" to see on public display the diminishing-sized bombs that bore his stamp (147).

On a different scale Taylor designed Hamlet, the most efficient fission bomb ever made in the kiloton range. Then he designed S.O.B., the Super Oralloy Bomb, which "was—and it still is—by far the largest-yield pure-fission bomb ever constructed in the world" (90). Of Emerson's *Representative Men*, Taylor most resembles Emanuel Swedenborg, of whom Emerson writes:

He was apt for cosmology, because of that native perception of identity which made mere size of no account to him. . . . The thoughts in which he lived were, the universality of each law in nature; the Platonic doctrine of the scale or degrees; . . . the fine secret that little explains large, and large, little.(106)

Taylor's method of thinking is to walk around and around his house "on an interior circuit through several rooms, and also around outside" (166). Between bombs he and his colleagues bowl snowballs the size of volleyballs down the E Building corridor "to see what would happen" (114). Indeed, Taylor's obsession with circles and spheres is more acute than McPhee's, who perceives the circle simply as the sum of many levels or as a frame defining his subject. As a boy in Mexico City, Taylor

would open [a book] to a picture of the full moon or of a planet—any dislike thing seen in full view—and his flesh would contract with fear. He could never look through a telescope without stealing himself against the thought of seeing a big white disc. He began to have recurrent dreams that would apparently last his lifetime, for he still has them, of worlds, planets, discs filling half his field of vision, filling all his nerves with terror. (12)

Plutonium, particularly, held for Taylor the same distressing attraction. He tells McPhee he had been "hopelessly drawn to the spectacular and destructive potentialities of plutonium, even from the first moment he had ever heard its name, and to the binding energy that comes out of the nucleus and goes into the fireball, even before he could come to grasp the stunning numbers that describe it" (159–160).

The irony of McPhee's title is that it is "binding energy," the energy equivalent to the strength of the forces that bind the parts of the atomic nucleus together, that, when converted from matter to energy, become the destructive nuclear blast. Binding energy thus destroys. Taylor tells McPhee that the "most astonishing" realization he has had in physics is that "when Fat Man exploded over Nagasaki the amount of matter that changed into energy and destroyed the city was one gram—a third the weight of a penny. A number of kilograms of plutonium were in the bomb, but the amount that actually released its binding energy and created the fireball was one gram" (163).

Taylor worked on only one hydrogen bomb during his seven years at Los Alamos, but such bombs, no matter what size, began to distress him. He came even to be sorry he had designed the Super Oralloy Bomb. In 1956 he left Los Alamos to turn his attention first to peaceful use of atoms for space exploration and then to safeguarding nuclear materials. Taylor has been prophetic in his fears regarding the role of bomb-making in individual and small-group terrorism. In an unnerving scenario involving the whole and its levels Taylor notes that

a one-kiloton bomb exploded just outside the exclusion area during a State of the Union Message would kill everyone inside the Capitol. . . . The bomb would destroy the heads of all branches of the United States government—all Supreme Court justices, the entire Cabinet, all legislators, and . . . the Joint Chiefs of Staff. With the exception of anyone who happened to be sick in bed, it would kill the line of succession to the Presidency—all the way to the bottom of the list. A fizzle-yield, low-efficiency, basically lousy fission bomb could do this. (222)

It is not surprising that McPhee would describe the safeguards required to protect nuclear materials as "ideally . . . a series of frames around the nuclear industry, expanding with it through time" (64). Taylor believed that the Atomic Energy Commission's requirements were little more than "veneer safeguards," inadequate for 1974, let alone for the future (65). In one of many anonymous representative quotes that McPhee employs to suggest the range of "official" opinion, the speaker suggests that in the nuclear industry, the simpler things are, the better. "We believe in the fulcrum, and we believe in the inclined plane," he explains. "The wheel we're not sure of" (141).

The challenge for Ted Taylor and John McPhee in *The Curve of Binding Energy*, therefore, is precisely that: to invent the wheel of nuclear safeguards. Because Taylor believes that public pressure is the only force to which the nuclear community responds (126–127), the wheel he and McPhee proffer is the encircling pressure of public opinion—created by the knowledge in McPhee's book. This is the saving rhetorical "bomb" they wish to explode. To this end, Taylor dares to describe how construction of a nuclear bomb might occur, from the molding of two hemispheres of plutonium in a $100 electric furnace, to soldering two wax-lined stainless steel mixing bowls together around the plutonium sphere. Spheres and levels are fundamental to this process. The fuel plates consist of an aluminum-uranium alloy "sandwiched between layers of uncomplicated aluminum," the whole thing whirling in a centrifuge (134). Perhaps even more unnerving is Taylor's confession that there exists a "level of simplicity" of bomb-making that is so simple, he would not dare explain (225).

Safeguards of nuclear materials are needed, but in this respect, McPhee writes, the United States is "in the foothills picking daisies and has not yet begun to climb the mountains" (227). The ultimate irony in this irony-laced volume is that it was the limited-test-ban treaty of 1963, forbidding nuclear explosions in space and in the atmosphere, that led to the suspension of Taylor's Orion project, which might have changed the entire dimension of nuclear activity.

When Taylor departed Los Alamos in 1956 he went to work for General Atomic, a "nuclear Xanadu of circular and curvilinear buildings" in California, and eventually developed his own project called Orion (176). America was engaged in the space race with the Soviet Union, and the Orion project was an effort to launch a spaceship with a nuclear bomb. Stanislaw Ulam, the emigrant Polish physicist who first conceived of the way to make the hydrogen bomb, speaks of Taylor as a quintessential American hero. "When I met Ted, he fitted the ideas I formed as a boy of Americans, as represented by Jules Verne," Ulam tells McPhee. "The trait I noticed immediately was inventiveness" (120). Freeman Dyson goes even further in suggesting Taylor as the thwarted Columbus of our future worlds.

Taylor and Dyson had wider goals in the Orion project than simply exploding a spaceship toward the moon. They were thinking of the long-term survival of the planet, and therefore, of course, of spheres. Their dream, cut short, was this: "to assure almost indefinite survival, [a planet] would send giant plates of materials into orbit around its sun, forming a great discontinuous shell, a titanic nonrigid sphere, conserving almost all the heat and light and photosynthetic sustenance the sun would give" (172). Musing about his dreams for large and inexpensive spaceships traversing space, Taylor confesses: "I never imagined myself sitting at the throttle. I dreamed of looking out a porthole at the rings of Saturn, sometimes the moons of Jupiter. . . . The remotest place I expected to see was Pluto, where the sun is a pale disc and there is deep twilight at noon" (177).

The inverse of the pale sun at noon is the glorious midnight sun of Alaska. If McPhee is concerned with the fate of the planet in *The Curve of Binding Energy*, in his 1977 *Coming Into The Country* it is the microcosm of Alaska that compels his concern. To McPhee, Alaska possesses the "beauty of nowhere else, composed in turning circles" (93). The three sections of the volume represent, not concentric, but interlocking circles, each with its representative Alaskan emblem.[8]

Alaska means "the great land." Perhaps one of its lures for a writer fascinated by levels is its location above the "lower forty-eight." McPhee begins his opening section, "The Encircled River," at the "upper limit of the Great North Woods." He is on the Salmon River of the Brooks Range, its watershed wholly above and within the Arctic Circle. Salmon, of course, are synonymous with rising, leaping, aspirations, and Mc-Phee begins his Alaska story by celebrating their circles within the Arctic Circle: "Everywhere, in fleets, are the oval shapes of salmon. . . . Looking over the side of the canoe is like staring down into a sky full of zeppelins. . . . There is a pair of intimate salmon, the male circling her, circling, an endless attention of rings" (6, 7).

McPhee recalls that for thousands of years, "to extents that have varied with cycles of plenty" (24), the woodland Eskimos have fished for these salmon, and he proceeds to depict Alaska as a system of interlocking natural spheres: "The river cycle is only one of many hundreds of cycles—biological, meteorological—that coincide and blend here in the absence of intruding artifice. Past to present, present reflecting past, the cycles compose this segment of the earth" (16). When McPhee and his friend John Kauffmann try to circumambulate an island they find moose tracks intertwined with wolf. "There were changes of direction, overlapping circles. No other sign" (29). The caribou cycle, "dearth to plenty and back again" (33), seems to complete itself in sixty to one hundred years, and it, in turn, effects the movements of the Eskimos, who also are part of the cycle.

Only by understanding Alaska as this land of expanding and contracting natural cycles can the full dimension of its current dilemma be understood, McPhee seems to imply. The 1971 Native Claims Settlement Act provided 70 million acres for 60,000 natives, and called for 80 million acres to be set aside for future national parks. The unwitting result of this seemingly fair and farsighted government action, McPhee notes, is that "boundaries now have to be adjusted, adjudicated, where boundaries never existed" (35). McPhee describes private property as an uncomfortable and incompatible jacket placed on the Alaskan natives, who, presumably, know how to dress themselves. In the current stage of caribou abundance, for example, the native hunters require less range, but they will need more again, McPhee explains. "It is impossible to draw lines around a situation like this one, but the lines are being drawn" (35).

Kauffmann and McPhee never succeed in circling their island, and in "The Encircled River" McPhee poses the final stakes in similar cautionary tableaus involving the Alaskan salmon and grizzly bear. He sounds the first note of dissonance in describing the effect of humans on the salmon. These fish "ignore the boats, but at times, and without apparent reason, they turn and shoot downriver, as if they have felt panic and have lost their resolve to get on with their loving and their dying" (6).

When McPhee leaves the river and ascends a mountain he encounters an Alaskan grizzly, the Great Bear, and in his presentation it becomes the emblem of North American wilderness, encircled, yet still holding its own:

What mattered was not so much the bear himself as what the bear implied. He was the predominant thing in that country, and for him to be in it at all meant that there had to be more country like it in every direction and more of the same kind of country all around that. He implied a world. He was an affirmation to the rest of the earth that his kind of place was extant. (62–63)

The grizzly possesses the qualities of independence and individuality that McPhee will later admire in the human beings who "come into the country" to *live*, rather than to impose divisions. He quotes photographer Andy Russell, who says of the grizzly: "The grizzly can be brave and sometimes downright brash. . . . Whatever he does, his actions match his surroundings and the circumstance of the moment. . . . His is a dignity and power matched by no other in the North American wilderness" (72, 63).

But the circle is closing on the grizzly. Once, McPhee recalls, "his race was everywhere in North America" (63). The state animal of California, "whose country was once his kind of place," the grizzly is there extinct (63). As *Coming Into The Country* unfolds, we see McPhee is paying homage to more than the endangered grizzly itself, but to the qualities of independence and self-reliance that it exemplifies. In the final tableau of the opening section he depicts the grizzly as a hirsute cowboy, high-spiritedly at home on his range:

[The grizzly] picked up a salmon, roughly ten pounds of fish, and, holding it with one paw, he began to whirl it around his head. . . . With his claws embedded near the tail, he whirled the salmon and then tossed it high, end over end. As it fell, he scooped it up and slung it around his head again, lariat salmon, and again he tossed it into the air. (94)

The question of the site of a new Alaskan state capital is in the air as well. In "What They Were Hunting For," *Coming Into The Country*'s second section, McPhee descends from the Arctic Circle to Anchorage and the southern terrain. Once again the seemingly impossible task confronting Alaskans is to select a capital site suited to the overlapping needs and interests of the state. Juneau, the current capital, is the former gold center in decline. Fairbanks is the "de facto" capital of the interior and the "pivot from which travellers fan out to the north," while Anchorage is the commercial center, "the central hive of human Alaska" (106, 129).

Employing the figure of the circle, McPhee presents the divergent attitudes toward use of Alaskan land as a wheel of public opinion. John Kauffmann, who wishes to preserve the Alaskan wilderness, "represented only a small arc or two in a wheel of attitudes toward the land" (83). Robert Weeden, Alaska State Policy Development and Planning director, tells McPhee the state has gone from a "development urge to development plus conservation, while the federal trajectory—in general—has been from neglect and preservation to exploitation of resources" (85). To McPhee, the state's development-plus-conservation posture is ninety degrees from Kauffmann's preservation stance, while Robert Atwood, editor and publisher of the Anchorage *Times*, articulates the national policy, which is to subordinate Alaska to national (oil) self-sufficiency. This development-intensive posture is 180 degrees from Kauffmann's preservation position, and Alaskan natives, McPhee writes, "were somewhere on the way back to Kauffmann" (86).

While McPhee withholds direct expression of his own views until the final section, he leaves little doubt in section two that no new capital should be modeled on Anchorage. In fact, he depicts Anchorage as an example of the development impulse at its most insensitive, and contrasts this major city with Mount McKinley, which joins the grizzly as an authentic Alaskan emblem.

Almost all Americans would recognize Anchorage, because Anchorage is that part of any city where the city has burst its seams and extruded Colonel Sanders. . . . Anchorage is the northern rim of Trenton, the center of Oxnard, the ocean-blind precincts of Daytona Beach. It is a condensed, instant Albuquerque. (130)

Most of all, Anchorage "is virtually unrelated to its environment"—the worst possible sin to a writer like McPhee (130). In section one he describes the native village of Kiana as a "dot" in the wilderness (39); in section two Anchorage, too, is a "dot," but it is also a "pustule," a city that "grew like mold" (133, 132).

The 50,000 acres that constitute Anchorage are called the Anchorage Bowl. In contrast to the awe and delight he feels in the Arctic Circle of section one, McPhee feels trapped in this lower sphere. He feels "penned in" with the other "inmates" of Anchorage, and plots a "breakout" (133, 134). McPhee wants to escape to find Alaska, and it is noteworthy that one of the few points the Capital Site Search Committee can agree on is that any new Alaska capital should be in sight of Mount McKinley, North America's highest massif. "In so many mountains, there was one mountain," McPhee writes, and McKinley becomes the symbol of "true

Alaska South" in section two, just as, in section one, the grizzly represents Alaska North (101). Like the elusive bear, "the mountain can emerge [from the clouds] as swiftly as it disappeared, and when it is out only the distant curve of the earth can reduce its dominance, for it is the most arresting sight from forty million acres around" (110). On an aerial inspection tour with the Site Committee, McPhee observes Mount McKinley "framed" in the window. "Sometimes bears were too," he adds (169), and on the ground, committee members frame one another in photographs—eating bearberries (122).

A massif is an independent part of a mountain range, and in this way, too, McKinley is linked with the self-reliant bear and the state in which they range. McPhee not only approves of a new capital in view of Mount McKinley, but he also recommends a name for such a city in the Indian name for the mountain, Denali, meaning The High One. But McPhee is apprehensive regarding the development process. Given his mythos of levels, it is not surprising he takes pains to describe the McHargian method employed by the Committee for Site Selection, a method in which each criterion, such as drainage or vegetation, is plotted on a clear plastic map overlay, and which, when all the layers are amassed, permit experts to see best and worst sites. "They had buried the map of central Alaska under layers of acetate," McPhee comments, and he hints that committee members are endangered species themselves amid all this plastic, "like a crane standing on one leg staring into a pond" (155).

Section two ends, not with the capital found, but with another cautionary image regarding Alaskan development. McPhee returns to the Anchorage Bowl with the Search Committee. Through the windows that had framed Denali and the Alaskan bear "the streets and buildings below appeared to be lying under ten layers of acetate" (178).

In the final, title section of *Coming Into The Country* McPhee escapes the imprisoning Anchorage Bowl to Eagle, Central, and Circle, Alaska, and comes full circle to the Alaskan rivers and mountains, salmon and bear, and enters himself into their natural cycles. If the grizzly bear is the dominant Alaskan image in section one, and Mount Denali in section two, Alaskan gold shares dominion in section three with the independent human Alaskans, whose self-reliance McPhee finally celebrates.

McPhee begins with the representative man of the river, Dick Cook, a man who has been in Alaska "long enough to cover a couple of the natural cycles" (204). Circles are involved in many of Cook's enterprises, as they are integral to all those dwelling within "the country." Cook lays out his traplines in loops, and has to camp out at least one night to "complete a circuit" (187). Elmer Nelson and his partner choose either loops or cloverleaves for their patterned traplines (211), and Ginny Gelvin tries to trap a bear by strewing grouse carcasses "in a tempting circle" (308). Some of the inhabitants use fish wheels to catch their daily meals, and these circular activities have their counterpart in conversation. "As the talk curved through its long ellipses," McPhee observes, "it turned and returned, as always, to the Yukon, to every gravel bar, rock, rip, eddy, and bend—free or under ice" (260). Here is another encircled river.

The fish wheel, though often associated with Indians, was actually invented by a white man, McPhee discovers, and this fact reflects one of the major insights in *Coming Into The Country*: that in the changing Alaskan cycles the white settlers "have taken up where the Indians left off," and are now, in many ways, the true natives of Alaska (258). McPhee passes fish camps "all down the river, for the most part established by Indians and abandoned now—places that once netted as much as thirty tons of salmon a year" (285). Mike Potts, the representative man of the mountains, continues the cycle by re-teaching native skills to the Indians.

Potts's chosen terrain, the mountains, is even more isolated than Dick Cook's river region. "Without circling twice," McPhee writes, Potts claimed the mountain summits in his imagination as a teenager, during a flight with his father (400). Immediately after high school graduation in Iowa, Potts left for Alaska and made his way to the Eagle Indian Village. "I was trying to learn to live like an Indian, and do things better than most," he tells McPhee in a line with the rhythm of Thoreau's "I went to the woods because I wished to live deliberately, to front only the essential facts of life" (402). Now a "seasoned performer—relaxed in the pleasure of his chosen life"—Potts teaches mountain skills to the Indians (423).

It was gold in these Klondike ranges and Yukon streams that first brought people into this country. In this final section McPhee proffers this scarce and noble metal as his third symbol of native Alaska, and links it with the Alaskans he most admires. "Gold is not merely rare," McPhee notes. "It can be said to love itself. In the idiom of science, it is, with platinum, the noblest of the noble metals—those which resist combination with other elements. It wants to be free" (221). Furthermore, gold exudes the traits of the stream from which it comes; it emanates, like the grizzly, a sense of where it was. "An experienced miner," McPhee writes, "can look at a nugget and name the stream" (226).

Two such miners are Ed and Stanley Gelvin, father and son, and the most complete and admirable Alaskans McPhee encounters. Nothing can go wrong that would cause Ed Gelvin to seek help elsewhere. Like the gold, he wants to be free, and he is totally self-reliant and skilled in every form of hunting and repair. While Ed pilots ably above, Stanley works a Caterpillar earthmover below, both with sure senses of pre-

cisely where they are. Readers expecting McPhee to criticize the Gelvins's mining the face of the earth are first surprised and then charmed
by his final verdict, with its Thoreauvian cast:

This pretty little stream is being disassembled in the name of gold. . . . Am I
disgusted? Manifestly not. Not from here, from now, from this perspective. . . . the relationship between this father and son is as attractive as anything I have seen in Alaska—both of them self-reliant beyond the usual reach
of the term, the characteristic formed by this country. Whatever they are doing,
whether it is mining or something else, they do for themselves what no one
else is here to do for them. Their kind is more endangered every year. Balance
that against the nick they are making in this land. Only an easygoing extremist
would preserve every bit of the country. And extremists alone would exploit it
all. Every one else has to think the matter through—choose a point of tolerance, however much the point might tend to one side. For myself, I am closer
to the preserving side—that is, the side that would preserve the Gelvins. To be
sure, I would preserve plenty of land as well. My own margin of tolerance
would not include some faceless corporation "responsible" to a hundred thousand stockholders, making a crater you could see from the moon. Nor would
it include visiting exploiters—here in the seventies, gone in the eighties—with
some pipe and some skyscrapers left behind. But I, as noted, am out of sync
with the day. Is it midnight? Is it morning? Is it late afternoon? Where on earth
could the Gelvins be? (430–431)

The Gelvins, like the grizzly, appear now to be only in Alaska. From
the elevation of their state and, further, elevated in the air the Gelvins
see and report to McPhee the "wolf-moose story in all its phases," an
Alaskan ring cycle that McPhee imaginatively joins (311). From the air
the Gelvins see

a ring of wolf tracks where a pack first encircled a moose, and a while later
another ring, and then another, another. Each time, the moose fended off the
wolves, recovered its wind, broke out, and ran on. . . . Returning later on,
they see nothing where the moose was but a hoof and some hair, within a
tracked circle. (311)

The Gelvins's dog, Tara, is half wolf and tied to a stake. "Whenever I
come near her," McPhee recalls, "she races around her stake in the
tight circles it prescribes. . . . I have no doubt that if Tara was to come
off that chain and out of that pen as I am passing by, there would be
nothing much left of me but a rubber hoof and a little hair on the
unencircled ground" (312).

McPhee continues this food cycle in an only slightly less whimsical
vein in the final pages of *Coming Into The Country* when he partakes of
his first meal of grizzly, an act of symbolic incorporation of Alaska. The
effect on him is one of expansion, yet also humble submission to the

cyclical Alaskan order: "In strange communion, I had chewed the flag, consumed the symbol of the total wild, and, from that meal forward, if a bear should ever wish to reciprocate, it would only be what I deserve" (421).

McPhee has submitted himself to Alaska as respectfully as one might who has not "come into the country" to stay, but only "to draw a circle around [himself] a very great distance from the rest of [his] life" (335). This is a Thoreauvian act, and *Coming Into The Country* is one of Mc-Phee's most overtly Thoreauvian volumes. McPhee goes to a cabin in the wilderness to confront the essential facts of Alaska. He finds and limns these facts, and pays homage to the individualistic human beings who have valued self-reliance and place over accumulation of wealth. The government restrictions on Alaskan land today make cabin-building settlers trespassers, and would make Thoreau's act (and McPhee's) an impossibility in the future, a fact that, to McPhee, imperils the national character. *Coming Into The Country*, in this respect, is a brave and anguished plea for preservation of the American character as defined by Emerson and Thoreau. He closes his volume with a new Thoreauvian man, and with the hope that the Thoreauvian cycle will continue:

Of the people I had seen coming into the country—particularly the young ones arriving in summer to seek the mountains and the river—the one I remember best was an immense young man in a blue parka and blue rain pants and a wide-brimmed black hat, who walked up to me, total stranger, and said he had heard I had maps. . . . He had been to the Eagle General Store, where he bought a standard gold pan and a length of gold nylon rope, which was coiled around his shoulder. He told me he had talked with someone named Cook and found him prickly. He took a close long look at the maps. He was as amiable as he seemed determined, and his manner suggested momentum—suggested that this was his time and his place and, from Doyon, Ltd., to the federal government, whoever didn't like it could step out of the way. Stuck in the band of his big black hat were a tall eagle feather and the dogtooth jaw of a salmon. I asked him where he meant to go.

"Down the river," he said. "I'll be living on the Yukon and getting my skills together."

I wished him heartfelt luck and felt in my heart he would need it.[9] I said my name, and shook his hand, and he said his. He said, "My name is River Wind." (437–438)

McPhee told an interviewer in 1986: "The common thread in everything I've done is that I'm interested in the worlds of individuals" (Dunkel 42). Unquestionably this is true. Circles provide him a way of prescribing individual achievement and placing that achievement in social context. Through expanding, shrinking, or overlapping circles McPhee can illustrate rising and falling, or overlapping and competing achievements as well as relate the one to the many and the many to the one.

This process is revealed elegantly in *La Place de la Concorde Suisse*, McPhee's 1984 paean to the Swiss Army. Here McPhee reveals his transcendental frame of mind in his description of Switzerland as the place "where trains run like clocks, and clocks run like watches, and watches are synchronous with the pulse of the universe" (50). The Swiss Army, similarly, is a unity of considerable diversity. Primarily a civilian army, it is composed of every level of Swiss society, and it abides, McPhee implies, by tolerating individualism.

Swiss defense, in fact, is predicated on the theory of concentric circles. The army is not conceding an inch of Switzerland, McPhee notes, and so is constantly in Basel, the most vulnerable of Swiss outer cities (29). If an enemy seizes Basel and manages to overwhelm or bypass the defenders of the Jura, he explains, the next several lines of resistance have been drawn in the Mittelland (29). McPhee quotes a Swiss officer as stating: "Our lines of defense are deep—one, two, three, four, five, six, seven. If all lines are penetrated, if the enemy comes into the Alps, guerrilla warfare follows" (32).

A sense of prickly individualism is seen in the Swiss Army as a whole in its unique posture as a defensive army only, as well as in many of its individual regiments and soldiers. Although the Army is willing to defend itself by withdrawing into progressively contracting circles, each circle itself is envisioned as a spiny "porcupine defense"—as Switzerland brandishing its quills. In recounting Swiss military history McPhee describes heroes who turned themselves almost literally into porcupines. In a fourteenth-century battle against Austria a Swiss soldier named Arnold Winkelreid "gathered to his body the pike points of many foemen, thus opening on either side of him holes in the Austrian line, through which the Swiss backfield poured, swinging six-foot halberds, while Winkelried died" (51). For every Swiss who died in this battle at Sempach, nine Austrians died as well. During the Renaissance the Swiss developed the Lucerne hammer, a poleax with a brass fist on its head with spikes protruding between the fingers, and later the Morgenstern, an eight-foot cudgel with a sixteen-spike pineapple head. They also, of course, invented the Swiss Army knife. In the twentieth century Swiss uniforms bear small imitation grenades called petards. Soldiers carrying fifty or more petards can be turned into literal exploding firecrackers should they be fused. This weaponry illustrates the Swiss philosophy, which is to be so well prepared and prickly that the price of entry will be too high for any enemy, and Swiss independence will be preserved.

As he did with Mount Denali in *Coming Into The Country*, McPhee posits La Place de la Concorde Suisse, the supreme glacier in Europe, as a grand natural emblem of this philosophy. A frozen porcupine or sparkler, La Place de la Concorde Suisse has "avenues of ice coming from six or eight directions to conjoin in a frozen intersection" (11). McPhee flies over La Place de la Concorde Suisse and describes the Sunday "spins" of Peter Keller, a Swiss Army pilot who makes weekly aerial circuits from Basel to the Bernese Oberland, over the La Place de la Concorde Suisse, and up the Mattertal "to circle the Matterhorn clockwise" (120).

Counterclockwise moves another Swiss ritual that joins the many into one circle of unity. This is the convivial wine-drinking ritual of Luc Massy, Swiss winemaker and taster supreme and a soldier in the recon- naissance division called the Section de Renseignements. Massy's ritual, repeated at intervals throughout *La Place de la Concorde Suisse*, brings unity to McPhee's volume as well, and is, in McPhee's telling, a poly- phony of spheres.

[Luc Massy] erects the corkscrew and revolves it into the cork. . . . We hear the sound of a tennis ball, well hit. . . . Massy fills the glass, holds it up to his eye. "Santé," he says, with a nod to the rest of us, and—thoughtfully, unhur- riedly—drinks it himself. . . . After finishing the glass, he fills it again and hands it to his right—to Jean Reidenbach. . . . After Pierre Pera, it is my turn to drink, and then Massy's, Reidenbach's, Schyrr's, Wettstein's, Pera's, mine, and Massy's. (34–36)

Massy is one of several representative men McPhee celebrates in this volume. McPhee shows how Swiss military service is integrated into Swiss daily life by showing Massy coming full circle from a wine cave in his native canton to a cave attached to an army bomb shelter built under a Swiss school: "To come into the army, he had left his cave, and now he was back in a cave" (101). McPhee makes of his own assignment to the Section de Renseignements a similar full circle incorporation of the military into his life as a writer. Like McPhee, the soldiers of the Ren- seignements are collectors of information and sketchers of terrain. By and large, he notes, they are miscellaneous "freelancing loners," and the officers at the command posts are "editors" trying to make sense of the information presented by the patrols (71). "We have inched our way down the valleyside and taken the Nussbaum bridge—that is, taken notes on its width, its tonnage, its lack of prepared demolition," Mc- Phee writes (124), and we see how he has prescribed a circle around the renseignements, taking notes and sketching them as they take notes and sketch the terrain.

Toward the end of *La Place de la Concorde Suisse* McPhee returns to the mountains and slowly moves his gaze "in full circumference" from mountain peak to peak (122). In the final scene Massy, McPhee, and the other soldiers of the Renseignements climb 1,400 feet to make an aerial sketch of the valley environs of Brig. "The view is now panoptic,"

McPhee writes as Pierre Gabus draws a deft sketch of the view—and McPhee of Gabus sketching (147). Then Massy begins the wine. "The army needs marginal people," Jean-Bruno Wettstein tells McPhee. "They know that in an emergency if there's a job to be done we'll do it. That's why they leave us alone" (149). The redoubtable Massy is sending mock messages by transceiver to the command post as his part in these mock military maneuvers. Between ritual drinks, and stirring the fondue with the transceiver antenna, Massy transmits his fictive war reports. McPhee closes his volume with a message that must have been particularly congenial to him, giving a nod, as it does, to atom bomb miniaturist Ted Taylor as well as to the staunch individualistic Swiss. "AN ATOM BOMB OF PETITE SIZE HAS BEEN DROPPED ON SIERRE," Massy improvises.

LEVELS

McPhee's interest in levels may be as inherent as his name. He no doubt grew up hearing of Scottish highlanders and lowlanders, and this gradient perception was reinforced by his Deerfield Academy teacher Frank L. Boyden, whom McPhee lionized in his second volume, *The Headmaster*. One of Boyden's oft-repeated precepts was "Keep it on a high level" (22); indeed, he invariably arranged boys according to height (77). A boy had a sense of where he was at Deerfield Academy.

"Eucalyptus Trees," an early McPhee short story, and the 1966 nonfiction *New Yorker* profile "Fifty-two People on a Continent" together hint that after college, McPhee was concerned about the barriers met by individuals seeking to rise through corporate strata. The young hero of "Eucalyptus Trees" is named Ian. His surname, Gibbons, suggests one indexing the decline and fall of American civilization. In this story Gibbons resigns his position in a petty corporation when the company refuses to approve a transfer that would allow him actually to see the eucalyptus trees about which he has been writing. "It's nothing personal," his immediate superior tells him. Policy "can't be swayed by individual cases" (38).

In contrast, in the nonfictional "Fifty-two People on a Continent," Carrol Wilson's African Fellows are sent with blessings to see sights equally as exotic as the eucalyptus. They are, in fact, individually screened and matched with positions of responsibility in emerging African nations. "I was somewhat oppressed by the difficulties young people faced on long ladders of progression," Wilson tells McPhee. "The structured quality of American business nowadays makes it hard to find a fast track for young talent" (AROH 139).

The new African governments were in need of temporary middle and lower administrators, making Wilson's program a perfect solution for both the one and the many, for American individuals and African nations. If Fellow Henry Thomas had gone to work for the Chase Manhattan Bank, McPhee notes, "it would have taken him at least five years to work his way up to the point where he could countersign a check, let alone shoot an oribi" (AROH 148). It is not surprising, McPhee remarks, that such a "highly creative use of both money and talent did not have its origin in the ruminations of a committee" (AROH 136).

Another celebrated mentor is Dr. Robert Johnson, the tennis-playing physician who created a program to place young black tennis players on a faster track to greatness. McPhee's 1969 volume *Levels of the Game* is his most direct exploration of levels until his recent geological series, yet it also looks back to his first volume, *A Sense of Where You Are*.[10] *Levels of the Game* is dedicated to Bill Bradley, and begins with a ball tossed in the air. In the course of the volume McPhee's representative man, Arthur Ashe, rises to higher and higher levels of achievement, just as Bradley does in *A Sense of Where You Are*.

"Tennis is a game of levels, and it is practically impossible for a player who is on one level to play successfully with a player on any other," McPhee explains (139–40). Dr. Johnson's level of tennis was of such height that he played in tournaments of the American Tennis Association, which was the black U.S. Lawn Tennis Association. A boys' mentor like *Headmaster* Boyden, Johnson establishes a Junior Development Team and vows to himself that if it takes the rest of his life, he will develop a young black tennis player who will become national interscholastic champion.

Arthur Ashe begins at the lowest levels of Dr. Johnson's team, cleaning the doghouse every day as his off-court duty. He rapidly rises, and by the age of fifteen, when the Middle Atlantic Lawn Tennis Association refuses to process his application, he is ranked fifth among boys in the United States and is "knighted" by Wilson with free racquets (45, 71). In 1960 Dr. Johnson sends Ashe to St. Louis for his senior year of high school, not because of his native region's racial slight, but because "by that time, there was no tennis player of any color in or near Richmond who could play points with him" (139).

Ashe graduates with the highest grades in his high school class and enrolls at the University of California, Los Angeles, where "the level of his game became so high" he is made an honorary member of the Beverly Hills Tennis Club (140). McPhee dismisses facile parallels with baseball's Jackie Robinson, noting that Ashe stood alone: "In tennis, the nearest black was light-years below him now, and he became, in his own words, 'a sociological phenomenon' " (141).

The structure of *Levels of the Game* resembles La Place de la Concorde Suisse, a central glacier and radiating ice floes. McPhee's centerpiece is the 1968 U.S. Open semi-final match between Ashe and Clark Graebner, but from it he digresses repeatedly to track each player's rise, and the psychological and sociological pathways that contribute to his highest level of play. "A person's tennis game begins with his nature and his background and comes out through his motor mechanisms into shot patterns and characteristics of play," McPhee explains in a sentence applying as well to the artful "game" of literary nonfiction (6).

McPhee poses the match as a conflict between a white Wagnerian Superman, Graebner, and the smaller, but, as it happens, more Emersonian figure of Ashe. Clark Graebner possesses "a facial bone structure that suggests heroic possibilities," McPhee observes. "It is doubtful whether a trimmer, healthier, better-built, or more powerful human being than Graebner has ever stood on a tennis court" (31, 119). Clark Graebner, in fact, looks like Clark Kent, Superman's alter ego, and when he writes his name his signature is "pi Hancock squared": the "G" is two and a quarter inches high (32, 19). Ashe's physical frame and signature are slighter and more ambiguous, the latter "halfway between bold and timid, and well within the sub-Hancock zone" (119).

Ashe signs his name Arthur R. Ashe, Jr., the Jr. acknowledging his respect for his father. In describing each player's father and home life McPhee gives clear evidence of which is truly representative of Jeffersonian and Emersonian values. Graebner's father is a dentist, and their home on Wimbledon Road is "almost too big for the parcels of land allotted" (59). Arthur R. Ashe, Sr., in contrast, is an Emersonian man-of-all-work. He has three jobs and five houses, four in Richmond and one in Gum Springs, Virginia, which he built with his own hands. Although this property is "bestrewn with automobile parts, miscellaneous cordwood, oil drums, scrap lumber, and gravel, . . . [Mr. Ashe] knows exactly what and where everything is and the use to which he intends to put it" (57). Mr. Ashe would be at home in Alaska. Like Emerson, he "set[s] maxims before his son like stepping stones," a habit that Arthur Jr. continues (63).

Clark Graebner reveals, however, even more audacious confidence in where he is and where he (and Arthur Ashe) will go in the future. He "knows the exact height and tensile strength of the corporate ladder," McPhee observes (10). Graebner predicts that his wife "will be active in the Junior League—that type of circle," while he will be president of Hobson Miller and on the board of Saxon Industries, the mother company (104). Ashe, he projects, will never be chairman of the board or president of Phillip Morris, but will be a brand manager or a vice-president in charge of marketing. "Even though Arthur is well accepted in a place like Phillip Morris," Graebner opines, "he's never going beyond that level" (103). Asked the same question, Ashe lacks such certainties. "I haven't the slightest idea what I am going to be doing twenty years from now," he states (103).

Dr. Johnson taught his Junior Development Team that "confidence goes back and forth across a tennis net much like the ball itself, and only somewhat less frequently. If two players are on about the same level, no matter what that level is, the player who experiences more minutes of confidence will be the winner" (32–33). Arthur Ashe, Jr., would appear to be at a disadvantage in this criterion as well as in size and strength, but he makes up for it with a daring, unorthodox style based on Emersonian intuition rather than on conservative, consistent play. Graebner's game, Ashe believes, is "steady, accurate, and conservative . . . Republican tennis" (90). In contrast, Ashe plays tennis, Graebner believes, "with the lackadaisical, haphazard mannerisms of a liberal" (93). Graebner's description, however, might more accurately define Emersonian intuition:

[Arthur] comes out on the court and he's tight for a while, then he hits a few good shots and he feels the power to surge ahead. He gets looser and more liberal with the shots he tries, and pretty soon he is hitting shots everywhere. He does not play percentage tennis. Nobody in his right mind, really, would try those little dink shots he tries as often as he does. . . . He plays to shoot his wad. . . . If he were more consistent, he might be easier to play. (93)

But Emerson has always had the last word on consistency, and in *Levels of the Game* Arthur Ashe's character and intuition prove more than a match for the arrogant Graebner. After losing the first set Ashe begins to feel the power within him. He tries a half-volley drop shot that, McPhee notes, "a person should try once a match, if at all, and hardly in the most vital moments of the second set, when—already losing—he is in imminent peril of falling almost hopelessly behind" (92). But Ashe's daring shot succeeds, and Graebner's shoulders droop as he walks back to the baseline.

Ashe wins this second set to tie the match, and in the third set "games pile up like pairs of blocks," until they stand at five-all (125). "Somewhere now," McPhee writes, "the blocks must fall" (126). Perhaps because of his fascination with levels, McPhee pauses for dramatic emphasis at this moment when the two players appear most even:

At this moment, this match, almost over, is as nearly even as any tennis match could be. There is a narrow statistical edge, though, and it is Graebner's. Graebner has won more points on service returns than Ashe has, he has hit more returns safely back than Ashe has, and he has hit more aces. Each has won one set. The present set is in balance. Ashe is ahead by one game. Graebner has the serve. A hundred and eighty-six points have been played by the two players so far. Ashe has won ninety-three. Graebner has won ninety-three. As it happens, the next four points they play will decide it all. (128)

At this balanced moment Graebner, playing smart percentage tennis, hits to Ashe's weakest stroke, his forehand, and from deep within himself Ashe pulls off "an all-time winner" (130). "Nothing has happened to Graebner's game," McPhee wants us to understand. "It continues at the level of solid excellence that has brought him, all even, to the present crisis. The level of Ashe's game, however, appears to have risen. He is playing with loose, all-out, fluid abandon—prudence be damned" (130).

Ashe's favorite stroke is the backhand, an affinity that "sets him apart from most tennis players on all levels," (130). In McPhee's description, this stroke is a stroke of liberation: "the follow-through does not cramp the arm into the body but . . . opens both arms wide and high, so that the stroke ends in the stance of the Winged Victory" (131–32). In the final point of the third set, leading the game fifteen-forty, Ashe tells himself to play it safe. He tells himself that he does not need a great shot.

But Graebner, for some reason, hits his second serve down the middle, toward Ashe's backhand. The temptation is much too much for Ashe, and the shot he hits is by far the greatest of the day. When the ball has left the cannon, Ashe stands on his toes with his arms spread-eagled in the follow-through. The shot is a crosscourt, in-and-out backhand that goes two zillion miles an hour—in. It goes past Graebner so fast that Graebner does not even move. (132)

In the fourth set Ashe "now begins to hit shots as if God Himself had given them a written guarantee" (137). His serve, the "roundhouse" with which McPhee started the volume, becomes even stronger. "He plays full, free, windmilling tennis," McPhee notes, inserting his mythos of circles (137). In fact, Ashe is now playing "almost consistently on the level he stepped up to in the last three shots of the third set" (138). He leads in the fourth set four games to one, and, McPhee states, "his game is so big now that it is beyond containment" (148).

In the final image of the volume, and of the match, McPhee depicts Ashe as the authentic American eagle—the Winged Victory:

Graebner hits the big serve into the net, then hits his second serve to Ashe's backhand. The ball and the match are spinning into perfect range. Ashe's racquet is back. The temptation is just too great, and caution fades. He hits for it all. Game, set, match to Lieutenant Ashe. When the stroke is finished, he is standing on his toes, his arms flung open, wide, and high. (150)

Although McPhee concludes *Levels of the Game* full circle with this image of liberated man in flight, as with *A Sense of Where You Are* he makes us aware of higher levels and a wider circle of achievement awaiting Ashe. Although Clark Graebner is presented by McPhee as narrower than Ashe and currently lacking the character to rise to Ashe's level, he is sportsman enough to join his fellow Davis Cup teammates in the press box the next day to root Ashe on to victory in the finals. Donald Dell, the Davis Cup Team coach, "has made a team out of a half-dozen blatantly individual tennis players," McPhee writes (135), and both Graebner and Ashe would rather win the Davis Cup for America than the individual U.S. Open championship. Arthur Ashe acknowledges this higher level at the moment he fulfills Dr. Johnson's dream in the finals. He turns and points his racquet to Dell and his Davis Cup teammates, and then bows to them, "giving them something of his moment as the winner of the first United States Open Championship" (149).

A subtler exploration of levels is *Encounters with the Archdruid*, McPhee's 1971 profile of environmentalist David Brower. The volume's three parts—"A Mountain," "An Island," "A River"—suggest declining rather than rising elevation, a movement that parallels Brower's decline as Sierra Club president.

David Brower is equated with the mountain. As a boy, he found an "escape zone" in the Sierra Nevada from the close-quartered California poverty in which he was raised (29). A quintessential Emersonian man, he dropped out of college at the age of nineteen to go into the mountains. "Before ten years had passed, it was being said of him that if he were to be set down at night anywhere in the Sierra Nevada, with the coming of morning he would know just where he was" (34). "Mountaineers are individualists—loners," observes one Sierra Club member. "Brower is an individualist, a loner" (214).

In McPhee's presentation Brower is also a religious visionary. The Archdruid of the title, his religion is conservation. Brower calls the speeches he gives "The Sermon," and in it he delivers "the gospel according to John Muir," the great nineteenth-century naturalist and Sierra Club founder (79, 84). Brower's own transcendental vision is suggested in McPhee's wry observation that Brower's "field, being the relationship of everything to everything else and how it is not working, is so comprehensive that no one can comprehend it. Hence the need for a religion and for a visionary to lead it" (83–84). Like Emerson, Brower believes in "feeling" rather than fact. The striking statistics in "The Sermon" are more "indices" than verifiable figures, he acknowledges. "What matters is that they feel right" (86). Brower "is suspicious of education and frankly distrustful of experts," observes McPhee. "His intuition seeks the nature of the man inside the knowledge. His sentiments are incredibly lofty" (86).

As a young boy, Brower would lead his blind mother on long walks in Grizzly Park, describing to her the terrain. This scene is emblematic of his later mission, leading the blind public to the beauties of the wilderness. McPhee writes that Brower "had spent his life defending mountain ranges and what, by extension, they symbolized to him" (6). Brower's wife tells McPhee: "Until you've seen him up there, you don't know him" (132).

McPhee achieves this knowledge in the first section of *Encounters with the Archdruid* by accompanying Brower and Charles Park, a geologist and mineralogist, through Washington State's Glacier Peak Wilderness. Park is one of Brower's "natural enemies," for he believes in mining mountains—to maintain high standards of human living. In this volume, as well as in his others, McPhee reminds us of Montaigne (one of Emerson's *Representative Men*) in his robust skepticism and ability to chart an individual moderating perspective. Though his final sympathies are always with Brower, McPhee gives full scope to Park's portrait and position; Park is not a simple villain. The mineralogist, McPhee notes, "is a man who knows what he is looking at in wild country. I have never spent time with anyone who was more aware of the natural world" (67). Nevertheless, Park's most characteristic act throughout the journey is to chip away at the mountain with his pick, an ominous act in light of Brower's equation with the mountain. Troubled by this seemingly indiscriminate undermining, McPhee asks Park what he is looking for in these random strikes at mountain outcroppings. "Nothing," Park replies. "I just haven't hit one in a long time" (18).

The journey through Glacier Peak Wilderness permits McPhee to contrast not only the two men, but also their representative emblems: the mine and the mountain. Brower wishes to reach Image Lake, which reflects and even magnifies Glacier Peak, the "scenic climax" of this wilderness. The trip is difficult, and when they finally arrive Brower arranges his pallet on top of a high promontory above the lake shore. McPhee and Park remain below, but as darkness descends McPhee climbs the slope "to witness in the water the fading image of the great mountain." "Objectively," he writes, "the reflection was all it was said to be" (59). In the morning he once again celebrates the mountain, "seven miles away—all ice and snow, and almost too dazzling to look at as it sprayed sunlight in every direction" (73).

Park is not interested in gazing upward at Glacier Peak, however; he prefers to look down for copper. The mine Park would place in this wilderness would mean a boring downward in spiraling circles rather than the upward striving of the mountain. McPhee reports that the largest copper mine in the United States, located in Bingham Canyon, Utah, "goes down into the earth in some fifty concentric circular terraces, so that from the air it looks very much like a thumbprint pressed into the ground—the thumbprint, it works out, of a man well over a hundred miles tall" (37). Such degrading of levels is necessary because of lowering standards of acceptable yield. McPhee explains that earlier in this century, if copper ore was not at least 2 or 3 percent copper, it was bypassed. "Now," he notes, "if it is seven-tenths of one per cent copper it is mined" (40). Brower worries that "if you start with point seven per cent and work down, say, to point three five—if that level becomes commercially feasible, then there's no telling *how* big the pit will be" (41).

The choice seems clear: lower our mountains or lower our standard of living. Brower (and McPhee) would favor the latter, "drop[ping] our standard of living, so that people a thousand years from now can have any standard of living at all" (21). The concentric circles, to Brower, are the circles of hell, and he says any mine would "puncture" this wilderness "like a worm penetrating an apple" (39). "If we're down to where we have to take copper from places this beautiful," he stresses, "we're down pretty far" (21).

But the temptation of glittering rocks and the high standard of wealth they represent is shown to be powerful. It affects Brower and McPhee as well as Park. In the following passage McPhee hints that the competing sights are a matter of long- versus short-term perspective:

The beauty of the mountain [Glacier Peak] was cool and absolute, but the beauty of the stone in Park's hand was warm and subjective. It affected us all. Human appetites, desires, ambitions, greeds, and profound aesthetic and acquisitional instincts were concentrated between the stone and our eyes. (52–53)

Even David Brower hunts for the green copper-filled rocks, but only for their beauty and to form them in a circle. In the final tableau in this section McPhee underscores Brower's greater spiritual elevation through another circular motion evocative of the feeding of the multitudes at the Sermon on the Mount:

Brower's [Sierra] cup was up to its brim, and before he ate any himself he passed them among the rest of us. It was a curious and surpassingly generous gesture, since we were surrounded by bushes that were loaded with berries. We all accepted.

"I just feel sorry for all you people who don't know what these mountains are good for," Brower said.

"What are they good for?" I said.

"Berries," said Brower.

And Park said, "Copper." (75)

In "An Island," the second section of *Encounters with the Archdruid*, Brower's "natural enemy" is an enlightened real estate developer whom he seeks to convert to a disciple. At stake is the future of Cumberland

Island, which, in 1971, lay virtually uninhabited off the coast of Georgia. Perhaps McPhee is easier on Charles Fraser because he is a fellow Scot. No doubt also he admired Fraser's eye for natural beauty, not so different from Brower's own. Fraser, too, is a "visionary"; he represents the highest levels of aesthetic real estate development (89). Personal profit is not paramount among his motives (95). McPhee appears also to have seen Fraser's work as that of a strong, not to say imperious, individual. The deeds he draws up for his Seaside Pines development on Hilton Head Island read like "a reverse bill of rights (ironclad), a set of ten times ten commandments—take it or leave" (92–93). Fraser is "Yahweh" to those living in this idyllic development. He is "not merely mayor and the zoning board, he is the living ark of the deed covenant" (94).

If Fraser assumes for himself attributes of the all-powerful Old Testament god, Brower represents both a Christ-figure and an older, pantheistic spirit. He is not the "angry Zeus" Fraser expected, but "the inscrutable lord of the forest, the sacramentarian of *ecologia americana*, the Archdruid himself" (103, 138). His impending decline is foreshadowed when he talks gently to a tame buzzard who nibbles at his basketball shoes, then his fingers, and then drapes a talon over his hand (148).

Though Brower appears to be strangely passive during this episode, he is actually putting himself in context. The surprising solution he finds is to incorporate Fraser into his religion. Throughout his visit Brower comments admiringly on Fraser's youth and energy (127). If Hilton Head had to be developed, Brower tells McPhee, "I'm glad it was developed by him" (147). Fraser's major failing, if any, is the speed with which he races across the terrain. In his final words to Fraser, Brower proffers an alternative style and a charge to discipleship:

On the beach, I could have stopped all day long and looked at those damned shells, looked for all the messages that come not in bottles but in shells. . . . You, Charles Fraser, have got to persuade the whole God-damned movement of realtors to have a different kind of responsibility to man than they have. If they don't, God will say that man should be thrown away as an experiment that didn't work. I have seen evidence of what you can do. Now make others do it. (144)

In the volume's final section, titled "A River," Brower floats the Colorado River in a rubber raft while the water level rises higher and higher. A metaphor for the sentiment that is slowly mounting against him, it (embodied in the Sierra Club) eventually engulfs him.

If Charles Fraser in section two represents a youthful competing deity, Floyd Dominy, Brower's "natural enemy" in "A River," suggests a full-circle return to the Devil-figure of section one. McPhee tries to

muster as much appreciation for Dominy as he can, by showing Domi-
ny's origins in the Great American Desert during the Great Depression.
Nevertheless, as Commissioner of the U.S. Bureau of Reclamation,
Dominy symbolizes the greatest scourge to conservationists: the dam.
Using yet again the figure of concentric circles, McPhee observes that

the outermost circle of the Devil's world seems to be a moat filled mainly with
DDT. Next to it is a moat of burning gasoline. Within that is a ring of pinheads
each covered with a million people—and so on past phalanxed bulldozers and
bicuspid chain saws into the absolute epicenter of Hell on earth, where stands
a dam. . . . The conservation movement is a mystical and religious force, and
possibly the reaction to dams is so violent because rivers are the ultimate metaphors of existence, and dams destroy rivers. Humiliating nature, a dam is
evil. . . . (158, 159)

Dominy escorts Brower and McPhee on a passage evocative of the
descent into the copper mine described in section one. Here the descent is into a dam, into the interior of Dominy's "indisputable master-
piece, the ten-million-ton plug in Glen Canyon" (190–91). Lake Powell
and the Glen Canyon dam represent a defeat for David Brower, yet
McPhee reminds us of Brower's grand victories in the past, employing
yet again the metaphor of levels: "Down the tiers of the Western states,
there are any number of excellent damsites that still contain free-flow-
ing rivers because of David Brower—most notably in the immense, arid
watershed of the Colorado" (161). The "Grand Canyon battles," over
two dams not built because of Brower, have been the bitterest fought
between Brower and Dominy's bureau, which concedes that because of
Brower, no dams will be built in the Grand Canyon for at least two
generations.

Dominy, however, has not been idle. "He had begun his career by
building dams seven feet high," McPhee notes, "and he would one day
build dams seven hundred feet high" (169). In fact, he and his bureau
"hope to see the Colorado River become a series of large pools, one
stepped above another, from the Mexican border to the Rocky Mountains" (162). Momentum in 1971 seems to be with Dominy. On the raft
trip down the Colorado they encounter layer after layer of land and
mountain mass now covered with water. In Brower's memory the most
beautiful place in the Glen Canyon region was a cavernous space, under vaulting rock walls called the Cathedral in the Desert. Once the
waterfall in the Cathedral fell sixty feet; now, only ten. "It had been
beautiful in there before the reservoir came," McPhee writes, "and it
would continue to be so, in successive states, until water closed the room
altogether" (201). Dominy speaks in jest of laying a wreath on Gregory
Arch, a large natural rock span now thirty-five feet under water. When

they come to Havesu Canyon, which McPhee describes in a symphony
of levels and circles (236–37), Dominy still wants to submerge it in the
backup waters from a dam, even though he describes it as "the prettiest
[canyon] in the West" (237). When the others on the raft learn that
Dominy's dam would cover Havesu Creek, Upset Rapid, and Lava Falls,
they "become a somewhat bewildered—perhaps a somewhat divided—
chorus" (226).

They are a Greeklike chorus to a confrontation of giants, yet there is
a touch of hubris in Dominy that marks him the inferior titan. Though
McPhee admires Dominy's enterprise, he notes that Dominy, as a young
county agent, "took it upon himself to overcome nature if the farmers
and ranchers could not" (156). Dominy calls Campbell County, Wyoming, his "kingdom" when he is twenty-four years old (157), and he
boasts to Brower: "I'm a greater conservationist than you are, by far. . . .
I make things available to man" (240). At Lake Powell, Dominy's creation, "[Dominy's] name spread everywhere within moments of his arrival, and as he moved along the nonskid marina decks he was regarded as a kind of god, creator of the unending blue waters" (205).
When a New Yorker says to Dominy, "I see God has given us good
water here this morning," Dominy replies, "Thank you," an overwean-
ing moment repeated three times in the journey (190).

David Brower, in contrast, sees God speaking through nature rather
than through Floyd Dominy. Pointing to the "strange striations" on a
canyon wall, he says to Dominy, "That is hieroglyphic, written centuries
ago by God Himself."

"Yeah? What does it say?" said Dominy.

"It says, 'Don't flood it' " (204).

Dominy's hubristic assumption of deity is contrasted with Brower's
modesty in a succeeding episode when it is Brower who is deified. Two
hikers emerge from a rugged overland journey from Navajo Mountain.
When introductions are made the two youths have never heard of Floyd
Dominy or his bureau, but when they hear the name David Brower,
McPhee wonders "if the hiker was going to bend over and draw a picture of a fish in the sand" (207).

On their own rugged journey to the mountain in section one Brower
yodels with happiness the closer he gets to Glacier Peak, causing Mc-
Phee to dub him Antaeus (58). According to Greek mythology, this
giant wrestler was invincible while he touched the earth. There is something fitting, then, in McPhee's entwining Brower's "expurgation" by
the Sierra Club with this river episode. "They are crucifying him, and
they are self-congratulating bourgeoisie," a Brower supporter tells
McPhee while the "high tribunal" of the Sierra Club meets to ratify
Brower's ouster (209, 213).

In McPhee's presentation Brower's defeat is a matter of circles and

levels. His loss is a cyclical repetition of the defeat of John Muir fifty-
five years before, and it comes, McPhee implies, largely because Brower
rises to higher and more inclusive levels than the remainder of the
Club. "I don't think the man changed so much as he developed," one
Sierra Club member tells McPhee (212). Brower, himself, defines the
conflict as "expansion cracking" (218). In McPhee's view,

a small, local organization had grown into a major national and international
force in the conservation movement, and at each stage there had been people
who had wanted to stop. Brower had come to see conservation as inescapably
a global and supranational matter. . . . The best of his opposition, not necessarily disagreeing, felt that the Sierra Club should have more limited objectives
if it was to reach any objectives at all, but Brower, meanwhile, was reaching
into the endangered stratosphere and beyond it for the sun and stars. (219)

In section one Brower's redwood home is described by McPhee as
clinging to a steep hillside overlooking San Francisco. On the day of
his defeat by the Sierra Club a giant redwood falls. But it will rise again,
and in his battle on the river with Floyd Dominy, Brower returns to
this knowledge of nature's sure triumph. On one hand, Brower notes,
silt will rise up behind the dams; on the other, the river will have its
way: "The lava dam of Quaternary time was eventually broken down
by the river. This is what the Colorado will do to the Dominy dams that
are in it now or are ever built. It will wipe them out, recover its grade,
and go on about its business" (242). McPhee sides with Brower on this
matter. "My own view," he writes, "was that the river would make all
the decisions" (244), and in the volume's final scene it is Brower, not
Dominy, who reads Lava Falls best.

McPhee's gradient way of seeing is that of a landscape painter. His
descriptions frequently capture foreground terrain and then ascend in
levels: "Red cliff walls met the dark-blue water, big buttes stood high
in the background, and above it all—immense and alone in the distance—was sacred Navajo Mountain" (EWTA 195–196). With almost
equal equanimity he can descend, as in his wry observation that "the
building as a whole rests on limestone, dolomite, and the People's Republic of China" (TCOPE 102).
This last citation foreshadows the expansion of McPhee's vision in
the past decade to include the unseen layers of the geological earth.
McPhee is like Talese and Wolfe in moving toward more direct exploration of the figures of his artistic imagination as his career develops.
In the first three volumes of a proposed six-volume series on geology
McPhee seeks to add another level to his vision: the dimension of time.
The geological charts on the inside covers of *Basin and Range* (1980),

In Suspect Terrain (1983), and *Rising From The Plains* (1986) are literally levels of the earth through time.

In *Basin and Range* McPhee presents roadcuts as "windows into the world as it was in other times" (33). They are landscape paintings framed by his eye. *Basin and Range* enables McPhee to celebrate James Hutton, the Scottish physician-turned-geologist considered the founder of modern geology. Hutton, like McPhee, was drawn to coastal outcrops and upland cliffs; he was preoccupied with the "dynamic cycles" of the earth (96). It was Hutton who, staring at a stream cutbank two centuries before McPhee, expanded the world's conception of earthly time. In McPhee's description, Hutton is unquestionably a representative man:

Alive in a world that thought of itself as six thousand years old, a society which had placed in that number the outer limits of its grasp of time, Hutton had no way of knowing that there were seventy million years just in the line that separated the two kinds of rock, and many millions more in the story of each formation—but he sensed something like it, sensed the awesome truth, and as he stood there staring at the riverbank he was seeing it for all mankind. (106)

McPhee's motive in *Basin and Range* is similar: to expand our comprehension of ourselves in time. From David Brower he derived the belief that human beings tend to think in five generations, "two ahead, two behind—with heavy concentration on the one in the middle":

Possibly that is tragic, and possibly there is no choice. The human mind may not have evolved enough to be able to comprehend deep time. It may only be able to measure it. . . . On the geologic time scale, a human lifetime is reduced to a brevity that is too inhibiting to think about. . . . Geologists, dealing always with deep time, find that it seeps into their beings and affects them in various ways. They see the unbelievable swiftness with which one evolving species on the earth has learned to reach into the dirt of some tropical island and fling 747s into the sky. They see the thin band in which are the all but indiscernible stratifications of Cro-Magnon, Moses, Leonardo, and now. (127, 128)

McPhee quotes several geologists on the benefits of this longer view. "You begin tuning your mind to a time scale that is the planet's time scale," says one. "For me, it is almost unconscious now and is a kind of companionship with the earth" (129).

The lesson of the American Basin and Range, like that of plate-tectonics theory in general, is a transcendental message regarding expanding and contracting levels. "The lesson," McPhee writes, "is that the whole thing—the whole Basin and Range, or most of it—is alive. The earth is moving" (48–49). Like human beings, the plates (which are the moving segments of our sphere) "grow, shrink, combine, disappear, their number changing through time" (183). This is our companion-ship with the earth.

In Suspect Terrain is McPhee's Thoreauvian minority report on plate-tectonics theory. This 1983 volume has for its representative figure An-ita Harris, a former map editor for the Geological Survey, who tells McPhee that the goal of many geologists is to make time-lapse maps of earth history (187). Harris carries many such maps in her head, and this may have been what drew McPhee to her, for he is clearly seeking this four-dimensional vision. He describes what he will assay in writing in the following discussion of landscape painting:

I have often thought of those [Hudson River School] canvasses—with their Durham boats on the water and cows in the meadows and chuffing locomotives on the Pennsylvania side—in the light of Anita's comment that you would un-derstand a great deal of the history of the eastern continent if you understood all that had made possible one such picture. She was suggesting, it seemed to me, a sense of total composition—not merely one surface composition visible to the eye but a whole series of preceding compositions which in the later one fragmentarily endure and are incorporated into its substance. . . . (77–78)

McPhee attempts such a portrait of Brooklyn and Manhattan by re-tracing in Harris's company her migrations as a young girl. McPhee portrays Harris as expanding like a glacier from the red Triassic stone of her tenement home on Brooklyn's terminal moraine across the Brooklyn Bridge and, in successive waves, as far as the micaceous out-croppings of Central Park. In these youthful explorations Harris "did not know from geology," but when she returns with McPhee "she ad-dresse[d] Fifth Avenue as the axis of the trough of a syncline. She knows what is underfoot. She is aware of the structure of the island" (32, 33). Anita Harris has a deep sense of where she is.

Harris's sense of deep time allows her to correct common misconcep-tions, and this seems to be the primary goal of In Suspect Terrain. If we were true to Manhattan geology, for example, we would call it not the Big Apple, but the Big Carrot (34). Similarly, diamonds are hardly for-ever:

At room temperature and surface pressure, diamonds are in repose on an ex-tremely narrow thermodynamic shelf. They want to be graphite, and with a relatively modest boost of heat graphite is what they would become, if atmo-spheric oxygen did not incinerate them first. They are, in this sense, unstable—these finger-flashing symbols of the eternity of vows. . . . (17)

Human beings rank with bats, starlings, and Pleistocene sloths as the "great messmakers of the world" (25), and the fact that the earth existed some 4,600 million years before the Judeo-Christian era forces us to see ourselves as "an *arriviste* species, an obviously unsettled obtruder" (38).

Most suspect, however, in Harris's view, is the terrain that in 1983 was being claimed by plate-tectonics theorists, those believing that the shell of the earth is divided into plates of varying size, "which separate to form oceans, collide to make mountains, and slide by one another, causing buildings to fall" (5). Anita describes herself as a protestor, and McPhee evokes the memory of Thoreau in his description of her late husband, Leonard Harris, as "a missionary of contrary opinion" (131, 132). The Harrises object not to plate-tectonics per se, but to those who overapply it without attention to geological details. The Harrises found that plate-tectonics theory does not explain certain facts about Appalachian geology. Anita has spent months measuring every foot of rock in Water Gap, and what troubles her is the new breed of geologists who never leave their computers. With plate-tectonics, Leonard explains, anyone can write a history of an area without having been there—and they have no way to evaluate what they are doing. Worst of all, many tectonic theorists are guilty of the arrogance McPhee portrayed in dambuilder Floyd Dominy:

The theory took a metaphysical leap into the sancta of the gods, flaunting its bravado in the face of Yahweh. . . . Instead of reaching back in time from rock to river to mountains that must have been there—and then on to inference and cautious conjecture in the dark of imperceivable unknowns—this theory by its conception, its nature, and its definition was applying for the job of Prime Mover. (121)

Clearly this is unsatisfactory to Anita Harris and to a writer like McPhee whose entire career is based on accurately re-presenting exhaustive data collected from exotic terrains. For a meticulous landscape artist like McPhee, Anita's analogy to modern art, which he places in the volume's concluding paragraph, is particularly apt. Much of the work by plate-tectonics theorists, she observes, is "like some modern art—done by people who throw paint at canvas and have never learned the fundamentals" (209).

David Love, the Rocky Mountain geologist McPhee celebrates in his recent volume, *Rising From The Plains*, has grown up in terrain that is the least explainable in the world in terms of plate-tectonics theory (29). This hardly bothers Love, however, for he is field-oriented; like Anita Harris and James Hutton (and John McPhee), he knows geology from having found it out himself.

In this portrait of Love many of the strains of McPhee's artistic vision unite. David Love is of Scottish ancestry. His grandfather was a physician, yet also a professional photographer and lecturer on world travel.[11] Love's father was born on the Wisconsin farm of environmentalist John Muir, his granduncle. This father records David's rising height on a board nailed to the inside of the kitchen door frame, and his mother notes his developing sense of "scale" (87). Although the Love family encounters cycles of plenty and drought, it never sells out its self-reliance or staunch individualism.

David Love, it is clear, is another of McPhee's representative men. Born in the center of Wyoming in 1913, Love grows up reading Emerson, Thoreau, and Shakespeare.[12] At the age of nine he reads his mother's copy of LeConte's *Elements of Geology*, and when McPhee asks him whether he grasped structure and stratigraphy then he replies, "After all, we could see it out in front of us" (106). Charles Lupton, the structural geologist, appears at the ranch during Love's youth, bringing ammonites from the mountains, index fossils of the Upper Cretaceous Period. He demonstrates to Love that these spiral cephalopods had once approached the size of wagon wheels.

Following a path also taken by David Brower and Alaska's Mike Potts, Love, at age twenty-one, goes off to work in the mountains. There he climbs the Tetons and rows the lakes, "like Thoreau sounding depths on Walden Pond" (130). His method, like McPhee's, is one of

gradually absorbing the country, sensing the control from its concealed and evident structure, wondering—as if it were a formal composition—how it had been done. . . . Having no way to know what would or would not yield insight, he noticed almost anything. . . . Over the decades, a stretch at a time, he completely circumambulated the skyline of Jackson Hole. (131, 132)

When Love comes to write his doctoral thesis, he does not "mark off a little basin somewhere and essay to describe the porridge it contained"; instead, he writes a "spinning pinwheel of geology," challenging and adding to the knowledge of the region (113). It contained the unabridged story, McPhee writes, noting its levels, from the surface to the fossil topographies exhumed far below (114).

David Love, thus, is the quintessential field geologist. There is stratigraphy even in his trifocal glasses (5). If James Hutton laid the foundation for the science of geology in the eighteenth century and Charles Lyell's *Principles of Geology* built on it in the nineteenth century, the work of David Love, McPhee insists, should set the standard for the twentieth century (168). McPhee quotes Malcolm McKenna of the American Museum of Natural History as saying: "When the solid foundations aren't there, geologists are talking complete mush. Dave is making sure the foundation is there" (144).

But David Love's realm, like David Brower's, is now endangered.

Stratigraphy, the study of the order or levels of the earth, is no longer taught in some colleges, and field geologists are on the decline (153, 147). Analog or "black-box" geologists, those whose noses are to the printout instead of the outcrop, tend to outvote field geologists on questions of curriculum and to outperform them in writing grants, McPhee notes—despite the fact that the museum samples they often use for field relations are secondhand and frequently out of context (148). Peerless time-lapse geological map-making, for which Love sets the standard, "is below the salt now," says Malcolm McKenna, and therefore Love, like so many of McPhee's representative men, represents a point of view at odds with his time (144). Brower refuses "to go up the ladder" in the corporate world, or even in the Geological Survey," preferring to remain in his own Wyoming terrain (124). As regional field offices close, his remains "vestigial in the structure of the Survey" (124). When he goes, McPhee tells us, the office in Wyoming will close.

McPhee borrows his volume's title, *Rising From The Plains*, from the pioneer journal of Ethel Waxham Love, David's mother. When, on her first journey across Wyoming, she wrote "Mountains were far away ahead of us, a range rising from the plains and sinking down again into them," she did not realize she had intuitively written in one sentence their geological history (14). The Wyoming ranges had come out of the plains, and into the plain had, in various ways, returned, yet this title also describes a man as well as his representative region.

At the close of *Rising From The Plains* McPhee returns with Love to his childhood home in central Wyoming. Through symbolic details he suggests that in the current conflict with computer geology, Love's vision may be the more enduring:

We could see in a sweeping glance—from the ranch southwest to Green Mountain—the whole of the route he had taken as a boy to cut pine and cedar for corral poles and fence posts. An hour before, we had looked in at the ranch, where most of those posts were still in use—gnarled and twisted, but standing and not rotted. . . .

Over the low and widespread house, John Love's multilaminate roof was scarcely sagging. . . . The kitchen doorframe was intact, and nailed there still was the board that showed John Love's marks recording his children's height. (211, 212)

THE SHRINKING CIRCLE

John McPhee is outward-tending. His primary instinct is to trace outward expanding levels of the earth, and in this he reveals his transcendental optimism and kinship in bonhomie with Ralph Waldo Emerson.

Proof of the flexibility of his vision, and also of his streak of Thoreau-vian iconoclasm, are his volumes documenting shrinking rather than expanding circles. These volumes also seek to preserve nineteenth-century values—values that to McPhee, seem endangered or even extinct.

Oranges, McPhee's third volume, mourns the contracting circle of fresh orange juice consumption owing to the rise of frozen orange juice concentrate. Oranges and orange blossoms have long been symbols of love; however, McPhee notes, their history has been one of steady decline from the time they were considered fruit of the gods. "Fresh, whole, round, orange oranges are hardly extinct, of course," he acknowledges, "but they have seen better days since they left the garden of Hesperides" (8).

McPhee is dismayed by the rise of frozen concentrate because it standardizes one of the most individual of natural beverages. Fresh orange juice, he explains, "is probably less consistent in flavor than any other natural or fermented drink, with the possible exception of wine" (8). The taste and aroma of oranges vary by country, state, and county, by season and by type, and even by location of individual oranges on the tree. In the heart of Florida orange country McPhee fails repeatedly to secure a glass of fresh orange juice—even from a restaurant encircled with laden orange trees. To achieve what he desires McPhee must buy a squeezer and squeeze his own.

Such lost regard for individual nuance in orange juice is not merely epicurean elitism. McPhee suggests it has had the effect of inverting previous standards in the industry:

Growers used to sell oranges as oranges. They now sell "pounds-solids". . . . Because the concentrate plants are making a product of which the preponderant ingredient is sugar, it is sugar that they buy as raw material. . . . Growers now worry more about the number of pounds of sugar they are producing per acre than the quality of the individual oranges on their trees. (127)

One researcher tells McPhee, "We are growing chemicals now, not oranges," and what was once a way of life has now become "just a way to make money" (136, 126).

In the long run, McPhee observes, those making short-term profits on uniformity rather than diversity and on quantity rather than quality may be doing themselves in. William Grierson, Florida's greatest fresh-fruit expert, tells McPhee: "I believe that if growers continue to neglect the fresh-fruit market, they may find, in the next ten or twenty years, that the market for all forms of orange products has suffered" (31–32). County agents believe the rise of concentrate "may be causing the end, in a sense, of the Indian River" (111).

McPhee characteristically takes a moderating Montaigne-like position by concluding *Oranges* with a "universal man of citrus, a fresh-fruit shipper and a concentrate maker—[a man with] one foot in the past and the other in the future" (141). Ben Hill Griffin, however, is a bit of an anachronism himself. He is the remaining example of the individual orange barons of Florida's past. He is named, in fact, for Georgia's nineteenth-century Senator Benjamin Harvey Hill, a rugged individualist and states' rights advocate "who regarded the federal government as a caged monster and delivered eloquent speeches recommending that the key be thrown away" (144). Outside his concentrate plant Ben Hill Griffin flies the flags of the United States and Florida, but his individuality is shown in the fact that he is having his own flag made, and "it would soon be flying there, too" (148–49).

The Pine Barrens (1968), which followed *Oranges* (1967), chronicles a shrinking circle closer to home: the 650,000 acres of New Jersey wilderness that, ironically, constitute the geographical center of the developing megalopolis between Boston and Richmond. The volume begins with a panoptic view from Bear Swamp Hill and moves (foreshadowing *Coming Into The Country*) to a celebration of the natural cycles of the "pineys," their independence and their self-reliance. But the "old-time pineys," those who lived wholly by the cycles, are gone (57). As with orange juice concentrate, artificial replacements have usurped seasonal products. Plastic moss has largely replaced the sphagnum moss grown in the spring, which was once used in boxes of cut flowers all over the East (43). The "modern briquette" has eliminated the market for bagged Pine Barrens charcoal, and Philadelphians no longer buy Pine Barrens turtles by the gross to keep their cellars free of snails (46–47).

Paradoxically, although the wilderness itself is shrinking, interest in the Pine Barrens is expanding. The Pine Barrens aquifer stores half of all the precipitation it receives—and it is pollution-free and potable. New York City could take all its daily water requirements from this aquifer without diminishing the basic supply. McPhee calls the Barrens "one of the great natural recharging areas in the world" (14), but with all its space and all its subsurface water it is vulnerable to developers. "Gradually," McPhee notes, "development of one kind or another has moved in over the edges of the forest, reducing the circumference of the wild land. . . . " (6). A jetport, on the planning boards, would eliminate "virtually all the Upper and Lower Plains, several ponds, a lake, an entire state forest, and Bear Swamp Hill" with its panoptic view (153–54).

When he published *The Pine Barrens* in 1968 McPhee had little hope for their preservation, and he closes the volume with an image of the shrinking circle:

It would appear that the Pine Barrens are not very likely to be the subject of dramatic decrees or acts of legislation. They seem to be headed slowly toward extinction. In retrospect, people may one day look back upon the final stages of the development of the great unbroken Eastern city and be able to say at what moment all remaining undeveloped land should have been considered no longer a potential asset to individuals but an asset of the society at large— perhaps a social necessity. Meanwhile, up goes a sign—"Whispering Pines, Two and Three Bedrooms, $11,900"—and down go seventy-five acres of trees. Up goes another sign: "Industry!! Jackson Township Has an Abundance of Water!," and another. . . . At the rate of a few hundreds yards or even a mile or so each year, the perimeter of the pines contracts. (156–57)

When McPhee turns from vegetation to human beings he often sees the shrinking circle as well. A final contracting circle is that of the dirigible and its "helium head" devotees honored by McPhee in *The Deltoid Pumpkin Seed*. Every facet of McPhee's artistic vision is present in this volume: circles and levels, Princeton, and preachers who are both individuals and representative men.

The hopeful experimental dirigible looks like an orange. It is, in fact, painted Princeton orange and is a practical compromise between an airfoil and a sphere. Like Ted Taylor's tiny bombs, these new blimps are designed to press the "inverse frontier," to explore the lowest, most economical limits of aerodynamic possibility. A fleet of such dirigibles could provide superslow transport, burning little fuel in low-cost, low-power engines. Such airships could also rise, however; they would be just as useful at 10,000 feet as at sea level (48).

This American aerodynamic dream is conceived as a Faith Fleet, and represents a full-cycle return to Solomon Andrews, the nineteenth-century minister's son and Renaissance man who designed and flew the first dirigible in 1863, decades before Germany's Count Zeppelin. McPhee notes that the invention came to Andrews during one of his father's sermons, and he always considered the sermon a direct inspiration. Although Andrews's legacy includes twenty-four inventions, this physician, who was also mayor of Perth Amboy, "always considered the Aereons to be the purpose of his life, his real destiny" (125). Andrews published a pamphlet titled "Without Eccentricity There Is No Progress," and McPhee quotes a sentence from the 1863 *New York Herald* describing Andrews's feat as "the greatest stride in invention ever made by a single individual" (97).

Andrews thought of his dirigible as a tremendous lemon seed rather than as a pumpkin seed, but its history seems to foreshadow the airship's twentieth-century fate. After Andrews received initial support from the government in 1863, the Civil War ended, the president was assassinated, and the government forgot Andrews (100). In the 1960s, after the assassination of President Kennedy, the government also withdraws financial support from the Aereon Corporation. Actually after World War II the Navy conducts "a rite of obsolescence" for the dirigible, despite its proven usefulness and safety record (33). The Hindenberg fire seems to have consumed all faith in the dirigible, and McPhee mourns this overreaction, observing that at the height of their development and performance, the rigid airships disappeared.

The representative men seeking to revive Solomon Andrews's nineteenth-century dream bring a religious dedication to the project. William Miller, a former classmate of McPhee's at Princeton and now Aereon's major financial backer, had wanted to be an aeronautical engineer, yet was "inexorably drawn to a higher calling" (142). He obtains a Master of Theology degree, yet recalls Emerson when he tells McPhee that he went to divinity school to learn how to help people spiritually, but not necessarily in a church (140). Miller sees Aereon as bringing a means of transportation of benefit to humanity. A small town in Ghana could afford to buy its own aerobody for commerce and transportation, and thus become more self-reliant. "We don't want people to be dependent on us," Miller explains, evoking Emerson's sense of true philanthropy (138).

Assisting Miller are three men who represent the highest levels of achievement in their respective fields. John Kukon is a master builder of aircraft models. Like Ted Taylor (and McPhee), Kukon moves up and down the various gradients of his realm, designing and building in his basement as a high school student Class A models, Class Bs, Class Cs, proto-speeds, and jets. He even makes his own fuels. Kukon makes Aereon 7 in his basement, and it is one of an ascending series of aerobodies, including a twenty-inch Aereon, a four-foot Aereon, Aereon 7, and, finally, Aereon 26, the proof-of-concept model. "As yet unbuilt, but much alive in Miller's imagination," McPhee notes, were a 52-foot Aereon, a 200-foot Aereon, a 340-foot Aereon, and an Aereon approaching 1,000 feet (6).

Aereon 26 is built by Everett Linkenhoker, a Heliarc welder who constructs the entire airship using neither bolt nor rivet. "The interior of the 26 seemed to have been composed rather than engineered," McPhee marvels. "Or it might have been some prize-winner's discovery in organic chemistry—a novel molecule magnified eight hundred billion times" (66). The aerobody is tested by John Olcott, who exemplifies the highest professional standards in a test pilot. Olcott has a sense of where he is. He tells McPhee that his experience hunting for thermal currents in an engineless glider has helped him develop a keen awareness of an airship in its environment. Like Miller, Olcott believes in increments, in "small and careful steps one at a time, toward a new level" (78).

The Deltoid Pumpkin Seed is structured upon the gradual rise of the

Aereons to higher and higher levels of flight, yet as with *Oranges* and *The Pine Barrens* (and *The Crofter And The Laird*), it ends with a shrinking and disbanded circle. In its initial *New Yorker* publication the first section of *The Deltoid Pumpkin Seed* concludes with the total destruction of the small Aereon 7—yet it had flown. Kukon's model had rotated around its center of gravity, lifted its nose wheel off the ground, and ascended to forty feet. But when Kukon tries to turn it around, to guide it in a circle, it spirals to its destruction.

McPhee's second *New Yorker* section chronicles the test flights of Aereon 26, the first piloted Aereon. Following his philosophy of small increments, pilot Olcott makes a first run without rotation, and then a second adding the rotation and ascending to ten feet. Beginning to loosen up (like Arthur Ashe in *Levels of the Game*), Olcott in his seventh test makes his move "for something or nothing," and the 26 climbed completely out of ground effect, and for the first time cleared the pines (93).

In the concluding section of *The Deltoid Pumpkin Seed* Olcott and Aereon 26 successfully complete the circle:

Olcott was now about to try the first significant turn the 26 had ever made. . . . he swung into a perfect hundred-and-eighty-degree turn and was now pointed again into the sun. He was five hundred feet over the broad white stripes from which he had begun his takeoff. He had completed a circuit of the field. . . .
    "Aereon is great," said NAFEC's chief executive officer. "Just look at it and you can see the potential." (169, 171–172, 173)

Despite this potential and the successful testing of Aereon 26, continued expansion remains difficult for Miller's Aereon Corporation. McPhee closes *The Deltoid Pumpkin Seed* by chronicling the disbanding, and thus the shrinking, circle of dirigible experimenters. In 1973,

Miller alone continued to work full time for Aereon. . . . Aereon attracted interest but no developmental contract, no developmental funds. The summary results of all tests, all flights, all briefings and debriefings, all computations, two configurations, three propellers, one founder, four presidents, twelve years, nearly one and a half million expended dollars, and a hundred miles of circuit flight had been reduced to data that could be expressed on a single sheet of paper. Miller travelled around the country holding up the data like a lamp. (183, 184)

Perhaps one purpose of McPhee's recent geological studies has been to help him gain the long view on such shrinking circles of individuality and enterprise. Through his use of the circle, the sphere, and levels, readers are also able to "take a view" of the natural world. McPhee's concrete forms guide his eyes and ours. They help us discriminate, and the forms themselves derive from the natural world and so are naturally suited to their subjects. By following rising or contracting levels of natural growth or human achievement McPhee derives an organic structure for his works that also is narratively dramatic, even (at times) suspenseful. Dramatic tension arises from overlapping circles and cycles as well. McPhee also uses his natural forms to make abstractions concrete, and thus more comprehensible, such as his presentation of the diverse views of Alaskan development as a wheel of public opinion.

In his aesthetic appreciations of "level number one," the natural world, McPhee strives always for the fullest, "panoptic" vision. Thus his works, characteristically, include not only natural description, but also the historical, scientific and technical, religious, sociological, biographical (and even autobiographical) dimensions that contribute to each scene. In this respect McPhee reveals his kinship with the transcendental perspective of Emerson and Thoreau, their rich appreciation of the relation of the many to the one and of all things to all things. McPhee underscores this point by frequently equating his representative men and women with natural phenomena—such as mountains, rivers, and gold—thereby asserting humanity's tie to nature. His canon, furthermore, is an assertion that representative men and women continue to exist in the twentieth century.

McPhee's persona is as beguiling as Thoreau's. He refuses to allow photographs of himself on his books, and is protective of his privacy and work. Nevertheless, his outlook and wit are somewhat more genial than Thoreau's, and he seeks a reasonable, moderating stance on public issues which represents a twentieth-century tempering of Thoreau's and Emerson's relentless idealism.

In recent years McPhee's work has shown a twenty-year, generational recycling to subjects of his earliest years. *Table of Contents*, published in 1985, collects new visions of Bill Bradley ("Open Man"), Ted Taylor ("Ice Pond"), Alaska ("Riding the Boom Extension"), and bears ("A Textbook Place For Bears" and "Under the Snow"). It contains McPhee's homage to his father ("Heirs of General Practice") and to his Maine woods kinsman, another John McPhee ("North of the C.P. Line"), and thus in a very real way is a table of McPhee's content.

What will be the future direction of McPhee's artistic vision once his geology series is complete? Theodore Taylor and David Brower offer, I believe, the surest indices. When he has completed his levels of the Earth, McPhee, with his remarkable gradient way of seeing, may turn his attention to the sea, or to the vaster atmospheric circles above. And who better to describe for us the troposphere and the stratosphere, the mesophere, ionisphere, and exosphere beyond?

4

Joan Didion's Lambent Light

Joan Didion's sensibility is highly literary. Her artistic vision has been shaped as much by the American (and English) literary tradition as by her own biology and by Western geography and history. This chapter might have been titled "Joan Didion's Certain Slant of Light," for it strikes me as surprising that no one has noted the similarities between Didion and that nineteenth-century petite-but-hard-edged wordsmith Emily Dickinson. It is not only that Didion possesses Dickinson's shy, reclusive personality, or that both produce works of high compression. It is that Didion shares Dickinson's interest in that "certain slant of light" as a metaphor for the elusive "glimmer" of truth.

Even more important is Didion's bond with F. Scott Fitzgerald, who toiled in Didion's own vineyards of fiction and nonfiction. Didion's early writings contain at least twenty references to Fitzgerald or his work. The bond, as with Dickinson, is more than parallel traits or personal histories—here of Westerners drawn and repelled by the East, of writers of Hollywood movies living in Malibu. It is more than their similar interests in wealth and illusion, the beautiful and the damned, the lost Eden of the American Dream and the dark night of the American soul. It is even more than Didion's willingness to follow Fitzgerald's advice of "tearing your . . . tragic love story out of your heart and putting it on pages for people to see" (Phillips 75). Didion's special affinity is with what Milton R. Stern has called Fitzgerald's "golden moments."[1]

In a lecture at Berkeley in 1976 Didion described an illustration of a cat that appears in many introductory psychology books. Drawn by a patient suffering from schizophrenia, the cat has a shimmer around it. "Writing is the attempt to understand what's going on in the shimmer," Didion explained. "To find the cat in the shimmer, if the cat is the important thing, or to find what the shimmer is."[2] Here, symbolically presented, is Didion's artistic vision. She employs the perceptions of her (often afflicted) nervous system as a metaphor for illusion and reality in the American experience. In some cases the shimmer she discovers is the false golden light of "mirage." In others her search yields neither cat nor shimmer, but only void. Didion craves the white light of truth, yet finds "truth" most often flickering and insubstantial, a lambent light, a "shimmer" hard to hold. Like Emily Dickinson, she locates "truth" obliquely, in the slippage or breakage, between the lines and over the border.

Didion begins to articulate this vision in her book and film reviews for the *National Review* and *Vogue* in the early 1960s. A Didion review most often is a contrast of false works with true, and her most frequent adjective for describing the latter is "brilliant." James Purdy is a "dazzling stylist" and his novel *The Nephew* "compels by the sheer brilliance of its telling."[3] Anthony Powell's *The Music of Time* is "brilliant," and John Cheever's "Torch Song" and "The Season of Divorce" are "as delicate and brilliant and suggestive and unforgettable as any [stories] written in English."[4] Repeatedly employing this metaphor of light, Didion admires the "brilliant stroke" on which Evelyn Waugh begins *Men at War*, and the "imaginative brilliance" of John Hawkes's *The Lime Twig*, its "appreciation of the possibilities that lurk somewhere outside Eliot House."[5] She finds *Rabbit, Run* "electric with Rabbit's own direct, mindless immediacy," and that Updike's milieu "radiates" a "grubby urgency."[6] The high praise she gives to Wright Morris's *Ceremony in Lone Tree* is that it is "illuminating," and her complaint regarding Claude Mauriac's *The Dinner Party* is precisely that "nothing amusing or illuminating happens."[7] She defines "nothing novels" as those that open "no windows" to light.[8]

Didion's interest in lambent light explains her romance with the "silver screen" in general, as well as her eccentric affection for certain film genres and films. It makes clear her rapture for science fiction movies, as she awaits "one more glimpse of the brain pulsing, . . . the Golden Gate dematerializing."[9] She likes, in fact, teen surfing movies for the opportunity "to spend forty unbroken minutes watching immense translucent combers rise and curl in the sunlight."[10] Among the things she likes about *Doctor Zhivago* are "the heat shimmering off the steppes, the chandelier in the abandoned summer house glittering with ice."[11] She takes note of "swans shimmering on a lake" in John Frankenheimer's *All Fall Down*, and admires the style of *Those Magnificent Men in Their Flying Machines*, "everything swimming in the . . . sweet lambent air of a 1910 that never was."[12] She mourns Billy Wilder's misapprehension of his genius for mirage and "desolate glare."[13] Such genius, of course, is also her own.

GOLDEN LIGHT: *SLOUCHING TOWARDS BETHLEHEM*

Didion's first three works of literary nonfiction—*Slouching Towards Bethlehem* (1968), *The White Album* (1979), and *Salvador* (1983)—can be understood as progressively starker explorations of lambent light.[14] Too often shimmering light can be the false light of mirage; therefore, much of Didion's nonfiction is devoted to exposing misapprehension and mirages of every American hue. It is as if Didion begins with Fitzgerald's "golden moments," only to expose them and skew away from them in perfect demonstration of Harold Bloom's anxiety of influence.

The first section of Didion's *Slouching Towards Bethlehem* is titled "Life Styles in the Golden Land," and we gradually perceive that "gold" in the Didion spectrum is synonymous with "mirage" and the past Edenic state Didion knows will ne'er return. Just as she first uses yellow paper in her writing as the color for "letting it run," Didion portrays the California dreamers as those who let their golden fantasies run, without the reining discipline Didion will apply to herself and her vision.[15]

Lucille Miller of Didion's opening article, "Some Dreamers of the Golden Dream," represents her fullest portrait of those rapt by that particularly persistent American mirage: the Fitzgeraldian dream of success and love. "This is a story of love and death in the golden land and begins with the country," commences Didion. Suggesting a parable of Eden lost, Didion observes that after the San Bernardino valley was abandoned by the Mormons, who planted the original orange groves, the land drew the kind of people "who imagined they might live among the talismanic fruit" (STB 4).

Lucille Miller's "private drive" is named Bella Vista and the subdivision flags advertise "TRAVERTINE ENTRIES," travertine being porous, light yellow crystalline limestone. By the summer of 1964 Lucille seems to have achieved all her golden wishes:

the bigger house on the better street and the familiar accouterments of a family on its way up: the $30,000 a year, the three children for the Christmas card, the picture window, the family room, the newspaper photographs that showed "Mrs. Gordon Miller, Ontario Heart Fund Chairman." (STB 8–9)

What, then, would drive such a woman, Didion inquires, "to . . . look our her new picture window into the empty California sun and calculate how to burn her husband alive in a Volkswagen"? (STB 15). Something is wrong with this picture. This American "mirage," like the porous, crystalline entrance to the dream house, is insubstantial. The future "always looks good in the golden land," Didion notes, "because no one remembers the past" (STB 4). The error is one of perception. Didion's description of Rabbit Angstrom's wife in her 1961 review of

Rabbit, Run applies equally to Lucille Miller: "[Rabbit's] wife . . . drinks too much and watches daytime television to blur the already fuzzy edges of her unfocused dissatisfaction."[16] The Janice Angstroms and Lucille Millers of America perceive fuzzily. Because they have no perceptions of the past, they derive their ideals from "the only places they know to look": television, the movies, and tabloid newspapers (STB 4). Everything, Didion writes, was "in the name of 'love'; everyone involved placed a magical faith in the efficacy of the very word" (STB 18–19). In the name of "love" anything went, including adultery and murder. Didion observes of the California Institution for Women at Frontera: "A lot of California murderesses live here, a lot of girls who somehow misunderstood the promise" (STB 25).

If they misunderstood, Didion did not—nor do we after reading this artful article. Not surprisingly, Didion locates the most profound truth of this story in the cracks and around the edges, where no one else saw light:

What was most startling about the case . . . against Lucille Miller was something that had nothing to do with law at all, something that never appeared in the eight-column afternoon headlines but was always there between them: the revelation that the dream was teaching the dreamers how to live. (STB 17)

Lucille Miller was "an erring woman, a woman who perhaps wanted too much . . . a woman motivated by 'love and greed,'" Didion makes clear (STB 22). Her golden dream is a mirage, the sign on her street telling:

> Private Road
> Bella Vista
> Dead End

The Millers never get their dream house landscaped, and their trash can is stuffed with "the debris of family life," including, ironically, what they need most: "a child's game called 'Lie Detector'" (STB 27). That their "mirage" will continue undetected, shimmering goldenly if destructively before a dazed American public Didion hints in the final lines of her article:

Some people . . . say that Arthwell Hayton [Lucille's lover] suffered; others say that he did not suffer at all. . . . In any case, on October 17, 1965, Arthwell Hayton married again, married his children's pretty governess, Wenche Berg. . . . The bride wore a long white *peau de soie* dress and carried a shower bouquet of sweetheart roses with stephanotis streamers. A coronet of seed pearls held her illusion veil.[17]

Lucille Miller has numerous sisters in the Didion canon. Her Nevada cousins are those whom Didion describes in ("Life Styles in the Golden Land's") "Marrying Absurd." Like Lucille Miller, the brides of Las Vegas are those for whom the golden mirage appears in the desire to wear "a candlelight satin Priscilla of Boston wedding dress" and have "Candlelight with Your Ceremony" (STB 81). Las Vegas merchandises "niceness" in its five-minute wedding ceremonies, Didion notes, "the facsimile of proper ritual, to children who do not know how else to find it" (STB 82). Like Gatsby pursuing the elusive green light, these young women stand "in the middle of a vast hostile desert looking at . . . sign[s] which blink . . . 'STARDUST' or 'CAESAR'S PALACE' " (STB 80–81).

Better educated and more privileged women than Lucille Miller and her sisters, however, can also fall victim to Golden American mirages. Didion depicts Joan Baez in thrall to a related American mirage: that golden dream of human improvability. That Didion did some of her most extensive rewriting in transferring her 1966 magazine article on Baez to "Life Styles in the Golden Land" suggests her ambivalent feelings toward the singer.[18] In many ways Didion admires Baez. "She has a great natural style, and she is what used to be called a lady," Didion writes (STB 44). Both compliments are of the highest order to Didion.

We gradually perceive, however, that, as with Jay Gatsby, it is the deluded dreamers surrounding Baez, and her own vague sense of self that place Baez in jeopardy. Ira Sandperl, the president of Baez's Institute for the Study of Nonviolence, possesses "glittering and slightly messianic eyes . . . and the general look of a man who has, all his life, followed some imperceptibly but fatally askew rainbow" (STB 51). Among the children attracted to the Institute is "a dreamy boy with curly golden hair," and the response of these children toward one another is "so tender that an afternoon at the school tends to drift perilously into the never-never" (STB 50, 49).

It is lack of self-knowledge, as well as ignorance of the historical past, that makes one susceptible to mirage, Didion seems to imply. "Joan Baez was a personality before she was entirely a person," Didion writes, recalling Fitzgerald's *This Side of Paradise*, "and, like anyone to whom that happens, she is in a sense the hapless victim of what others have seen in her, written about her, wanted her to be and not to be" (STB 47). One can, as in Baez's case, be turned into a mirage oneself—"the Madonna of the disaffected"—and Didion's vision of lambent light and her final indictment of Baez are revealed in the passage she quotes from Baez's own concert program: "My life is a crystal teardrop. . . . If I were to look into the teardrop for the next million years, I might never find out who the people are, and what they are doing" (STB 47, 57).

"Of their peculiar light," Didion might say with Emily Dickinson, *"I keep one ray/To clarify the Sight/To seek them by."* Three of the remaining five articles in "Life Styles in the Golden Land" trace other forms of California mirage—all related to human improvability. Didion is gentle with Michael Laski, the twenty-six-year-old general secretary of the Central Committee of the Communist Party U.S.A. (Marxist-Leninist) whom she portrays in "Comrade Laski, C.P.U.S.A.(M.-L.)." Didion confesses:

I know something about dread myself, and appreciate the elaborate systems with which some people manage to fill the void, appreciate all the opiates of the people, whether they are as accessible as alcohol and heroin and promiscuity or as hard to come by as faith in God or History.

But of course I did not mention dread to Michael Laski, whose particular opiate is History. (STB 63)

In the end, after revealing that Michael's world of "labyrinthine intricacy and immaculate clarity" is reducible to $9.91, Didion credits Laski with at least achieving "a minor but perilous triumph of being over nothingness" (STB 65, 66).

Didion is more severe with Michael's elders, the liberal ideologues at California's Center for the Study of Democratic Institutions, whom she skewers in "California Dreaming," perhaps because they traffic in millions rather than tens. She employs her metaphor of lambent light in the article's first sentence by ironically juxtaposing natural light with the ideologues' hubristic mirage: "just about the time the sun burns the last haze off the Santa Barbara hills, fifteen or twenty men gather . . . and begin another session of what they like to call 'clarifying the basic issues' " (STB 73).

Didion, in fact, treats the Center as if it were science fiction fantasy. The Center, she notes, is the current "mutation" of the Fund for the Republic; its rhetoric "has about it the kind of ectoplasmic generality that always makes me sense I am on the track of the real soufflé, the genuine American *kitsch*" (STB 73, 75). Ectoplasm, indeed, *means* "mirage," being a substance held to produce spirit materialization and telekinesis. Telekinesis means "unaccountable shimmer." The Center's "visionaries who never met a payroll" believe that everything they say "mystically improves the national, and in fact the international, weal" (STB 77, 75). They portray themselves as "besieged by the forces of darkness," and Didion exits this flying saucer soiree with a quote from the wife of a big contributor: "These sessions are way over my head, but I go out floating on air" (STB 77, 78).

Much more is serious and at risk in the concluding article in "Life Styles in the Golden Land," Didion's title piece "Slouching Towards Bethlehem." In 1967 Didion visited the Haight-Ashbury district of San

Francisco to report on the political and social revolution within the "hippie generation." In 1960 Didion had called San Francisco "a city dispossessed."[19] That article must have seemed hauntingly prophetic when she returned to study the love children assembling in Golden Gate Park. In "San Francisco Job Hunt" Didion had written: "When you drive into San Francisco, across the Bay Bridge from Oakland or the Golden Gate from Marin County, the city seems to float ahead like a mirage, white and shimmery, looking the way Atlantis should have looked" (128). Some are drawn to San Francisco "under the pervasive delusion that the Western cities are still wide open," she continued (128). If these glittering images are what draw the flower children in 1967, they, too, will be disappointed, although like America's other mirage-seekers many will continue rapt by their shimmering ideal.

Didion employs the trope of lambent light to expose the mirages of these golden children. The love children seek fulfillment through artificial means, she implies. They ingest "crystal" and mesmerize themselves with strobe lights and Day-glo, in fact "light shows" of every variety, to give them an external "flash" while they await the internal chemical "flash" from LSD. "When you're strung out on crystal, you don't need *nothing*," the aptly named Deadeye tells Didion (STB 109). Even the artificial "high" of LSD is often "simulated"—by Methedrine. The result, not unsurprisingly, is confusion as thousands of young people gather in Golden Gate Park to hear the Grateful Dead.

Didion contrasts the misperceptions of these young people and their parents with the sad truth she repeatedly perceives between all the lines:

the market was steady and the G.N.P. high and a great many articulate people seemed to have a sense of high social purpose and it might have been a spring of brave hopes and national promise, but it was not, and more and more people had the uneasy apprehension that it was not. All that seemed clear was that at some point we had aborted ourselves and butchered the job. . . .

Of course the activists . . . had long ago grasped the reality which still eluded the press: we were seeing something important. We were seeing the desperate attempt of a handful of pathetically unequipped children to create a community in a social vacuum. Once we had seen these children, we could no longer overlook the vacuum. (STB 84–85, 122)

Once again Didion perceives, not mirage, but void. Yet the children of Haight-Ashbury and the media watching them persist in seeing not the void, but the crystal. Didion ends with an emblematic fire started by a child earlier riding a wooden rocking horse in a blue spotlight. His burning and the screams of his mother go unattended "because they were in the kitchen trying to retrieve some very good Moroccan hash. . . . " (128)

If six of the eight essays in her opening "Life Styles in the Golden Land" section expose innocent and not-so-innocent mirages of American love and politics, Didion acknowledges how glittering such illusions can be by including two articles on figures of her own fantasy: John Wayne and Howard Hughes. Like the child on the rocking horse in the blue spotlight, Didion as a teenager was captivated by artificial blue rain falling behind an Officers' Club bar in Colorado. Because she could not stare at this shimmering water forever, she confesses at the opening of "John Wayne: A Love Story," she went instead to the movies, and it was there that she saw John Wayne. Suggesting how prone we are to illusion, she states: "I tell you this neither in a spirit of self-revelation nor as an exercise in total recall, but simply to demonstrate that when John Wayne rode through my childhood, and perhaps through yours, he determined forever the shape of certain of our dreams" (STB 30).

Didion is aware that the dream world of a Wayne western, a world of "cottonwoods shimmering in the early morning sun," is a mirage lacking historical validity (STB 31). Her response, however, is more lament than exposé, "In a world we understood early to be characterized by venality and doubt and paralyzing ambiguities, he suggested another world, one which may or may not have existed ever but in any case existed no more" (STB 30–31). Directors, in fact, sensed that into Wayne's "perfect mold might be poured the inarticulate longings of a nation wondering at just what pass the trail had been lost" (STB 31). Even Wayne's biography fueled this fantasy, "for it was no history at all," Didion explains, "nothing to intrude upon the dream" (STB 31).

When Didion goes to meet Wayne he has just come from Durango (Colorado), "the very country of the dream" (STB 32). She knows it is, in part, mirage: "The very name hallucinates. Man's country. Out where the West begins. There had been ahuehuete trees in Durango; a waterfall. . . . 'You really missed something, *Durango*,' they would say, sometimes joking and sometimes not, until it became a refrain, Eden lost" (STB 35). That something is amiss with this Dream is seen both in the reason for Didion's article and in her final evocation of the Dream. Didion pens her "Love Song" because the perfect mold has been stricken by cancer. "It did not seem possible that such a man could fall ill," Didion writes, "could carry within him that most inexplicable and ungovernable of diseases" (STB 30). But he does, and although in her final evocation, when three guitars play "Red River Valley," Didion is momentarily able to resurrect the Dream, its rhythm is not quite true, and in any case it was a Dream, even from its inception, gone.

"I have as much trouble as the next person with illusion and reality," Didion writes in this article, a confession that enlists reader sympathy and identification (STB 32). She confesses in fact to harboring certain illusions "deep in that part of [her] heart where the artificial rain forever falls" (STB 30). Howard Hughes represents, like Wayne, another

California myth of which Didion is inordinately fond. Though "7000 Romaine, Los Angeles 38," Hughes California address, is locked and abandoned, Didion insists even more emphatically than she does with Wayne that her secret affection for Hughes is a national one. In speaking of this Midas of the West, Didion evokes the national pastime: "The stories [of Hughes] are endless, infinitely familiar, traded by the faithful like baseball cards, fondled until they fray around the edges and blur into the apocryphal" (STB 69). One shimmering story involves a former Hughes contract starlet "fingering a diamond as big as the Ritz"; another a business deal discussed only between midnight and dawn in the municipal dump—by flashlight (STB 69, 70). The truth Didion locates around these dazzling edges is that Howard Hughes represents something we do not easily acknowledge, that "in a nation which increasingly appears to prize social virtues, Howard Hughes remains not merely antisocial but grandly, brilliantly, surpassingly, asocial. He is the last private man, a dream we no longer admit" (STB 72).

In truth it is not only Hughes's asociability that Didion admires; it is his ambition. An ambitious woman herself in an era when naked ambition is both unfashionable and discreetly clothed, Didion gravitates toward golden myths surrounding such disparate insatiates as Hughes, William Randolph Hearst, and Joseph Kennedy. In her 1964 review of Richard J. Whalen's *The Founding Father: The Story of Joseph Kennedy* Didion described Kennedy as "an organism pulsing with visceral want":

Fired by old passions, seizing new opportunities. They are phrases which seem to materialize between the lines on page after page of this fine and hauntingly detailed study of Kennedy, evoking the image of a man whose most stunning characteristic was the naked and sustained force of his want.[20]

Didion knows well such sustained want, and if her opening section of *Slouching Towards Bethlehem* explores such mirages of the "Golden Land," including her own, in the volume's final section, "Seven Places of the Mind," she seeks to penetrate the golden shimmer to discern starker truths. The three sections of *Slouching Towards Bethlehem* can be understood as signifying the false (section one), the true (section three), and "Personals" (section two)—the only way to get from the false to the true.

In "Notes from a Native Daughter," the first of the seven places of Didion's mind, she seeks to go beyond the golden mirages of California that she exposed in section one, to the harsher reality of California as she perceives it. From her opening sentence she undercuts popular illusions regarding the Golden State:

It is very easy to sit at the bar in, say, La Scala in Beverly Hills, or Ernie's in San Francisco, and to share in the pervasive delusion that California is only five

hours from New York by air. The truth is that La Scala and Ernie's are only
five hours from New York by air. California is somewhere else.

Many people in the East . . . do not believe this. They have been to Los
Angeles or to San Francisco, have driven through a giant redwood and have
seen the Pacific glazed by the afternoon sun off Big Sur, and they naturally
tend to believe that they have in fact been to California. They have not been,
and they probably never will be, for it is a longer and in many ways a more
difficult trip than they might want to undertake, one of those trips on which
the destination flickers chimerically on the horizon, ever receding, ever diminishing. (STB 171)

California, in short, is lambent light. Repeatedly in this article Didion
stresses the difficulty of proper knowing. "It should be clear by now
that the truth about the place is elusive, and must be tracked with caution," she stresses (STB 178). "It is hard to *find* California now, unset-
tling to wonder how much of it was merely imagined or improvised"
(STB 177). When Didion tries out "a few irrefutable statements" she
finds herself talking about the Central Valley, which is, for her, the lost
Eden of a former golden time (STB 179). Indeed, Sacramento came
into being with the discovery of gold in 1848. Although Didion believes
that Sacramento lost its character after 1950, the only truth she can
vouchsafe of California is the personal truth of lambent light, that "all
that is constant about the California of my childhood is the rate at which
it disappears" (STB 176).

"Letter from Paradise, 21° 19′ N., 157° 52′ W." reveals that Hawaii,
like California, also exists in its truest form for Didion as lambent light.
As a child she sat on California beaches and imagined that she saw
Hawaii, "a certain shimmer in the sunset, a barely perceptible irregu-
larity glimpsed intermittently through squinted eyes" (STB 188). Hawaii represents endless summer and escape from adult problems and
harsh realities for many Californians—and for Didion in particular. She
begins this article by confessing:

Because I had been tired too long and quarrelsome too much and too often
frightened of migraine and failure and the days getting shorter, I was sent, a
recalcitrant thirty-one-year-old child, to Hawaii, where winter does not come
and no one fails and the median age is twenty-three. There I could become a
new woman, there with the . . . children who have never been told, as I was
told, that golden lads and girls all must as chimney sweepers come to dust. I
was to lie beneath the same sun that had kept Doris Duke and Henry Kaiser
forever hopeful. . . . I was to see for myself that just beyond the end of the
line lay not Despond but Diamond Head. (STB 187–88)

A glittering mirage once again. It is because Hawaii represents such
an attractive mirage, such a paradise of escape for Didion that she must

penetrate its mist and find, as with California, its sharper realities. In point of fact, a tidal wave is threatening during a "restorative week" Didion and family spend in paradise,[21] and in "Letter from Paradise" she acknowledges that although she possesses that Fitzgeraldian yearning for Eden, she lacks, in truth, "all temperament" for it. (STB 188).

In "Letter from Paradise" Didion connects the three disparate images of Hawaii she held as a child: the Hawaii that meant Pearl Harbor and war and her father going away and "nothing the same ever again"; Hawaii's past, a "gentle idyll" also gone, but preserved in such accents as "flat silver for forty-eight and the diamond that had been Queen Liliuokalani's and the heavy linens embroidered on all the long golden afternoons that were no more"; and the current Hawaii, the "big rock candy mountain in the Pacific" for vacationing middle-class godmothers (STB 189, 190). The bleak truth Didion comes home to is the first Hawaii of her childhood, the Hawaii that meant war: "if there is a single aura which pervades Honolulu, one mood which lends the lights a feverish luster . . . that mood is, inescapably, one of war" (STB 190).

The harsh truth Didion perceives is that most Hawaiians consider war an "instrument for social progress" (STB 198). It was the war that opened up the contracting economy and the immobile colonial society and made possible the middle-class godmothers and the current rhetoric that Didion exposes as false paradise: "they talk, in a kind of James Michener rhetoric, about how Hawaii is a multiracial paradise and a labor-management paradise and a progressive paradise in which the past is now reconciled with the future . . . " (STB 203). What reconciles Hawaii's past to its future, for Didion, however, is war, and she offers this specter of true Hawaii in an image of shimmering light:

in the peculiar and still insular mythology of Hawaii, the dislocations of war became the promises of progress. Whether or not the promises have been fulfilled depends of course upon who is talking . . . but in any case it is war that is pivotal to the Hawaiian imagination, . . . war that seems to hover over Honolulu like the rain clouds of Tantalus.[22] (STB 202–3)

War and death are not congenial clouds when one is sunning oneself on the beaches of Waikiki. Yet they are the reality, Didion insists, and as she comes to the end of *Slouching Towards Bethlehem*, to the sixth and seventh "Places of the Mind," we see her continue bold, even defiant, in stripping away the auras of paradise to reveal death and corruption. In "Los Angeles Notebook," the sixth place of her mind, Didion returns to California, as if she had not told it all in "Notes from a Native Daughter." The California she returns to is the California of the Santa Ana and its arid fires, the California of catastrophe and apocalypse:

The city burning is Los Angeles's deepest image of itself; Nathanael West perceived that, in *The Day of the Locust*; and at the time of the 1965 Watts riots what struck the imagination most indelibly were the fires. For days one could drive the harbor Freeway and see the city on fire, just as we had always known it would be in the end. (STB 220)

The Santa Ana winds "dry the hills and the nerves to the flash point," Didion notes (STB 217). The fires in the San Gabriel Mountains go out of control. "The wind," Didion writes, "shows us how close to the edge we are" (STB 221).

By positioning the Helen Gurley Brown story after the eerie revelations of the Santa Ana in "Los Angeles Notebook," Didion offers a method of regaining control. "Bosses Make Lousy Lovers," Didion's original article on Brown, exposes the hard truth behind a Golden Dream that works. Helen Gurley Brown, and her "very sincere . . . little pippypoo books" *Sex and the Single Girl* and *Sex in the Office* (36), is precisely a Lucille Miller who makes the Golden Dream come true. It is for this reason that Didion places Brown in the closing pages of *Slouching Towards Bethlehem* rather than with the misperceivers.

Didion admires Brown for the same reason she admires Howard Hughes, William Randolph Hearst, and Joseph Kennedy—for her ambition:

There runs through [Brown's history] a thread of old-fashioned ambition so increasingly uncommon that her younger readers will recognize it only from early Joan Crawford movies on the *Late Late Show*. . . . She is the small-town girl who wanted to be the toast of Big Town. . . . *Some day I'll be rich and famous and have champagne for breakfast and then good-bye Sauk Center, good-bye Little Rock, good-bye C. K. McClatchy High.* (37)

C. K. McClatchy High was Didion's own high school, and Didion cannot talk about this Fitzgeraldian dream without evoking her mythos of lambent light. "It is a vision which has shimmered through restless hearts straight across the Republic," she writes (37). Helen Gurley Brown, however, possesses something that Lucille Miller and her sisters lack. While Brown presents herself as a forty-two-year-old Cinderella replete with Prince Charming, this fairy-tale existence is sustained by exacting and exhausting discipline: "What is it like to be the little princess, the woman who has fulfilled the whispered promise of her own books and of all the advertisements, the girl to whom things happen? It is hard work" (37). Didion was discovering this truth herself, and thus is in sympathy with *individual* "self-improvement" such as Brown's "curiously refreshing exhortations [to women] to stop 'being a slug' and get out there and work for what [you] want" (37).

Didion was doing just that in Los Angeles, and the final section of her "Los Angeles Notebook" foreshadows the defiance she will show the East and New York City in the concluding article in *Slouching Towards Bethlehem*, titled revealingly "Goodbye to All That." When a friend in New York City inquires of Didion *why* she is in a piano bar in Encino, Didion's insouciant response is "Why not?"

Slouching Towards Bethlehem is a book about childish illusions and, in its final section, about childhood remembered but left behind. That Didion chose to end her first collection of nonfiction with an article originally titled "Farewell to the Enchanted City" but retitled more cavalierly "Goodbye to All That" suggests her conscious separation from Fitzgerald's "golden moments," her continuous refinement toward truer light.

In 1961 Didion found New York City less of a "mirage" than San Francisco or Washington, D.C., in respect to career opportunities for women. Yet in "N.Y.: The Great Reprieve" we see that New York also possessed for Didion that romantic charm known to Nick Carraway and Jay Gatsby, the "special promise—of something remarkable and lively just around the corner," the "freedom to start over, to make mistakes and erase them".[23] Yet, even in 1961, Didion makes a distinction between her vision and Fitzgerald's in her awareness that New York was reprieve, not reality: "Make no mistakes: what [young women] have in mind is a sabbatical, not a break with anything; their intentions, however vague, have more to do with exploration than with rebellion, more to do with making themselves 'ready' for something than with splashing in the Plaza fountain" (150).

Six years later "Goodbye to All That" will be Didion's *Great Gatsby* and "Babylon Revisited" combined. The naive speaker of the opening refrain "How many miles to Babylon?" seems eager to reach this gilded city, not knowing perhaps of its negative associations. Not surprisingly, the query is a nursery rhyme filled with images of golden light:

How many miles to Babylon?
Three score miles and ten—
Can I get there by candlelight?
Yes, and back again—
If your feet are nimble and light
You can get there by candlelight.

Didion's feet were nimble and light when she arrived in New York City at the age of twenty. She was, as she confesses, "in love with New York" (STB 228), despite her growing sense of its Babylonian "vices" and analogous Fitzgeraldian mirage:

Wall Street and Fifth Avenue and Madison Avenue were not places at all but abstractions ("Money," and "High Fashion," and "The Hucksters"), New York was no mere city. It was instead an infinitely romantic notion, the mysterious nexus of all love and money and power, the shining and perishable dream itself. (STB 231)

As she continues delineating her gilded fantasy, we see that New York also represented, for Didion, a peculiar literary and film "nexus" of T. S. Eliot and Marilyn Monroe and Fitzgerald:

I stopped at Lexington Avenue and bought a peach and stood on the corner eating it and knew that I had come out of the West and reached the mirage. I could taste the peach and feel the soft air blowing from the subway grating on my legs and I could smell lilac and garbage and expensive perfume and I knew that it would cost something sooner or later—because I did not belong there, did not come from there. . . . (STB 228)

Didion engages our sympathy by demonstrating one last time that she is as susceptible to mirage as any. Despite her growing sense of living in Babylonian exile in New York City, she still clings fervently to every ephemeral glimmer: the weather signal beaming across town and the lambent lights that alternately spell out TIME and LIFE above Rockefeller Plaza. "That pleased me obscurely," she confesses, "and so did walking uptown in the mauve eight o'clocks of early summer evenings and looking at things . . . all the sweet promises of money and summer" (STB 235). Living in Babylon, she never feels poor; she imagines she can always "smuggle gold into India" or become a $100 call girl, "and none of it would matter" (STB 229).

Surely it is revealing that when the shimmer starts to fade from the mirage, Didion's response is to hang fifty yards of yellow theatrical silk across her bedroom windows. What ensues is an apologue of human miscalculation. "I had some idea that the gold light would make me feel better," Didion states, "but I did not bother to weigh the curtains correctly and all that summer the long panels of transparent golden silk would blow out the windows and get tangled and drenched in the afternoon thunderstorms" (STB 232–33).[24]

Didion ends, like Fitzgerald's Nick Carraway and Charlie Wales, by fleeing the golden city. Her characteristic insistence on the personal nature of this act belies its signal importance in terms of both literary allegiance and her mythos of lambent light. "All I mean," she writes, "is that I was very young in New York, and that at some point the golden rhythm was broken, and I am not that young any more."[25]

WHITE LIGHT: *THE WHITE ALBUM*

How scant, by everlasting Light
The Discs that satisfied Our Sight—
How dimmer than a Saturn's Bar
The things esteemed, for Things that are!

Emily Dickinson wrote these lines in 1866, but they perfectly describe Didion's exposé of the false golden "Discs" in *Slouching Towards Bethlehem*. If her first collection of literary nonfiction disabuses us of Fitzgeraldian gold, Didion's revealingly titled second collection, *The White Album*, enters a starker light. *Slouching Towards Bethlehem* begins with "Some Dreamers of the Golden Dream" and ends with Didion, the true perceiver. That *The White Album* begins with Didion suggests she may be taking up where she left off, yet it is with telling difference. In the opening "White Album" essay Didion has lost the cavalier confidence of "Goodbye to All That." In its stead are confessions of breakdown, uncertainty, and the ambiguity of white.

In *The White Album* white can suggest the blank page, tabula rasa, the null and void, and death—and it can represent the immaculate white light of truth. If Didion begins with yellow paper as the color for "letting it run," she progresses to pale blue when she starts "getting closer to it, to find the shape of the thing—the grain in the wood."[26] Last, however, is white. Didion explains that she dares the white paper "when it seems that if, if only I could commit myself to use this expensive paper, this sixteen-weight bond with a watermark on it, maybe if I make that commitment I could get it almost right" (Braudy 109). These painful hesitations and qualifications reveal how elusive the white light of truth is for Didion. Her posture is as tentative as the Dickinson persona who queries: "Dare you see a Soul *at the White Heat?*/Then crouch within the door."

In the title essay, "The White Album," experience is now a ghostly form of lambent light. "We live entirely, especially if we are writers, by the imposition of a narrative line upon disparate images," Didion writes, "by the 'ideas' with which we have learned to freeze the shifting phantasmagoria which is our actual experience" (TWA 11). Didion has begun to doubt the validity of any imposition, of any freezing. If her inaugural *Life* column in 1969 was called "A problem of making connections," in 1979 she will look back to the 1960s and confess to an *inability* to do so: "All I knew was what I saw: flash pictures in variable sequence, images with no 'meaning' beyond their temporary arrangement. . . . " (TWA 13).

These images, with increasing frequency, are of murder and suicide.

Didion reads the transcript of the Ramon Novarro murder trial several times, "trying to bring the picture into some focus," but is unsuccessful (TWA 17). She is amazed at the ability of Gary Fleischman, lawyer to Charles Manson devotee Linda Kasabian, to remain "cheerful, even jaunty, in the face of the awesome and impenetrable mystery at the center of what he called 'the case' " (TWA 43). For Didion, the Manson family heart of darkness remains an impenetrable mystery, and her own personal associations with it "an authentically senseless chain of correspondences" (TWA 45). While living in New York City Didion had been pleased to see the flashing TIME and LIFE signs. In California in "The White Album" Eliot's "Hurry up please, it's time" is pressing on Didion, who is interested now only in the image of the suicidal surrogate on the window ledge, a replica of Eliot's woman whose hair is all spread out in points. Didion's woman is also a vision of shimmering light: "her hair incandescent in the floodlights" (TWA 44).

"The White Album" represents Didion's most extensive effort until *Salvador* to articulate this shimmer at the edge of the void, at the window ledge of death. Her earlier writings reveal fleeting perceptions of the void in images primarily associated with California's bleached sky. In Didion's spectrum "bleached" shades to "bleak" and then "blank." Perhaps it is because nature deplores a vacuum that Californians fill the void with mirages of gold.

The vast bleached blankness that is the western sky encourages the related sense of tabula rasa that Didion also abhors. The three sections that follow the despairing "White Album" opening—"California Republic," "Women," and "Sojourns"—explore both tabula rasa fallacies and truer visions and visionaries. Following the method of *Slouching Towards Bethlehem* Didion interweaves her own fantasies, yet moves toward ever starker perceptions.

The title "California Republic" itself suggests tabula rasa insularity, a denial of historical and geographical ties with America proper. In her opening article in this section, "James Pike, American," Didion reasserts the tie. Bishop Pike represents, for Didion, a signal example of fatal tabula rasa mentality. Her experience with Pike was personal to the degree that he not only treated his own past marriages and religious affiliations as if they had never existed, but also encouraged other Episcopalians (like Didion) to do the same:

I was struck dumb by Bishop Pike's position, which appeared to be that I had not only erred [in marrying a Catholic] but had every moral right and obligation to erase this error by regarding my marriage as null, and any promises I had made as invalid. In other words the way to go was to forget it and start over. (TWA 56)

Pike's smug and narrow ahistorical philosophy leads to his death.

In "Many Mansions" Didion challenges the tabula rasa vision of the Reagans, who wish to forget the historical California governor's mansion—not to mention the American River—and, like Bishop Pike, start anew. The "Bureaucrats" of the California Department of Transportation similarly wish to alter the historical driving patterns of California motorists with message boards, diamond lanes, and car pools just as if they could "eradicate a central Southern Californian illusion, that of individual mobility, without anyone really noticing" (TWA 81). In "Good Citizens" Didion finds that the Jaycees lack all historical consciousness of 1960s political movements, just as the Hollywood "Good Citizens," who perceive every social problem as a playable script, lack any historical sense of politics as sometimes irreconcilable and unglamourous disagreement.

In contrast, what Didion admires about "The Getty" Museum in California is its refusal to take a tabula rasa perspective, its refusal to dim its historical spotlight:

The Getty tells us that the past was perhaps different from the way we like to perceive it. Ancient marbles were not always attractively faded and worn. Ancient marbles once appeared just as they appear here: as strident, opulent evidence of imperial power and acquisition. Ancient murals were not always bleached and mellowed and "tasteful." Ancient murals once looked as they do here: as if dreamed by a Mafia don. Ancient fountains once worked, and drowned out that very silence we have come to expect and want from the past. . . . The Getty tells us that we were never any better than we are and will never be any better than we were, and in so doing makes a profoundly unpopular political statement. (TWA 76)

It is a historical statement, however, to which Didion subscribes.

As noted earlier, one reason Didion creates reader sympathy for her views is that she does not present herself as completely free of the errors she criticizes in others. In "Holy Water" she confesses to being as rapt by pulsing light boards as the Caltrans "Bureaucrats," but here by the flashing boards of the California State Water Project. Yet a crucial difference is Didion's recognition that although she yearns for that godlike tabula rasa power of starting over, her attempts to make the California deserts fertile are, like those of the Water Project, meager efforts to control the uncontrollable.

In "On the Mall," in the "Sojourns" section, Didion confesses as well her temporary subscription to the suburban shopping center mirage, with its tabula rasa underpinnings: "The frontier had been reinvented, and its shape was the subdivision, that new free land on which all settlers could recast their lives *tabula rasa*. For one perishable moment there the American idea seemed about to achieve itself, via F.H.A. housing and the acquisition of major appliances . . . " (TWA 181). An "esplanade," one of several synonyms Didion uses for the shopping mall, is a flat, open stretch of white pavement, a literal *tabula rasa*, used for shopping mall promenades. Didion implies that these flat, white spaces produce the same mesmerizing trances as bleached California sky or the white slabs of U.S. Highway 99. Quoting Robert Penn Warren on the latter, she notes that "if you don't . . . slap yourself hard on the back of the neck you'll hypnotize yourself" (STB 180). Similarly, mall esplanades induce such a "sedation of anxiety" that consumers move for a while "in an aqueous suspension not only of light but of judgment, not only of judgment but of 'personality' " (TWA 186). They are thus programmed for "impulse buying."

Didion knows that both subdivision and shopping mall are impermanent, and she will insist that life is not tabula rasa. In her 1976 *Esquire* column "Thinking About Western thinking" she asserts:

Many people find the mention of family history obscurely offensive, an affront to their conviction that social virtue resides in a tabula rasa cosmopolitanism. Perhaps they are right. Since I share the common Western indifference to social virtue, I have no way of telling. All I know is that my own experience was not tabula rasa, that I came into adult life either equipped or afflicted with a specific narrative about the nature of life as the women in my family had understood it.[27] (10)

In "On the Road," which precedes "On the Mall" in the "Sojourns" section, Didion particularly satirizes the "tabula rasa cosmopolitanism" of New Yorkers, whose penchant is to fill the white void with "opinions." She does this, of course, through her metaphor of lambent light:

At the time I left New York many people were expressing a bold belief in "joy". . . . Lapidary bleakness was definitely rote. . . .
   I lost track of information.
   I was blitzed by opinion.
   I began to see opinions arcing in the air, intersecting flight patterns. The Eastern shuttle was cleared for landing and so was lapidary bleakness. (TWA 177, 178)

Perhaps it is because Didion perceives New Yorkers as rapt by their arcing opinions (and too dismissive of lapidary bleakness) that she calls them to task for their willful "blankness" when it comes to the truth "In Hollywood." One final time she will call on Fitzgerald, primarily to suggest that Hollywood, like California proper, is lambent light. Didion's sojourn "In Hollywood" begins with this quotation from *The Last*

Tycoon: "You can take Hollywood for granted . . . or you can dismiss it with the contempt we reserve for what we don't understand. It can be understood, too, but only dimly and in flashes" (TWA 153). Later she quotes this pointed criticism from Fitzgerald's Hollywood notes:

People in the East pretend to be interested in how pictures are made. But if you actually tell them anything, you find . . . they never see the ventriloquist for the doll. Even the intellectuals, who ought to know better, like to hear about the pretensions, extravagances and vulgarities—tell them pictures have a private grammar, like politics or automobile production or society, and watch the blank look come into their faces. (TWA 164)

Didion's "In Hollywood" attempts to penetrate both the flashy myths and the blankness to disclose the starker reality.

Blank looks have come into the faces of many reading Didion's attacks on "The Women's Movement" and "Doris Lessing" in her central section titled "Women." This is largely because they have not seen how these criticisms relate to Didion's artistic vision. Didion reacts, and perhaps overreacts, to Lessing and the Feminist Movement precisely *because* she perceives them succumbing to tendencies prevalent in herself, tendencies that she must continually struggle to subdue. I am speaking of the adolescent wail, the childish longing for the past. This is the facet of the Women's Movement on which Didion particularly fastens: "More and more we have been hearing the wishful voices of just such perpetual adolescents, the voices of women scarred not by their class position as women but by the failure of their childhood expectations and misapprehensions" (TWA 117).

This same criticism propelled Didion's 1965 attack on the "new fiction," which she described as having an "aggrieved, done-to" tone connoting "a failure not only of the imagination and the intelligence but of the maturation process."[28] It explains her 1979 recoil from the films of Woody Allen:

the paradigm for the action . . . is high school. . . . The message that large numbers of people are getting from *Manhattan* and *Interiors* and *Annie Hall* is that this kind of emotional shopping around is the proper business of life's better students, that adolescence can now extend to middle age. . . .
Most of us remember very well these secret signals and sighs of adolescence, remember the dramatic apprehension of our own mortality and other "more terrifying unsolvable problems about the universe," but eventually we realize that we are not the first to notice that people die.[29]

Death, childhood expectations, and misapprehensions, of course, have been the major subjects of the self-confessed "recalcitrant . . . child," Joan Didion. The energy of her attacks is revealing. These jibes are those of a writer frequently slapping herself on the back of the neck in an effort to reach moral toughness.

Similarly, Didion's attack on Doris Lessing stems from her identification with the British author. Those aware of Didion's mythos of lambent light would not be surprised that the Lessing works Didion favors are the early *African Stories* set against the hot and empty African sky, "What British Africa gave [Lessing], besides those images of a sky so empty and a society so inflexible as to make the slightest tremor in either worth remarking upon, was a way of perceiving the rest of her life," Didion notes (TWA 123). Lessing's error, in Didion's mind, was to leave this empty sky and dwell permanently in Babylon (England) without making the requisite return. Having chosen Babylon instead of home, Lessing must, of necessity, adopt the "starting over" mind-set. "Even given Mrs. Lessing's tendency to confront all ideas *tabula rasa*, we are dealing here [in *Briefing for a Descent into Hell*] with less than astonishing stuff," Didion cracks (TWA 121).

Given its title, it is not surprising that Didion's strongest criticism is for *The Golden Notebook*. What is noteworthy is that the Lessing Didion attacks is a persona only a hair's breadth from the Didion of "The White Album":

The Golden Notebook is the diary of a writer in shock. . . . [It represents] the fracturing of a sensibility beginning for the first time to doubt its perceptions. . . . Mrs. Lessing looms through *The Golden Notebook* as a woman driven by doubts not only about what to tell but about the validity of telling it at all. (TWA 124, 125)

This last sentence perfectly describes the Didion of the opening "White Album" despair. That through writing *The White Album* Didion is seeking to bring the lie to the concluding sentence of her opening essay— "writing has not yet helped me to see what it means"—shows her slight lead on the Lessing of *The Golden Notebook*. Didion, of course, is also wary of Lessing's quest for "final answers."

Georgia O'Keeffe, in the concluding essay on "Women," shows the proper way. Like Didion (and Fitzgerald), she was drawn to the East but then abandoned it. "At twenty-four," Didion observes, "she left all those [New York] opinions behind and went for the first time to live in Texas, where there were no trees to paint and no one to tell her how not to paint them" (TWA 130). Didion also shares O'Keeffe's obsession with light, and with the Dickinson/Fitzgerald "edge."[30] Didion reports that O'Keeffe liked to look at "the line of the Blue Ridge Mountains on the horizon," and that in Texas "there was only the horizon she craved" (TWA 129, 130). O'Keeffe made ten watercolors from lambent light, from a star appearing in the evening sky, and Didion's admiration for this, and for O'Keeffe's "Sky Above Clouds," can be sensed from her description of the canvas as "float[ing] over the back stairs in the Chicago Art Institute . . . dominating what seemed to be several stories of empty light" (TWA 126).

Georgia O'Keeffe was a hard woman, a tough Western woman who insisted on the personal, on seeing and painting things her way. She was, Didion tells us, an "angelic rattlesnake" in the midst of the Eastern male art scene (TWA 128). This wonderful Western metaphor reveals the role Didion has chosen for herself as a writer. Given in the central section of *The White Album*, it explains her orientation to her own lost Golden Eden as well. Rattlesnakes are noisome Western inhabitants, and they left a lasting imprint on Didion's own childhood. She recalls swimming as a child in that emblematic American River, which ran clean and fast until July, "when it would slow down, and rattlesnakes would sun themselves on its newly exposed rocks" (STB 173). Didion confesses she was a nervous child, "afraid of sinkholes and afraid of snakes, and perhaps that was the beginning of my error" (STB 173). When she returns home from New York and wishes to visit the family graveyard, she remains in the car because she had once seen a rattlesnake in that grass (STB 167). "What does [the fear of snakes] mean?" she inquires in "On Morality." "It means nothing manageable" (STB 161).

One way to manage is to become one's fear. As the "angelic rattlesnake" in our blighted Edens, Didion repeatedly proffers the hard realities. "To sit by the Royal [Hawaiian Hotel] pool and read *The New York Review of Books* is to feel oneself an asp, disguised in a voile beach robe, in the very bosom of the place," she confesses in the "Sojourns" section of *The White Album* (140).[31]

As she does with false and true light, Didion will expose American efforts to ignore or disguise the rattlesnakes—the wormy truths of sin, evil, and death—in our gardens. Blighted Eden, rife with snakes, is the reality to Didion, and she is particularly opposed to those who try to disguise the rattler by calling it garter snake: "There can be no real snakes in Eden any more; there must be instead, to account for unpleasantness and violence and Seconal, a Problem. A Problem is like a defanged snake in a bag, and can be exorcised, as sin cannot be, by A Liberal Education (words and music by Mark Van Doren)."[32]

California dreamers particularly, almost willfully, ignore the rattlesnake, according to Didion. "This was Los Angeles, where misinformation about rattlesnakes is a leitmotiv of the insomniac imagination," she observes.[33] At the Reagan's tabula rasa mansion "three maintenance men try to keep the bulletproof windows clean and the cobwebs swept and the wild grass green and the rattlesnakes down by the river and away from the thirty-five exterior wood and glass doors," Didion notes in "Many Mansions," doubting whether death in the form of bullet or snake can be so easily circumvented (TWA 67).

Didion, in fact, is hard pressed to describe a Californian or Western landscape without placing a rattlesnake there. When she escapes from Los Angeles to that illusory Eden called Malibu, it is to find the hills "infested with bikers and rattlesnakes"; indeed, to find that "a rattlesnake in my driveway meant its mate in yours" (TWA 209, 222). Even the dried bougainvillea drifting in her driveway duplicates the sound of the rattlesnake "a hundred times a day" (TWA 64). Snakes, then, are constant reminders of human error and mortality to Didion. In 1961 she was drawn to these questions in a John Cheever story: "Our ideas of castles, formed in childhood, are inflexible, and why try to reform them? Why point out that in a real castle thistles grow in the courtyard, and the threshold of the ruined throne room is guarded by a nest of green adders?"[34] Didion will reform and refine her childhood visions in the name of just these bleaker truths.

Yet, though she knows snakes are both precursor and fate, shimmering through the desert and the prairie grasses, Didion still longs for that snakeless, immaculate deathless valley of her imagination. In the final section of *The White Album* she is drawn to the "primeval silence" of greenhouses; yet, as with "Holy Water," she knows that this Eden is artificial and impermanent:

In the rain forest these orchids get broken by wind and rain. They get pollinated randomly and rarely by insects. Their seedlings are crushed by screaming monkeys and tree boas and the orchids live unseen and die young. There in the greenhouse nothing would break the orchids and they would be pollinated as full moon and high tide by Amado Vazquez, and their seedlings would be tended in a sterile box with sterile gloves and sterile tools by Amado Vazquez's wife, Maria, and the orchids would not seem to die at all. (TWA 219–20)

The orchid Amado Vazquez named after his daughter is *Phal. Linda Mia* "Innocence," and this snakeless orchid paradise with its "particular light" has every attraction for Didion (TWA 220, 216).

The Hoover Dam, however, comes even closer to symbolizing Didion's purest white light of truth. In "At the Dam," the concluding essay in the "Sojourns" section, she shows through images of bronze how the original bright promises of the dam turned to mirage:

Hoover Dam [is] . . . the several millions tons of concrete that made the Southwest plausible, the *fait accompli* that was to convey, in the innocent time of its construction, the notion that mankind's brightest promise lay in American engineering. . . . The bronze sculptures at the dam itself evoke muscular citizens of a tomorrow that never came. (TWA 199)

Yet, though this bronze Eden never materialized, Didion finds her own truth regarding the dam in an image of the "pristine concave face [of the dam] gleaming white" that materializes repeatedly in her mind (TWA 198). If the "gorgeous dream" of Jay Gatsby was dragged down by the dust of maculate men, Didion's dream remains immaculate, for "out at the dam there was no dust, only the rock and the dam" (TWA 200).[35] Indeed, she associates the dam with a star map, key to true lambent light and to the assuring non–tabula rasa promise "As it was in the beginning is now and ever shall be." She closes with this nod to Henry Adams: "Of course that was the image I had seen always, seen it without quite realizing what I saw, a dynamo finally free of man, splendid at last in its absolute isolation, transmitting power and releasing water to a world where no one is" (TWA 201).

Eden can exist for Didion, but only without Adam and Eve. Given human voices, we waken to drown in error and illusion. Didion might have ended *The White Album* with this radiating energy "free of man," but she does not. She might even have closed her final section, "On the Morning After the Sixties," with the greenhouse Eden and Amado Vazquez's proud "I will die in orchids" (TWA 221). But she does not.

Only the center section of *The White Album* concludes affirmatively with O'Keeffe's ten watercolors from a star. The four sections radiating outward from this center close on various shades of bleak despair. The opening title section ends with Didion's assertion that writing has not helped her see what her experience means. She chooses to end "California Republic" with Brother Theobold, motorcycle mayhem, Dallas Beardsley, California Gamblers Anonymous, and the suggestion that she does know the elected representatives to the "invisible city" in which these people dwell. If Didion has tried to keep one ray of "each peculiar light" to track the misperceivers, by *The White Album* she is closer to the Dickinson line "For every Lunacy of Light/I had not power to tell."

Didion chooses to close her fourth section, "Sojourns," with "the sun dropping behind a mesa with the finality of a sunset in space"—and thus with an image of the void—and with Hoover Dam releasing water to "a world where no one is" (TWA 201). She closes the volume proper with the contrasting specter of fire. Her "Quiet Days at Malibu" end with the destruction of Amado Vazquez's Eden of orchids, and the awareness that the fire had come to within 125 feet of her former property and "then stopped or turned or [was] beaten back, it was hard to tell which."

LIGHT AS DARKNESS: *SALVADOR*

"The Color of the Grave is white—/The outer Grave—I mean," wrote Emily Dickinson. The movement of Didion's artistic vision from the

1979 *White Album* to the ironically titled *Salvador* in 1983 is ineluctably toward the more interior gravity of death. If truth is ambiguous white in *The White Album*, it is the heart of darkness, "true noche obscura," in *Salavador*.

"In Bogotá," in *The White Album*, anticipates the truth as darkness in *Salvador*, and serves the same summary and pivotal functions in that collection as "Goodbye to All That" does in *Slouching Towards Bethlehem*. If New York was the enchanted city of the United States, Bogotá represents the golden city of the hemisphere, the literal source of all New World dreams of gold: the origin of "El Dorado." This work begins with Didion on the Colombian coast, surrounded by white:

In my room in Cartagena I would wake to the bleached coastal morning and find myself repeating certain words and phrases under my breath, an incantation: *Bogotá, Bacatá.* . . .

Maybe that is the one true way to see Bogotá, to have it float in the mind until the need for it is visceral, for the whole history of the place has been to seem a mirage, a delusion on the high savannah, its gold and emeralds unattainable. . . . (TWA 187, 188)

Didion's pilgrimage to Bogotá is a search for the source of golden dreams. She visits the Gold Museum and "looked at the gold the Spaniards opened the Americas to get" (TWA 188). She hears tales of Indian rulers covered with gold dust until they gleamed like golden statues, and considers this and other stories hallucinations, "stories a child might invent" (TWA 189).

Once again Didion will say "goodbye to all that" childish fantasy, and present the truth behind the mirage. Prefiguring her lengthier characterization in *Salvador*, she finds the "American presence" in Bogotá a "phantom colony," and the moral power of the church a dimming lambent light (TWA 191). The Cathedral of Salt in Bogotá is *underground*, is in darkness. Didion notes that "recessed fluorescent tubes illuminate the Stations of the Cross, the dense air absorbing and dimming the light unsteadily" (TWA 195). In another emblematic moment, which also anticipates *Salvador*, Didion watches a stewardess press buttons on a map of Colombian cities: "I watched her press the buttons one by one, transfixed by the vast darkness each tiny bulb illumined. The light for Bogotá blinked twice and went out" (TWA 190).

The light has gone out in *Salvador* as well, Didion's 1983 transport of Conrad's *Heart of Darkness* from the Old World to the New. Here El Salvador represents the Congo (the darkness of sin and death), and the United States, the deluded imperialists from the "white city." Didion begins the volume with the famous passage from *Heart of Darkness* that concludes with a metaphor of fatal light: "at the end of that moving

appeal to every altruistic sentiment it blazed at you, luminous and terrifying, like a flash of lightning in a serene sky: 'Exterminate all the
brutes!' "

Didion starts her sojourn in the "glassy and white" El Salvador International Airport, a monument to the Molina and Romero regimes'
"central hallucination," which was to establish "beach resorts, the Hyatt,
the Pacific Paradise" on the El Salvador coast (13). That the death squads
in El Salvador have depressed the tourist industry is an understate-
ment.

Thus the United States is not the only party guilty of misperception
in El Salvador. Didion implies that part of El Salvador's "problema" is
its lack of national identity. She notes that "so attenuated was El Salvador's sense of itself in its moment of independence that it petitioned
the United States for admission to the union as a state" (72). The materials for "indigenous" El Salvadoran crafts are imported from Gua-
temala, and native rituals have been rendered so impotent by the presence of death as to become obscene.

"If the country's history as a republic seems devoid of shared purpose or unifying event, a record of insensate ambitions and their accidental consequences, its three centuries as a colony seem blanker still,"
Didion finds (72). What remains in historical memory, what stands out
from this blankness, is death, "La Matanza," massacre. Death is the only
reality, the only "salvador," Didion insists, and her volume is a rosary
of incidents revealing terror, death, and the fallacy of the American
position.

"Terror is the given of the place," Didion discovers. "If it is taken
for granted in Salvador that the government kills, it is also taken for
granted that the other side kills; that everyone has killed, everyone kills
now, and, if the history of the place suggests any pattern, everyone will
continue to kill" (14, 34). In this light it is not surprising that Didion's
attention is drawn to a woman driving back and forth toward the edge
of a cliff: "We did not speak, and it was only later, down the mountain
and back in the land of the provisionally living, that it occurred to me
that there was a definite question about why a man and a woman might
choose a well-known body dump for a driving lesson" (21). The "woman
on the edge" in Salvador is related to the suicidal "woman on the ledge"
in The White Album, the one with "incandescent" hair. Both dissolve into
the image of the "famous beauty" in Bogotá whose "pale red hair was
fluffed around her head in an electric halo," and finally to the skulls in
El Salvador "surrounded by a perfect corona of hair" (TWA 192, 17).
In a fifth image of female immolation, the "corona" desired by the
contestants in the "Senorita El Salvador 1982" competition, the night
of the earthquake, is another mirage, golden life insurance as Didion
suggests in this description laced with irony:

[e]ach of the finalists was asked to pick a question from a basket and answer it. The questions had to do with the hopes and dreams of the contestants, and the answers ran to "Dios," "Paz," "El Salvador." A local entertainer wearing a white dinner jacket and a claret-colored bow tie sang "The Impossible Dream," in Spanish. . . . The four runners-up reacted, on the whole, with rather less grace than is the custom on these occasions, and it occurred to me that this was a contest in which winning meant more than a scholarship or a screen test or a new wardrobe; winning here could mean the difference between life and casual death, a provisional safe-conduct not only for the winner but for her entire family. (57–58)

The corona-skulls, however, place even this vision in question.

Such desire for golden protection, for mirages of tantalizing hue, is underscored by a discovery Didion makes regarding General Maximiliano Hernandez Martinez, El Salvador's dictator from 1931 to 1944 and the author of "La Matanza." General Martinez not only had a program for building schools, a program for increasing exports, and "La Matanza" for eliminating life's other irritations, but during an epidemic of smallpox in the capital, Didion writes, "he attempted to halt its spread by stringing the city with a web of colored lights" (54). As we have seen, Didion herself is not immune to such shimmering fantasy, and she confesses: "Not a night passed in San Salvador when I did not imagine it strung with those colored lights" (54).

Light is desired, but nowhere existent. In a third emblematic incident, the "literary coffee," Didion hears these words straight from Salvador's artists and intellectuals: "Los muertos, you know? We are the only ones left. There is no one after us, no young ones. It is all over, you know?" (84).

Didion knows, and tries to tell us, but, as with Kurtz and Marlow, her dark vision is unacceptable to those forming and implementing national Salvadoran policy. In three separate tableaus Didion presents images of the floundering U.S. position. America's effort in El Salvador is likened to crossing the Rio Seco. The name itself is an oxymoron and is, like most names and facts in El Salvador, misleading, for this river is "*seco* enough in the dry months but often impassable in the wet" as it is during Didion's June visit (40). In this tableau America is the earthmover and the foundered truck El Salvador:

We stood for a while on the bank and watched a man with an earthmover and winch try again and again to hook up his equipment to a truck that had foundered midstream. . . . It did not seem entirely promising, but there it was, and there, in due time, we were: in the river . . . stuck, the engine dead. (42–43)

Similarly, during the June earthquake that kills a dozen people, the one major building to suffer extensive damage is the one building specifically designed to withstand earthquakes: the American Embassy. Didion's history of this structure is a parable of American policy gone wrong:

When this embassy was built, in 1965, the idea was that it would remain fluid under stress, its deep pilings shifting and sliding on Teflon pads, but over the past few years, as shelling the embassy came to be a favorite way of expressing dissatisfaction on all sides, the structure became so fortified . . . as to render it rigid. (59–60)

So fortified from reality is American policy, in fact, that it is transacted not only in this rigid edifice, but also in the idyllic ambassador's residence far away from the terrors and body dumps of San Salvador. Reflecting on her luncheon with the American ambassador, Didion notes that

The sheep dog and the crystal and the American eagle together had on me a certain anesthetic effect, temporarily deadening that receptivity to the sinister that afflicts everyone in Salvador, and I experienced for a moment the official American delusion, the illusion of plausibility, the sense that the American undertaking in El Salvador might turn out to be, from the right angle, in the right light, just another difficult but possible mission in another troubled but possible country. (87–88)

This factitious luncheon stands in sharp contrast to Didion's experience of true terror, the true reality of Salvador, while dining on the veranda of a San Salvador restaurant. Significantly, this incident occurs during a "blackout," and Didion barely resists (once again) snuffing out her own candle:

on an evening when rain or sabotage or habit had blacked out the city . . . I became abruptly aware, in the light cast by a passing car, of two human shadows, silhouettes illuminated by the headlights and then invisible again. One shadow sat behind the smoked glass windows of a Cherokee Chief parked at the curb in front of the restaurant; the other crouched between the pumps at the Esso station next door, carrying a rifle. It seemed to me unencouraging that my husband and I were the only people seated on the porch. In the absence of the headlights the candle on our table provided the only light, and I fought the impulse to blow it out. (26)

This early experience of terror is duplicated in the final pages of *Salvador* in another seemingly meaningless incident that Didion makes meaningful. Here she, her husband, and an American journalist visit the San Salvador morgue. That seven unidentified bodies "bearing evidence of *arma de fuego*" did not constitute a newsworthy story in El

Salvador at that time seems revelation enough, but they return to find their car hemmed-in, just like America's Salvadoran policy: "This was a kind of impasse. It seemed clear that if we tried to leave and scraped either motorcycle the situation would deteriorate. It also seemed clear that if we did not try to leave the situation would deteriorate" (103, 104).

This is America's position in El Salvador precisely, and in *Salvador* Didion is more explicit than in any of her other nonfiction in criticizing America's misperception:

"anti-Communism" was seen, correctly, as the bait the United States would always take.

That we had been drawn, both by a misapprehension of the local rhetoric and by the manipulation of our own rhetorical weaknesses, into a game we did not understand, a play of power in a political tropic alien to us, seemed apparent, and yet there we remained. . . . At the heart of the American effort there was something of the familiar ineffable, as if it were taking place not in El Salvador but in a mirage of El Salvador, the mirage of a society not unlike our own but "sick," a temporarily fevered republic in which the antibodies of democracy needed only to be encouraged. . . . (95, 96)

Just as Didion believes that there are no "solutions" for her own migrainous and nerve-tortured body, she insists there is no "cure," no salve for Salvador; the best we can do is cure our misperceptions and begin to accept the darkness of death, of moral extinction. Once again, she uses herself as a model and illustrates not only her increasing proximity to ultimate darkness, but also the terror it entails. After leaving the grandson of General Martinez, Didion confesses, "this was the first time in my life that I had been in the presence of obvious 'material' and felt no professional exhilaration at all, only personal dread" (56).

Similarly, when Didion purchases Halazone tablets (for the tap water) at a San Salvador shopping center, she starts to take notes of the Manhattan beach towels for sale, the bar equipment, and the Muzak of "American Pie," but then abandons the effort:

This was a shopping center that embodied the future for which El Salvador was presumably being saved, and I wrote it down dutifully, this being the kind of "color" I knew how to interpret, the kind of inductive irony, the detail that was supposed to illuminate the story. As I wrote it down I realized that I was no longer much interested in this kind of irony, that this was a story that would not be illuminated by such details, that this was a story that would perhaps not be illuminated at all, that this was perhaps even less a "story" than a true *noche obscura*. As I waited to cross back over the Boulevard de los Heroes to the Camino Real I noticed soldiers herding a young civilian into a van, their guns at the boy's back, and I walked straight ahead, not wanting to see anything at all. (36)

No light will be found in this recent Didion work of literary nonfiction; or, rather, the illumination will be that of darkness. If the reality of *Salvador* is death, its corollary is moral extinction. Echoing in stronger tones her visit to the underground Cathedral of Salt in Bogotá is Didion's description of the Metropolitan Cathedral in San Salvador. Like the outer city in *Heart of Darkness*, the countryside Franciscan parish house has appeared to Didion to be "civilization's last stand," but in San Salvador the church no longer offers refuge, for more than twenty persons have been slain at the Cathedral (46). One last time Didion focuses on lambent light, only to reveal her ominous current posture:

The cross on the altar is of bare incandescent bulbs, but the bulbs, that afternoon, were unlit: there was in fact no light at all on the main altar, no light on the cross, no light on the globe of the world that showed the northern American continent in gray and the southern in white; no light on the dove above the globe, *Salvador del Mundo*. In this vast brutalist space that was the cathedral, the unlit altar seemed to offer a single ineluctable message: at this time and in this place the light of the world could be construed as out, off, extinguished. (79)

FUTURE NONFICTION

The Poets light but Lamps—
Themselves—go out—
The Wicks they stimulate—
If vital Light

Inhere as do the Suns—
Each Age a Lens
Disseminating their
Circumference

Where next for Joan Didion? Has the lambent light gone out? Is *noche obscura* the end of the line? Clearly Didion could continue indefinitely exposing golden American mirages. Her projected title of a future volume of literary nonfiction, *Fairytales*, suggests that may be precisely the path she will pursue.[36] She has also expressed a desire to write a book about water, a hint that she may be backtracking to that central "blue water" stage of the subconscious. Several critics have suggested that Didion has become more confident and less despairing during the 1970s and 1980s. Her movement away from Malibu, the site of Fitzgerald's early death, might be taken as such a sign. We might also note that Didion presents death and moral extinction not everywhere, but only in El Salvador: "at this time and in this place."

Yet those following Didion's vision of lambent light cannot help but be apprehensive about the future direction of her work. Though she may retreat to the gold or the blue/white, any important work will continue the limning of darkness—and beyond. Didion hints as much in her 1977 tribute to John Cheever, whose work she admired early and long, for his subject matter and imagery are very like her own. Indeed, one might say that after *Slouching Towards Bethlehem* in 1968, Cheever replaces Fitzgerald for Didion, just as black replaces gold. The following lengthy excerpt from Didion's 1977 review of Cheever's novel *Falconer* reveals the similarity of their artistic journeys:

Their best light [Cheever's characters'] was that which dapples lawns on late summer afternoons, and their favorite note was "plaintive" . . . and served to remind them that life and love were but fleeting shadows, to teach them to number their days and to call them home across those summer lawns. They yearned always after some abstraction symbolized by the word "home," after "tenderness," after "gentleness," after remembered houses where the fires were laid and the silver was polished and everything could be "decent" and "radiant" and "clear." . . .

Yet Cheever has persisted throughout his career in telling us a story in which nostalgia is "real," and every time he tells this story he refines it more, gets closer to the bone, elides another summer lawn. . . . In this sense of obsessive compression and abandoned artifice *Falconer* is a better book than the *Wapshot* novels, a better book even than *Bullet Park*, for in *Falconer* those summer lawns are gone altogether, and the main narrative line is only a memory. . . .

"When do you think you'll be clean?" Marcia asks. "I find it hard to imagine cleanliness," Ferragut answers.[37]

Joan Didion is finding it harder and harder to imagine "cleanliness" as well, and her best work will elide earlier lights and define what spare flickerings can yet be seen.

Didion's artistic gift has been to enrich the autobiographical strain in American literary nonfiction. She uses herself as both a probe and a model of American society. Her confessions of personal illusions both encourage reader sympathy and identification with her views, and demonstrate how prone Americans are to illusion. Her effort to discipline her illusions likewise becomes a model for reader behavior. Most cleverly, her assertions that she can find no meaning have the effect of spurring readers to moral understandings she herself refuses overtly to claim.

Didion's work offers the clearest illustration in this study of how writers' artistic visions may be inescapable embodiments, not only of their personal histories, geographies, and literary assimilation, but of their very corporal being. Those who have read Didion's descriptions of her migraine attacks and her possible multiple sclerosis cannot help but wonder if her artistic vision is a reflection of her unusual sensory condition. Michido Kakutani has reported that Didion wears oversized sunglasses even indoors to protect her light-sensitive eyes.[38] Furthermore, an "aura" (shimmer) is a documented early stage in most migraine attacks, preceding the actual headache. Didion herself has written:

Migraine gives some people mild hallucinations, temporarily blinds others, shows up not only as a headache but as a gastrointestinal disturbance, a painful sensitivity to all sensory stimuli, an abrupt overpowering fatigue, a strokelike aphasia, and a crippling inability to make even the most routine connections. When I am in a migraine aura (for some people the aura lasts fifteen minutes, for others several hours), I . . . lose the ability to focus my eyes or frame coherent sentences. . . . (TWA 170)

In the first known description of migraine, Hypocrates noted that "most of the time [the sufferer] seemed to see something shining before him like a light" (Critchley 28). Blaise Pascal, a probable migraine sufferer, not only was prey to periodic illusions, but also would imagine that a cavity was yawning on his left-hand side (Critchley 34). Thus Didion's obsession with light and with the Fitzgeraldian precipice may have neurological as well as literary origins. Furthermore, excessive water has been found to be bad for migraine sufferers and dehydration beneficial (Dunlop 80). Didion's obsessions with water and deserts may, therefore, have physical as well as spiritual nuance. Additionally, weariness with life and a wish to die are oft-reported experiences of migraine sufferers.

Joan Didion's mythos of lambent light thus may be an exquisitely rendered translation of her physical condition. Certainly her struggle with and acceptance of her physical affliction have influenced her adamant stance against "human improvability." By extension, Didion sees no promise of melioration for America. Her truest vision is of the void, with life, love, and national greatness only ephemeral shadows. Lacking all faith in human improvability, Didion's vision is primarily backward-looking rather than forward-looking, and her characteristic tone lament for moments all too soon gone.

This description by the twelfth-century Abbess Hildegard of Bingen of the visual phenomena recurring throughout her migrainous life seems vividly to capture the movement of Didion's artistic vision: "I saw a great star, most splendid and beautiful, and with it an exceeding multitude of falling sparks with which the star followed southward . . . and suddenly they were all annihilated, being turned into black coals . . . and cast into the abyss so that I could see them no more" (Critchley 35). Joan Didion is at the point of tracing those last sparks, the last lambent light, into the abyss. We await, almost with dread, her continuingly more rarified perceptions.

5

Norman Mailer's Ages of Man

Norman Mailer is an artist of epic prose.[1] Across his career he has insistently described himself as a novelist rather than as a nonfiction artist, despite the fact that in both quantity and quality his greater contribution has been to literary nonfiction. Mailer's remarkable achievement has been to explore and expand the boundaries of many of the nonfiction genres: autobiography (*Advertisements For Myself*); biography (*Marilyn, The Executioner's Song, Of Women and Their Elegance*); history (*The Armies of the Night*); the essay (*The Prisoner of Sex*); scientific and technical writing (*Of A Fire On The Moon*); and travel, political, and sports writing (*Miami and the Siege of Chicago, St. George and the Godfather, The Fight*).

Perhaps one reason Mailer insists he is a novelist is that he knows his strength is not in research, in the fact-gathering side of literary nonfiction. His greatest works of nonfiction have come from events in which he was an active participant (*The Armies of the Night*), or when extensive research has been done for him (*The Executioner's Song*). Indeed, in *Miami and the Siege of Chicago* so uncommitted to legwork was Mailer that he chose to stay home one evening and watch the 1968 Republican convention on television rather than experience the event firsthand. At this and other conventions he admits to missing the import of key events.

If Mailer is not a dedicated fact-gatherer, he compensates with his genius for shaping and styling the facts, once they are amassed. His greatest gift as a writer is for metaphor, which he employs as a probe of his subject and as a tool for enhancing intimacy with his readers and stimulating mental and social activity. Mailer's metaphors are his means of enlarging his subjects and introducing new ideas. As Aristotle observed, "it is from metaphor that we can best get hold of something fresh" (*Rhetoric* 1410b 13).

Through metaphor Mailer also establishes intimacy with his readers. Indeed, it is the forced intimacy of the metaphoric transaction that causes such disproportionate reader reactions to Mailer's texts—reactions usually of supreme admiration or distaste. As Ted Cohen has explained in "Metaphor and the Cultivation of Intimacy," in metaphorizing, the writer issues a kind of concealed invitation (the metaphor); the reader expends a special effort to accept the invitation (i.e., to "unpack" or understand the metaphor); and this transaction constitutes the acknowledgment of community. The two become "an intimate pair" (9). Problems arise for Mailer because some readers do not wish this kind of intimacy. Because metaphors involve the transference of thought from one idea to another, the invitation of metaphor involves a kind of journey. Mailer takes his readers repeatedly on trips, often (for this is the very nature of metaphor) against their will. Thus if one simply *understands* such a Mailer metaphor as "Man might be a fool who peed in the wrong pot" (TAOTN 44), and one does not wish to think of "man" that way, one nevertheless has done so. Metaphor is coercive. It does not give readers a choice. One fails to make the trip, or avoids intimate understanding, only if one fails to comprehend the metaphor. Add to this the fact that so many of Mailer's metaphors are elaborate trips and are designed to stimulate or activate the reader (i.e., they are good metaphors), and one has the natural irritation of conservatives, of those who do not wish to move. As Cohen has noted: "When the device is a hostile metaphor [or, I would add, a stimulating one] . . . requiring much background and effort to understand, it is all the more painful because the victim has been made a complicitor in his demise" (12).

Through metaphor Mailer is able to stimulate the human activity that he desires. We often forget that Aristotle described "activity" as one of the premier qualities of metaphor:

By "making them see things" I mean using expressions that represent things as in a state of activity. Thus, to say that a good man is "four-square" is certainly a metaphor; both the good man and the square are perfect; but the metaphor does not suggest activity. On the other hand, in the expression "with his vigour in full bloom" there is the notion of activity. (*Rhetoric* 1411b 26–29)

Paul Ricouer has carried Aristotle's reflection on metaphoric action even further, concluding that "the 'place' of metaphor, its most intimate and ultimate abode, is neither the name, nor the sentence, nor even discourse, but the copula of the verb *to be*" (7). This, I submit, is Norman Mailer's most profound wish as a writer: to bring life, to animate both individual bodies and the "body politic" into greater being. He is, therefore, more socially responsible than many readers think.

Metaphor, thus, is essential to the acts of animation and regeneration

that constitute Mailer's oeuvre.[2] What remains for me to outline is the
special form his vision has taken across his career in nonfiction. Mailer's
body of nonfiction in the twenty-year period from 1959 (*Advertisements
For Myself*) to 1979 (*The Executioner's Song*) comprises, not a geographical territory like Faulkner's fictional Yoknapatawpha County, but a
temporal odyssey, the pattern of the human lifespan compressed within
a generation. *Advertisements For Myself*, like Whitman's "Song of Myself,"
records Mailer's birth as an original American voice.[3] *The Armies of the
Night* (1968) marks his coming of age, his rite of passage from adolescence to maturity as a nonfiction writer. *The Prisoner of Sex* (1971), *Marilyn* (1973), and *Genius and Lust* (1976) chronicle adult love affairs (with
women and literature), but with *The Fight* (1975) Mailer's thought increasingly turns from love to death, a subject, in truth, never far from
his (or any great writer's) mind. *The Fight* commemorates the triumph
of art over death, while in the remarkable 1979 volume *The Executioner's Song* a somber Mailer seems to have lost faith in the regenerative
power of metaphor. Death and banality are recorded with only the
slightest hints of possible resurrection.[4]

HEALTH AS METAPHOR:
ADVERTISEMENTS FOR MYSELF

"Do not understand me too quickly," Mailer (quoting Gide) wrote as
the epigraph to *The Deer Park* (1955). A paradox of Mailer's critical
reception has been that readers not only have failed to understand the
most profound implications of his work, but have often overlooked the
most obvious surface clues. *Advertisements For Myself*, Mailer's first major
work of nonfiction, published in 1959, is a case in point. Although numerous critics have remarked on Mailer's salute to Walt Whitman in
his volume's title, no one as yet has pursued the hint deeply, deeply
enough to appreciate *Advertisements For Myself* as Mailer's inspired twentieth-century re-modeling of *Leaves of Grass*.[5]

Because Mailer is supremely conscious of his predecessors in the
American literary tradition, it is not surprising that at the age of thirty-
six, after both critical and popular failures of his second and third novels (*Barbary Shore* and *The Deer Park*), he should turn to Whitman, the
poet of great good health, for resuscitation. Whitman, from Mailer's
own Brooklyn borough, was thirty-seven when he wrote, "I, now thirty-
seven years old in perfect health begin." Mailer may have wondered if
he, in less-than-perfect health, could do the same.

The substitution of the commercial metaphor "advertisements" for
Whitman's lyrical "song" underscores Mailer's sense of decline (in himself and in America) from Whitman's robust anthems of 1855. In 1959
an American writer cannot simply sing; he must advertise himself. On

the literal level, therefore, Mailer's work is a forthright advertisement for his novel in progress, yet his metaphor also reminds us of the literal self-promoting Whitman himself was forced to undertake because the public failed to understand his work.

But Mailer does more than merely re-model the title "Song of Myself." His entire volume is a recasting of *Leaves of Grass*. Before addressing the major metaphor of *health* in *Advertisements For Myself*, I will briefly cite other noteworthy similarities between the two works to suggest that, in actuality, Mailer's volume is a large-scale metaphoric "model" of Whitman's opus.[6] To begin with, Mailer models Whitman in choosing to use his "personality as the armature" of his work (219). The metaphor *armature* evokes Whitman through its biological connotation of strong bone and musculature as well as in its resonances from the field of electronics. Here *armature* denotes that part of a relay, such as a buzzer or bell, that vibrates when activated by a magnetic field. Thus it is not only Whitman who speaks of his "electrical self" and who sings the "body electric." In *Advertisements For Myself* Mailer asserts that his senses "were still electric," and speaks of the "electric present" and "electric vivaciousness" near the sea (282, 342, 522).

Choosing his personality as the armature of his work permits Mailer to showcase his entire body of work from his Harvard undergraduate days to 1959. Like Whitman, he can be large and celebrate his own diversity. Mailer warns in his First Advertisement that he has "a changeable personality" (21), and in "The White Negro" he insists that his own diversity is a mere model of humanity's. "Therefore, men are not seen as good or bad (that they are good-and-bad is taken for granted)," Mailer writes, "but rather each man is glimpsed as a collection of possibilities. . . . Yet in widening the arena of the possible, one widens it reciprocally for other as well." (353, 354). Thus Mailer makes a virtue of diversity, of including the worst as well as the best of his work (219). Like Whitman, he inquires: "Wouldn't it be dishonest and a fraud on the public, as well as deeply un-American, to present myself as better than I am?" (313).

In *Advertisements For Myself* Mailer also re-models Whitman's tantalizingly equivocal relationship with his readers. In *Leaves of Grass* Whitman draws us close, hooks us about our waists, whispers in our ears, yet also at times holds us at arm's length, pushes us away. Mailer constructs an even larger tension—between intimacy and insult—across his *Advertisements*. In his first "Note to the Reader" he expresses his "desire to please" (7), and he increases this sense of intimacy in his second *Village Voice* column when he writes: "I will try to write for you . . . as if I were talking in my living room, or in yours" (287). In his Advertisement for his final section he deigns to give us "an easy time for awhile" (390), yet such efforts to approach readers and court their favor are lost on many who remember only his verbal assaults.

Mailer defines "hip" as the "affirmation of the barbarian" (355), and, like Whitman, who unabashedly sounds his barbaric yawp, Mailer hesitates not to "flesh the bold loud air [with] his pronouncements" (335). Thus in his first *Village Voice* column he bluntly writes: "That many of you are frustrated in your ambitions, and undernourished in your pleasures, only makes you more venomous" (279). If this snake metaphor does not completely alienate us, he offers more to make us wary: "At any rate, dear reader, we begin a collaboration which may go on for three weeks, three months, or, the Lord forbid, for three-and-thirty years. I have only one prayer—that I weary of you before you tire of me" (280). This clever insult (coupled as it is with the ironically obsequious "dear reader" and pompous—but Whitmanian—equation of himself with Christ) has the perverse effect of quickening our interest in what is to come. It spurs our attention, if only in defensive anger, as when (in his second column) he both patronizes and admonishes us: "If you are not in the mood to think, or if you have no interest in thinking, then let us ignore each other until the next column. And if you do go on from here, please have the courtesy to concentrate" (281). Later he confesses his wish to "ambush" us (391). Thus, just as Whitman makes us yearn all the more for his encompassing embrace by occasionally holding us away, Mailer makes it hard for us to ignore him, and places us on our guard by suggesting that *he* will ignore, grow weary, or ambush us.

Mailer's seventeenth and final column for *The Village Voice* echoes the close of "Song of Myself," and (through two metaphors) hints at an important difference in his re-fashioning of Whitman. "We may not have had the most pleasant of relationships, but it has been *stimulating* for me, and perhaps *stimulating* for some of you," Mailer writes. "So, regretfully, good-bye for awhile. I wonder in which form some of us will *swing* into communication again" (318, emphases added). Whitman would seem to "sit content" if he can embrace us all; this, however, is not enough for Mailer. He must "stimulate" us. And here we see Mailer's profound emphasis on action: he wishes to arouse the body to the action so vividly imaged in his metaphor *swing*.

Once one entertains the notion that Whitman provides the model for *Advertisements For Myself*, many other features of Mailer's opus assume richer significance. We see, for example, Mailer stretching himself to be a writer of the commonplace. "To sense what is real in the commonplace is not easy when one is young, shy, half in love and certainly self-beloved, sex-ridden . . . ," he writes in the Advertisement for his early short story "A Calculus at Heaven" (27). Mailer's final persona further recalls the Whitman of "things" when he insists: "I will leave the oceans then, I will leave the flowers and the bees and the trees, reminding you that the extraordinary can hide in the meanest maggot" (515).

And even though Mailer will choose for the flag of *his* disposition a maggot, a metaphor even meaner (and more active) than grass, his volume contains suggestive references to Whitman's own famous emblem. In his "Last Advertisement For Myself Before the Way Out" Mailer evokes the grass metaphor to discuss America's harshness toward its writers:

America is a cruel soil for talent. It stunts it, blights it, uproots it, or overheats it with cheap fertilizer. And our literary gardeners, our publishers, editors, reviewers and general flunkeys, are drunks, cowards, respectables, prose couturiers, fashion-mongers, old maids, time servers and part-time pimps on the Avenue of President Madison. . . .
So the strong talents of my generation, those few of us who have wide minds in a narrow overdeveloped time, are left to wander through a landscape of occult herbs and voracious weeds, ambushed by the fallen wires of electric but meaningless situations. (475)

Whitman's grass has been overgrown; his electric messages fallen. Yet in re-making Whitman in America of 1959 Mailer will not let this inhospitable climate stay him. He writes of the three pieces he admires most in *Advertisements For Myself* ("The White Negro," "The Time of Her Time," and "Advertisements For Myself on the Way Out"): "With these three seeds, let us say the book has its end" (335). And on the penultimate page of the volume, in a metaphoric salute to Whitman, he projects the seeds even further:

The fats, the blood, the muscles and the bone sink into the earth again . . . yes, with the pores of a pinewood box, we give of our poor soured flesh to the wistful cemetery grass—in a century or two perhaps they will let the cows enter there to eat and make the milk and give the meat which will permit one distant relative of a molecule, ten hundred dynasties of family removed, to slip into a human body again. . . .
And is that all? . . . Or is there more?
And if I say I think there is, I turn the key into the category of my own secret. . . . (530–31)

Thus Mailer models (in truth, re-models) Whitman in his acceptance of and triumph over death.

And here we approach the profound importance of Whitman as a model for Mailer: the great good health Whitman offers to those who come near him. The overwhelming preponderance of metaphors in

Advertisements relate to bodily disease and health. "I shall be good health to you, And filter and fibre your blood," Whitman promises at the close of "Song of Myself." That Mailer in 1959 felt the need for this great Respirator can be seen in the fact that he makes more than a thousand references to bodily health (the majority of them metaphorical) in the 532 pages of *Advertisements For Myself.*

Mailer's concern for his own (and the nation's) exhausted spirit can be gauged from his employment of at least ninety-three synonyms for ill health. That he considers himself a mere exemplum of the general disease of the "social body" or "body politic" is apparent in the fact that he refers to the ill health of others, and of America personified, at least as frequently as to his own malaise. "I have been dying a little these fifteen years, and so have a good many of you, no doubt," is typical of this equation (18–19). However, Mailer, drawing on and re-modeling the spirit of Whitman, will address our wounds, will revive himself and us. "Dying," in truth, is the most frequent trope in *Advertisements For Myself,* alluded to at least 169 times. Yet much of the interest of the volume lies in the prodigious range of illness that Mailer diagnoses, illness progressing from mere exhaustion (twenty-five references), to metaphorical cramps and nausea (four each), to metaphorical starvation (seven), mutilation (five), and sterility (six)! All readers can locate their own ills in Mailer's anatomy.

Mailer diagnoses a general fatigue, a weariness in the American spirit. "Nineteenth-century capitalism exhausted the life of millions of workers," he insists in "From Surplus Value to the Mass-Media" (436–37). The characters in the majority of fictional works in *Advertisements* exude this essential weariness. These include the Chaplain, Wexler, and Rice in "A Calculus at Heaven" (34, 57, 69); Brody in "The Dead Gook" (140, 144, 146); Sam Slovoda, whose job as a comic strip artist seems to "exhaust his imagination" in "The Man Who Studied Yoga" (163); and both Denise and Sergius in "The Time of Her Time" (492, 502). Even the "tireless" Pierrot in "The Patron Saint of MacDougal Alley" becomes tired after his first day of factory work (395, 396, 401).

The nonfiction in *Advertisements* engages this theme directly. In "David Riesman Reconsidered" Mailer describes the Left Liberal as "progressively more exhausted" (202); in "The White Negro" the atheist suffers "spiritual fatigue" (342); and Mailer even speaks of the deity as "Our weary Father" (508). Mailer himself suffers this same fatigue. "I contain within myself the bitter exhaustions of an old man, and the cocky arguments of a bright boy," he confesses in his First Advertisement For Myself (17), and in one of the most suggestive metaphors of illness (again associated with grass) he worries that he "may have fatigued the earth of rich language beyond repair" (22).

Disclosed here is the serious consequence of such personal and national weariness, that the nation and its artists will be worn out, and thus Mailer's metaphors of exhaustion (twenty-five), tiredness (twenty-five), fatigue (twelve), and weariness (eight) give way to at least ninety-four references to wearing out (or down), burning out, being "ground down," "pooped out," depleted, broken. Looking back on his predecessors, Mailer characterizes Thomas Wolfe as a "burned-out rocket" (474) and insists that James T. Farrell "wore down with dignity" because he was "cheated of a recognition which could match his size" (475).

It is when we follow the metaphors of *burn-out* and their synonym "collapsed" that we gain a full appreciation of the desperate straits from which Mailer brought forth his *Advertisements.* Personifying his second novel, *Barbary Shore,* Mailer writes: "toward the end the novel collapsed into a chapter of political speech and never quite recovered" (94). Mailer then "tried to start a novel too soon, a rather mechanical novel about Hollywood, which collapsed after a month of the worst writing [he had] ever done" (106–107). He tries to write a journal, but it "wore down" by February 1956 (235), and when he tries to write his newspaper column for *The Village Voice,* his wit "ran out" (282). Mailer then assays the drama only to discover the mood of his play "shattered beyond repair" (411).

It is thus poignantly ironic that the mass media commit their first "murder" of him by recording him with run-down batteries. "The tape had expressed a sad comedy of vanity and worn-out tools," Mailer writes (406). Mailer's collapse, in point of fact, was literal as well as figurative. In August of 1958, he reports, he "fainted dead away" for the first time in his life (404). In two passages he ties this collapse to loss of personal courage and integrity. Looking back on his fainting spell, he suggests that "the reason was that something honorable had worn out in me, and I knew I was going to sell my book [*The Naked and the Dead*] (which I loved so much) to a man who didn't know the difference between the Army and the Marines" (404). When, in desperation, he seeks Hemingway's endorsement of *The Deer Park,* he notes that "a day or two after the book went off to Hemingway, the broken shell of my pride collapsed into powder" (267).

In *Advertisements* Mailer places the blame for the *wastings* and *sappings* of human energy on American society as well as on himself. Enforced conformity is the external cause of human desiccation most frequently cited by Mailer. In his reply to Harvard's 15th Anniversary Report, which he includes in his First Advertisement, he writes: "But, given the brawl, the wasting of the will, and the sapping of one's creative rage by our most subtle and dear totalitarian time, politely called the time of conformity, I do not know that I would be so confident as to place the bet on myself any longer nor indeed on any of my competitive peers" (18). That Mailer felt impelled to explain his metaphor suggests the intensity of his concern. He notes that much of the meaning of his Harvard reply "depended on the word 'sapping' with its connotations of weakening, enervating, deadening—that word was the nerve of my paragraph" (19). Later, in his *Village Voice* columns, he stresses that "it was rage for what had been wasted in me, and conceivably there was equal rage for what had been wasted in others. If I had one noble emotion it was rage against that national conformity which smothered creativity" (283). In "The White Negro" he continues to bewail that "slow death by conformity with every creative and rebellious instinct stifled" (339).

Mailer, however, perceives the wastings and sappings of national conformity as damage individuals do one another; they are actions under individual control. In one of his characteristically dense metaphorical passages he discloses his grandest literary ambition, with its focus on action:

It is almost beyond the imagination to conceive of a work in which the drama of human energy is engaged, and a theory of its social currents and dissipations, its imprisonments, expressions, and tragic wastes are fitted into some gigantic synthesis of human action where the body of Marxist thought, and particularly the epic grandeur of *Das Kapital* (that first of the major *psychologies* to approach the mystery of social cruelty so simply and practically as to say that we are a collective body of humans whose life-energy is wasted, displaced, and procedurally stolen as it passes from one of us to another). (358)

In *Advertisements*'s short fiction Mailer's stress is on just such individual, damaging transactions. Bowen Hilliard says to his wife, Cova, in "A Calculus at Heaven," "Maybe two people do suck each other dry" (49), and in many ways Denise Gondelman and Sergius O'Shaunessy *are* perfect mates for each other in "The Time of Her Time." Sergius wishes to "lay waste to her little independence" (490) while Denise "drained" the best half of Sergius's desire (488). Much political rhetoric can have the same "sapping" or stifling effect, and thus Mailer nominates Hemingway for president because he believes Hemingway might speak simply and freshly "and the energy this would arouse in the minds of the electorate, benumbed at present by the turgid Latinisms of the Kefauvers, the Stevensons, and the Eisenhowers, is something one should not underestimate, for almost never has the electorate been given the opportunity to have their minds stimulated" (311–12).

Yet if individuals, through their language and actions, can benumb or sap other's energies, they can also stifle their own, and Mailer forthrightly confesses his own responsibility for his wasted condition. He admits that his fear of homosexuality as a subject was "stifling [his] creative reflexes" (222), and that the "warning" he wrote prefacing his second *Village Voice* column "sap[ped] the column for the next sixteen weeks" (281). In time he came to see that his involvement with *The Village Voice* resulted (like the Civil War) in "too many energies . . . wasted in internal disputes"(317), and that he would have to proceed in his working life without this *Voice* and without the "wastes" of drugs (248). Indeed, drugs have been his worst enemy, and he writes: "With each week of work, bombed and sapped and charged and stoned with lush, with pot, with benny, saggy, Miltown, coffee, and two packs a day, I was working live, and overalert, and tiring into what felt like death . . . " (243).

The sappings of energies lead, then, to a panoply of metaphors of diminishment—shrinking (eight), withering (seven), reducing (seven), starving (seven), deteriorating (two), attenuating (two), dwindling (one), and shriveling (one). Metaphors such as shrinking and shriveling carry a sexual resonance and thus lead to and interact with sixty-six references to impotence in the volume. A careful scrutiny of Mailer's metaphors of impotence in *Advertisements* reveals that he primarily employs these sexual metaphors to speak, not of sex itself, but of cerebral power. Twice in his *Village Voice* columns he castigates the "mental impotence" of his readers (281, 298), and he speaks of the "impotent imagination[s]" of the admirers of *Waiting For Godot* as well (321). In other contexts he speaks of "slack" instincts and wit (390, 474), and the "flaccid taste of these years" (466).

Nor is Mailer, himself, immune from this pervasive impotency. He acknowledges that Gore Vidal was able to spot what was "slack" in his play *The Deer Park* (479), and he prints a letter from a *Village Voice* reader that speaks of his columns as a "castrated bellow" (326). The thousand references to health in *Advertisements For Myself* thus reduce to the perpetual struggle between potency and impotency, life and death, which are at the heart of the volume. Mailer surpasses his precursor, Whitman, as a connoisseur of death. The collective condition, he writes, "is to live with instant death by atomic war, relatively quick death by the State as *l'univers concetrationnaire,* or with a slow death by conformity with every creative and rebellious instinct stifled" (339). He finds organized religions "morally dead" (384), Freud's answers "deathlike" (273), and all the Democratic party candidates suffering an "unfortunate resemblance to a prosperous undertaker" (311).

Mailer's vision of death-in-life can be seen in many of his short stories. His 1939 three-paragraph story "It" concludes: " 'My god, I'm dead,' my head said. And my body fell over" (391). When Bowen Hilliard (in "A Calculus at Heaven") confesses he is not an artist any longer, his friend replies: "You can't paint when you're dead" (48). Weary Sam Slovoda in "The Man Who Studied Yoga" says to himself, "My toes are dead," as if death were creeping up his body (185), and perhaps the most stunning figurative use of death is in "The Dead Gook," when Mailer personifies a gun as the dead "Gook" Luis: "And the gun hugged him, a dancing skeleton, jiggling its death's-head in his face" (144).

Mailer presents himself as fending off just such (metaphorical) death glances from others and from himself. He speaks of *Time* magazine's response to *Barbary Shore* as a "Death-To-Norman-Mailer" review (409), and prints a letter from a *Village Voice* reader "saying a prayer over his departed literary genius" (326). He laments that his novel *The Deer Park* "never came alive" for Hiram Hayden (230) and confesses that he could feel the "deadness of [his] style" in 1954 and knew that this style was "strangling the life" of his novel (106, 235).

But Mailer will not submit to death (of spirit, of work, of action) without a struggle. It is no accident that the central section of *Advertisements For Myself,* called (significantly) "Births," contains both extended treatment of Samuel Beckett's *Waiting For Godot* as the central expression of post-modern impotence/death, and his own rejection of this vision and triumph over impotence through the ordeal of *The Deer Park* revision. It is not too much to say that Mailer recognized in Beckett's drama the fatigue, impotency, and death that he had been facing in himself and decrying in others. Characteristically, he evaluates the play in terms of potency and action:

[Vladimir and Estragon] are . . . looking for the Life-Giver. They are so desperate they even speak wanly of hanging themselves, because this at least will give them one last erection. But they have not the power to commit suicide, they are exhausted and addled by the frustration of their failures to the point where they cannot even commit a despairing action. (322)

God, Mailer is quick to stress, is in similar paralyzed condition. When Vladimir asks the boy what Godot does, the boy answers, "He does nothing, Sir" (324).

Although Mailer pays tribute to Beckett's gifts, he also argues that his vision need not prevail

because finally not everyone is impotent, nor is our final fate, our human condition, necessarily doomed to impotence, as old Joyce knew, and Becket I suspect does not. When it comes to calling a work great one must first live with the incommensurable nuance of the potent major key and impotent minor key. (316)

Waiting For Godot, for Mailer, is a great work in the impotent minor key. Mailer aspires, of course, to the potent major key. The multi-vocal metaphor "key" merits analysis, for it, like electricity, is one of Mailer's central metaphors of action, appearing repeatedly across Mailer's non-

fiction in passages of critical revelation. The context above would lead
readers to associate major and minor keys with music, and this is certainly appropriate. For Mailer, however, the metaphor *key* also evokes
both the idea of opening, disclosing, or solving something (as in the *key*
to a puzzle or code) and the literal instrument (key) that *moves* the bolt
or tumblers in the lock. *Key* is thus another metaphor that images action. I have earlier quoted the crucial concluding passage in *Advertisements* in which Mailer (through his persona Marion Faye) achieves victory over death. It is here that the metaphor emerges: "And is that all?
. . . Or is there more? And if I say I think there is, I turn the key into
the category of my own secret" (531). Freudians, of course, would be
quick to note that key carries phallic suggestion, an additional field of
active meaning that Mailer certainly evokes with the adjectives "impotent" and "potent." A final semantic field evoked, which will return us
to Whitman, is that of telecommunications where a *key* is a circuit-breaker
or opener.

Thus Mailer rejects Beckett's vision of impotence and offers instead
his own sexually potent, electric, and musical Whitmanian key. His victory over his impotency as an artist comes through his struggle to write
The Deer Park and with publishers' criticisms of its obscenity. Through
this trial Mailer is able to give birth to a new writer in himself in a
manner similar to Whitman's repeated birthings of Walt, the poet, the
Real-Me in *Leaves of Grass*. In "Out of the Cradle Endlessly Rocking"
Whitman writes of his birth as a poet:

> The love in the heart long pent, now loose, now at last tumultuously
>   bursting, . . .
> My own songs awaked from that hour,
> And with them the key . . .

Mailer both echoes and revises this passage in his Fourth Advertisement for Myself: The Last Draft of *The Deer Park* in describing his
recognition that he was out of fashion and that the publishing habits
of the past were going to be of no help to his *Deer Park*: "And so as the
language of sentiment would have it, something broke in me, but I do
not know if it was so much a loving heart, as a cyst of the weak, the
unreal, and the needy, and I was finally open to my anger" (234). Whitman's bursting or breaking forth is always with love; Mailer's with anger. This is why it is so much easier for readers to love Whitman than
Mailer.

Mailer notes that this sudden liberation of his anger allows a first-
person hero, "bigger than myself," to come alive and speak: "I was
able, then, to create an adventurer whom I believed in, and as he came
alive for me, the other parts of the book which had been stagnant for

a year and more also came to life . . . " (237). This new persona is Mailer's "Real Me," his more muscular voice, and when comparing excerpts from the two drafts of *The Deer Park* that Mailer includes in *Advertisements*, the reader can sense more than just Sergius's less effete style. Also apparent is the fact that in his revisions, Mailer makes his metaphors more concrete—and active. Here are three short examples:

Rinehart edition: I had discovered that to make love to Lulu was to make myself an accessory to the telephone.

Revised Putnam edition: I had discovered that to make love to Lulu was to make myself a scratch-pad to the telephone. (252, 253)

Rinehart edition: One time it would be her father who was marvelous.

Revised Putnam edition: One round it would be her father who was marvelous. (254, 255)

Rinehart edition: . . . she lay beneath me like a captive, pallid before the fury she aroused.

Revised Putnam edition: . . . she lay like a cinder under the speed of my sprints. (258, 257)

Mailer models Whitman in his ability to agitate this more muscular voice into being across *Advertisements*, and particularly in the three pieces ("seeds") he admires most. A new active figure, "The White Negro," is brought to life by that essay, and has stimulated considerable reaction. The potency of Sergius O'Shaugnessy in "The Time of Her Time" has been equally controversial. At the close of *Advertisements For Myself* Marion Faye (*Advertisements*'s strongest Real Me) is able to transcend death.

Without straining too much, I think it can be seen that Mailer's *Advertisements For Myself* represents a re-fashioning of Whitman's *Leaves of Grass* in the manner Harold Bloom describes in *The Anxiety of Influence* and *The Map of Misreading*. *Advertisements* reveals all six of Bloom's stages of creative mis-reading. Mailer's *clinamen*, or creative swerve from *Whitman*, is his emphasis on *stimulation* rather than on love. In the second stage of *tessera* or completion Mailer illustrates Bloom's contention that American writers (after Emerson) tend to "complete" their precursor's work by implying that the precursor did not dare enough. Thus, as I have earlier noted, Mailer moves beyond *grass* to *maggot* (as if grass isn't mean enough), and pushes his speculations on death to reincarnations far beyond Whitman's "I bequeath myself to the dirt to grow from the grass I love." As Bloom observes:

What the strong [writer] thus does is to transform himself into a fouled version of himself, and then confound the consequence with the figure of the precursor. . . . Yet the strong [writer's] imagination *cannot see itself as perverse;* its own inclination must be health, the true priority. (TAOI 62, 85)

Thus, in Bloom's third stage of *kenosis,* Mailer, through his endless repetitions regarding fatigue and illness, empties himself and prepares himself for the fourth stage of *daemonization,* in which he withdraws from society only to expand through the voice of the daemon, the Real Me. In this voice Mailer enters Bloom's fifth stage of *Askesis,* which Bloom characterizes as "peculiarly a lie against the truth of time" (TAOI 130). When this happens the final stage of *Apophrades* or the return of the dead occurs, in which one hears Whitman in Mailer's text: "The mighty dead return, but they return in our colors, and speaking in our voices, at least in part, at least in moments, moments that testify to [the later writer's] persistence, and not to their own" (TAOI 141).

Bloom has written of the "extraordinary obsessiveness with health and cleanliness that oddly marks Whitman's poetry."[7] In *Advertisements For Myself* Mailer demonstrates that by re-modeling Whitman's master-piece he is able to draw off, siphon that "great good health," and use it to regenerate his own writing. Simultaneously he provides a model for us (as readers) to do the same. As he writes in his poem "Dead Ends," employing a lively metaphor of action:

> Consciousness is the breath
> with which we breathe
> our sickness away. (508)

RITE OF PASSAGE AS METAPHOR:
THE ARMIES OF THE NIGHT

Once Mailer has birthed himself in *Advertisements For Myself* his next stage is the adolescent rite of passage. The controlling metaphor of *The Armies of the Night,* Mailer's Pulitzer prize-winning account of the 1967 anti-war march on the Pentagon, is the rite of passage. Taken in its most profound anthropological sense, this metaphor makes coherent many passages in *Armies* that too often have been dismissed as merely "Maileresque" excess. Mailer's genius was to perceive the October march on the Pentagon as a rite of passage, not only for himself, but for the American middle class.

In describing Mailer's rich use of the rite-of-passage metaphor, I will draw extensively on the work of Dutch anthropologist Arnold van Gen-nep and British anthropologist Victor Turner, who promulgated and extended van Gennep's theories. After studying hundreds of seasonal and "life crisis" rites van Gennep, in his seminal 1908 volume *Les rites de passage,* distinguished three stages that, he claimed, all rites of pas-

sage share: separation, transition, and re-incorporation.⁸ In the first
stage of *separation* the subject is severed from ordinary secular relationships. In the rich *transitional,* or "liminal," stage the individual undergoes ritual humiliation and ordeals and tests of various kinds, and the
rites conclude with symbolic birth or *re-incorporation* into society. Book
One of *The Armies of the Night* follows this pattern precisely.

Victor Turner drew on van Gennep's theories in elaborating his own
highly useful four-stage theory for understanding social drama. Metaphor is at the heart of such drama, which Turner defines as occurring
when "conflicting groups and personages attempt to assert their own
and deplete their opponents' paradigms" (DFM 15). Certainly this is
the situation when the doves confront the hawks at the Pentagon, and
Turner has insisted that social drama can be isolated for study in societies at all levels of scale and complexity. The four stages of Turner's
social drama include (1) the breach of a social norm (analogous to van
Gennep's first stage of *separation*); (2) mounting crisis and (3) redressive
action (both characteristic of van Gennep's *transitional* stage); and (4)
re-integration of the disturbed social group (van Gennep's re-incorporation) or recognition and legitimation of irreparable schism between
the contesting parties. All of this occurs in *The Armies of the Night.*

Book One, Part 1: Thursday Evening—Mailer's Separation and Breach

A rite of passage rarely occurs capriciously; a stage in the seasonal or
life progression must be reached, or a certain evil befall an individual
or group, to warrant a ceremonial rite. In primitive societies such evils
might include a famine or disease affecting the whole tribe, or a series
of miscarriages affecting a single woman. In *The Armies of the Night* Mailer
posits a disease that affects both Americans as a group and America
personified as a pregnant woman.

The disease he diagnoses is an advanced cancer traceable largely to
American technology. Because the twentieth century has left "its technological excrement all over the conduits of nature," America, the former young beauty, is in danger of dying of the "disease of her dowa-
ger," a metaphor that suggests America's *advanced* and *elevated* status in
technology (114). In words thought (but never spoken) Thursday evening Mailer criticizes poet Robert Lowell for ignoring this reality: "How
dare you condemn me! You know the diseases which inhabit the audience in this accursed psychedelic house" (41). Later he criticizes the
U.S. marshals for believing America was threatened by a "foreign disease," when in truth "the evil was within" (144, 145).

Some rite must be assayed, therefore, to heal this evil, this diseased
condition. Mailer clearly believed that technological balms were not

working. "America ripped itself apart and then dressed the wounds with television," he complains (169). Significantly it is the war in Vietnam that has made America's disease apparent: "Now there was no room for the sore beneath the skin. A new sore, Vietnam, had pushed the old sore into the light" (101). The 1967 March on the Pentagon is thus transformed by Mailer's metaphor from a political protest against the Vietnam War to a series of rites to exorcize the disease of American technology.

Book One, "History As A Novel," recounts Mailer's personal rite of passage; Book Two, "The Novel As History," describes the collective rite for the middle class. Part I, titled "Thursday evening," marks Mailer's separation from society and first breach of social norms. When Mailer removes himself from his work and family in New York City his separation is both spatial and temporal. He flies from New York to Washington and checks in at the Hay-Adams Hotel, a symbolic association with the reformative ideals of Henry Adams. "Alienation from the immediate environment can mean continuity with an older ideal," Turner explains (DFM 288), and this seems to be what Mailer is seeking. His beginning *Armies* with the *Time* magazine account of his Thursday night misbehavior not only permits him to castigate journalism for its shallow perception of truth, but (more important) also permits him to make a further symbolic separation from temporal order. As his concluding line in Chapter 1 makes clear, "Now we may leave *Time* in order to find out what happened" (4). The reader is hereby invited to accompany Mailer in separation from the social status quo.

As Thursday evening progresses Mailer's acts of separation continue. He refuses food, an act of abstinence common in religious rites, and at the Ambassador Theatre he separates himself from the public address system (modern technology). Taken as a whole, his outrageous behavior at the Ambassador Theatre can certainly be seen as a breach of social norms and thus initiation of social drama, yet, in terms of rites of passage, it is infinitely more complex. At first one is tempted to interpret Mailer's acts of rapid metamorphosis Thursday evening as inauthentic rites preceding the authentic transformation of spirit that occurs in Parts 2, 3, and 4 Friday through Sunday. Yet I think this would be a mistake. Mailer's Thursday actions should be seen as vital preliminary rituals making the later transformation possible.

Turner has observed that passage from one status to another is often accompanied not only by geographical movement, but also by smaller parallel symbolic actions, such as crossing thresholds or opening doors (FRTT 25). After his acts of separation from society Mailer's first crossing occurs in the balcony of the Ambassador Theatre: "[He] stepped off into the darkness of the top-balcony floor, went through a door into a pitch-black men's room, and was alone with his need" (31). Ambiguity is an intrinsic feature of the transitional or liminal stage of a rite of passage, but the humorous ambiguity of Mailer's line should not keep readers from recognizing this moment in the dark as important to the ritual action. Being alone in the dark with his need not only allows Mailer to discover a "restorative view of man" and to emerge "illumed" by the first stages of "Emersonian transcendence," but it also offers him an "utterly non-Sisyphian release," which appears to be the function of the entire first evening of preliminary rites (31, 32).[9]

Indeed, Mailer's preliminary balcony rite brings about his metamorphosis into that aspect of the shaman that is "the Beast" (30). Here the controlling rite-of-passage metaphor makes meaningful what has seemed to many readers to be merely Mailer's rationalization of drunken misbehavior. Turner has noted that an important component of the transitional (or liminal) stage that follows separation from society is an enhanced stress on nature at the expense of culture:

[The transitional stage] is also replete with symbols quite explicitly relating to biological processes, human and nonhuman [such as urination], and to other aspects of the natural order. . . . Thus it is in liminality and also in those phases of ritual that abut on liminality that one finds profuse symbolic reference to beasts, birds, and vegetation. . . . Thus, symbolically, [the human neophytes'] structural life is snuffed out by animality and nature, even as it is being regenerated by these very same forces. . . . Structural custom, once broken, reveals two human traits. One is liberated intellect, whose liminal product is myth and proto-philosophical speculation; the other is bodily energy, represented by animal disguises and gestures. The two may be recombined in various ways. (DFM 252–53)

Mailer's breach of social decorum (after the appearance of the shamanic Beast) liberates both his intellectual and physical energy. He is impelled to extensive "proto-philosophical speculation" as well as toward forceful bodily action at the Pentagon.

Robert Lowell, at one moment, seems caught up in Mailer's rite. At the close of Chapter 5, just prior to the final chapter of Part I, in which Mailer's most dramatic possession occurs, Lowell throws up his eyes "like an epileptic as if turned out of orbit by a turn of the vision" and falls backward (41). Although Mailer clearly prefers Allen Ginsberg's poetry, with its unreserved immersion in the deeps, to Lowell's polite "pirate's patrols" (125), he still credits Lowell with sensitivity to the psychic currents underlying events, and twice finds himself aided by Lowell acts, as if Lowell, too, fellow artist, were a fellow shaman. In Chapter 5 the possessed Lowell enacts a literal "turn of vision" analogous to that which Mailer hopes will seize the Hawks. In Chapter 6, titled "A Transfer of Power," Lowell's poem *Near the Ocean* provides Mailer with a vivid metaphor for the national rite of passage in progress. "O to break loose, like a chinook," Mailer quotes, underscoring the social *separation* required:

> . . . stopped by ten
> steps of the roaring ladder, and then
> to clear the top on the last try,
> alive enough to spawn and die. (45)

This poem is one likely source of the metaphor of the moral "ladder" that Mailer will use so effectively later. Furthermore, the poem dramatizes the active meaning of a rite of passage: death to one order of being but birth to another.

Lowell serves another function in *Armies* as well. In his role as "Poet" to Mailer's "Novelist" he is part of the rich play of oppositions within the volume. *The Armies of the Night* is filled with such inversions and oppositions struggling for reinterpretation. They include the Hawks and the Doves, the two armies of the night (the army of the Pentagon and the army of protestors), History as a Novel and The Novel as History, and American nobility and American obscenity, both exemplified in Vietnam. Inversions and reversals, and the positing and manipulating of oppositions in the phases of *separation* and *transition* lay the groundwork for new forms—of thought, of literature, indeed of social order.

In the final chapter of Part I, called "A Transfer of Power," Mailer makes a dramatic attempt at synthesis. In his shamanic state he invokes Abraham Lincoln (who succeeded in preserving the union from civil war) and stresses that the protestors are "gathered here . . . to invest the Pentagon" (46–47). This cunning metaphor activates at least three connotations of *invest*. The military meaning of *invest* is to surround, hem in, or besiege, and this, of course, is the literal design of the march. Yet *invest* can also mean to cover or surround with a garment: to shroud. Thus Mailer invokes a sense of symbolic death to the Pentagon. Even more suggestive is a third meaning of *invest*, which is to endow with qualities or traits. Thus in literal and figurative senses Mailer is calling for a civilian military siege designed to destroy the paradigms of the Pentagon and to endow those in the Pentagon with the pacifist qualities of the marchers.

Time magazine described Mailer's action as incoherent. It is more interesting, however, to think of Mailer's Thursday night behavior as a ritual shamanistic performance in a rite of passage. Edward de Grazia, Mailer's lawyer and an important character in *Armies*, has spoken of that Thursday evening in just this sense:

Without him the evening would have been a flop. His excitement and his energy—however much it was fueled by the bourbon—but also this particular genius he has when he's drunk probably was the most important thing going on. The act he put on, however incorrigible he seemed, really tied the thing together. (Mills 316)

Book One, Part 2: Friday Afternoon—Mailer's Transition

Thursday evening's ritual activities, then, serve vital functions of continued *separation* from and *breach* of social structures. As Turner so clearly recognized: "Dismembering may be a prelude to re-membering" (FRTT 86). Thursday evening's exertions deliver Mailer from the rage, violence, and frustration that had been gathering inside him for weeks, like an infectious disease (56). They permit—as does all symbolic behavior—a union of internal forces with external action. As Mailer notes:

It was . . . as if two very different rivers, one external, one subjective, had come together; the frustrated bile, piss, pus, and poison he had felt at the progressive contamination of all American life in the abscess of Vietnam, all of that, . . . represented one river, and the other was the frustrated actor in Mailer. . . . (51)

As a result of Mailer's Thursday actions, his rites of exorcism, Friday morning he feels cleansed of hatred. "To his surprise, Mailer realized he felt gentle—in fact, this morning, he felt like a damn Quaker," he notes, establishing his tie with the Quakers, whose martyrdom will cap the rites of passage in Book Two (57).

Thus Friday will mark a new stage in Mailer's personal rite of passage. He is now in the long *transitional* or liminal stage where many rites of redressive action will occur. Appropriately the first events take place in the Church of the Reformation. If Mailer's personal *breach* of social norms occurs Thursday evening, the march's first public *breach* occurs Friday at the church. The formal breach is of a law, section 12 of the National Selective Service Act, which declared that anyone "who knowingly counsels, aids, or abets another to refuse or evade registration or service in the armed forces . . . shall be liable to imprisonment for not more than five years or a fine of ten thousand dollars or both." In their leaflets and their speeches the marchers make it clear that they will publicly counsel young men to continue in their refusal to serve in the armed forces as long as the war in Vietnam continues, and that they will aid and abet them in every way they can. Thus the stage is set for confrontation, for social drama. Significantly the protestors seem to require not just leaflets and private counseling, but also "a clear, simple ceremony" (ritual action) to "make concrete" their opposition to the

war (59), and the thirty to forty men volunteering to turn in their draft
cards in this ceremony sit apart at the church. In short, they are in the
stage of separation entered by Mailer Thursday, "indifferent to the numerous onlookers" (61).

Though feeling cleansed of his former rage, Mailer persists in his
own phase of separation Friday morning. He feels a "great wall of total
miscomprehension" between himself and the press (65), and he feels
slighted and ignored by the others at the church meeting (63). His ambiguous feelings of being in and out of the experience simultaneously
are part of the ambiguity of the entire event, which he discusses at
length in Part 2. Noting that the march on the Pentagon was "an ambiguous event whose essential value or absurdity may not be established
for ten or twenty years, or indeed ever," he insists that its chronicler
must be an eyewitness who is a participant, yet not a vested partisan:
"he must be not only involved, but ambiguous in his own proportions,
a comic hero . . . a ludicrous figure with mock-heroic associations" (53).

Many critics have noted that Mailer's assumption of the role of comic
hero in *Armies* endows him with the power of the ancient fool to shock,
unsettle, and criticize the social powers with impugnity. He is endowed
with the "power of the weak," usually visionary in nature. Mailer's controlling rite-of-passage metaphor impels us to probe these ideas deeply.
Turner observes that "cognitively, nothing underlines regularity so well
as absurdity or paradox" (TRP 176). Thus Mailer's comic stance increases the reader's consciousness of the very social structures he is
mocking. Parody, which he employs in Parts 2, 3, and 4, has a similar
cognitive function. Because readers are manipulated by the mock-hero
to be acutely aware of traditional structures (of the novel and American
society), they become more receptive to the criticisms and new paradigms also being offered. The word "ambiguity" in fact is derived from
the Latin word *agere*, meaning "to act." Thus Mailer's transitional ambiguity is a necessary stage of metaphoric social action.

Despite his initial feelings of alienation and ambiguity, Mailer does
undergo a profound spiritual experience during the Friday afternoon
ceremony. William Sloane Coffin, the Yale chaplain, perhaps initiates
Mailer's experience with his discussion of the important ritual concept
of *sacrifice*. Robert Lowell follows, speaking with "a pilgrim's passion,"
proclaiming that those against the war will not try to avoid "whatever
may arise in the way of retribution" (73, 74). This notion of sacrifice
and a martyr's acceptance of retribution impresses Mailer. As the ritual
begins, with each student filing up the steps to drop his draft card in
the bag, Mailer's language discloses his recognition that each individual
action represents a social breach and separation: "So they came up one
by one, not in solidarity, but as individuals, each breaking the shield or

the fence or the mold or the home or even the construct of his own security" (77).

And this effects a profound change in Mailer. If his Thursday night rites were rites of exorcism, then Friday's rites are those of initiation:

[As they filed forward] a deep gloom began to work on Mailer, because a deep modesty was on its way to him, he could feel himself becoming more and more of a modest man as he stood there in the cold with his hangover . . . he had lived long enough to know that the intimation one was being steeped in a new psychical condition (like this oncoming modest grace) was never to be disregarded, permanent new states could come into one on just so light a breeze. . . . there was no escape. As if some final cherished rare innocence of childhood still preserved intact in him was brought finally to the surface and there expired, so he lost at that instant the last secret delight he retained in life as a game where finally you never got hurt if you played the game well enough. (77, 78)

The new modest Mailer has discovered that his role in the coming action is not to be that of either gamesplayer or leader, but that of "victim" (78), that his role will be that of one undergoing sacrifice. And when eventually he is called to make a speech his behavior is the opposite of his Thursday evening bravado. In a "modest" speech he states: "The war in Vietnam [is] an obscene war, the worst war the nation had ever been in, and so its logic might compel sacrifice from those who were not so accustomed" (79). Turner stresses that rites of initiation humble people before permanently elevating them to a higher status (FRTT 25). Indeed, an appropriate analogy to the initiation process Mailer undergoes Friday is the vigil required of the medieval knight the night before his anointing. During this vigil the knight must pledge to serve the weak and the distressed and to meditate on his own unworthiness. His subsequent power as a knight, Turner explains, "is thought partially to spring from this profound immersion in humility" (TRP 105).

And Mailer's vigil at the steps of the Justice Department, and his rite of initiation, like that of the newly dubbed knight, is celebrated by a "merry meal" (79). He receives the congratulations of his fellows, particularly Robert Lowell, in what seems to be a final rite of the day—a ritual of reinforcement:

Through the drinks and the evening at dinner, [Lowell] kept coming back to the same conversation, kept repeating his pleasure in Mailer's speech in order to hear Mailer doggedly reaffirm his more than equal pleasure in Lowell's good words. Mailer was particularly graceless at these ceremonious repetitions by which presumably New England mandarins (like old Chinese) ring the stately gong of a new friendship forming. (84)

But Mailer is learning, and the evening ends with avowal by Mailer, Lowell, and Macdonald to go out together Saturday and get arrested.

Book One, Part 3: Saturday Matinee—Mailer's Crisis

Saturday morning begins, Mailer tells us, with the mood of "collective celebration" (81). Here Mailer begins to suggest a particularly American quality to the rites in progress, for he likens the mood to that of a homecoming game, civic testimonial, or class reunion. (Later, after his arrest, he will equate the mood on the prison bus to that of a high school football team journeying to a game.) And yet beneath the American celebratory spirit exists the older, more universal link of the political with the primitive. Mailer reflects that

what possibly they shared now between them at the morning table of the Hay-Adams was the unspoken happy confidence that politics had again become mysterious, had begun to partake of Mystery; that gave life to a thought the gods were back in human affairs. . . . The new generation believed in technology more than any before it, but the generation also believed in LSD, in witches, in tribal knowledge, in orgy, and revolution. . . . In the capital of technology land beat a primitive drum. (86, 93–94)

In Mailer's description, the march takes on the quality of a ritual dance, with the "hollow square" of monitors in front, followed by lines of notables and un-notables linking arms, wavering, buckling, undulating across the Arlington Memorial Bridge into the Pentagon's north parking lot.

If Mailer's Thursday night shamanistic possessions at the Ambassador Theatre have been personal rites exorcising his own angers and frustrations (and perhaps those in his audience), the public exorcism at the Pentagon conducted by Abbie Hoffman and the Fugs is designed to rid the Pentagon of evil. What is significant is that here we have an actual rite of exorcism, not actions that are "like" ritual activity. While cymbals clang and a triangle is rung the protestors call on the gods of ancient and modern cultures to "raise the Pentagon from its destiny" and rid it of demons (121). And again Mailer is caught up in a rite against his will:

He detested community sing . . . but the invocation delivered some message to his throat. "Out demons, out," he whispered, "out demons, out." And his foot—simple American foot—was, of course, tapping. "Out, demons, out." Were any of the experts in the Pentagon now shuddering, or glory of partial unringed exorcism—even vibrating? Vibrating experts? "Out, demons, out! Out, demons, out!" (122)

And the rite of exorcism is followed by a sexual rite. Ed Sanders of the Fugs terms it "seminal culmination in the spirit of peace and brotherhood" and calls on all who wish to protect this "rite of love" to form a circle of protection around the lovers (122). But Mailer, who has on the bridge already liberated his love for America, is distracted from this rite by the first wedge attack by the National Liberation Front. Suddenly, seeing the charge repelled, Mailer relives the Civil War experience of Henry Fielding in *The Red Badge of Courage* and turns to run in order not to be overtaken. He admits that panic is upon him. He sprints a few steps, abruptly stops, and then, recognizing his fear, determines to delay his arrest no longer. Significant in respect to Mailer's belief in the constitutive power of words, he states: "Stating the desire [to get arrested] created it, and put a ligature across the rent in his nerve" (128).

This, then, is Mailer's crisis on the third day of his rite of passage. In the rich context of the rite-of-passage metaphor his actions of stepping over a rope and crossing the military police line become more than routine "transgressions." Van Gennep insists that the "prohibition against entering a given territory is . . . intrinsically magico-religious" (16), and Mailer reports that when he steps over the rope: "It was as if the air had changed, or light had altered; he felt immediately much more alive—yes, bathed in air—and yet disembodied from himself" (129). This magico-religious power seems to follow him, for when he confronts a black MP, the soldier quivers and (significantly) turns in the psychic field. And Mailer ponders: "Secret military wonder was [Mailer] now possessed of a moral force?" (130). Eventually, however, he is arrested. He has made his own literal *breach* of the law, his small action symbolically signaling his rejection of the constituted order.

Book One, Part 4: Saturday Night and All of Sunday— Mailer's Redressive Action and Re-incorporation

Mailer has passed through many tests and ordeals in his rite of passage. He has moved from shamanistic exorcism Thursday to ritual humbling Friday and liberation of both love and the power of action Saturday. Part 4 of Book One will carry him through his last *redressive actions* to final sacrifice and *re-incorporation* into society.

Readers would be remiss, however, if they fail to notice that they are undergoing the process with Mailer. At the opening of Part 4 Mailer reminds us that he has employed one of the oldest devices of the novelist, which is to bring his story to a pitch of excitement where the reader "no matter how cultivated is reduced to a beast" panting to hear what occurs next (133). We, like Mailer, are now reduced to beasts; we, too, are in the liminal, *transitional* stage, seeking redressive action.

After his arrest Mailer crosses a second bridge, a ramp into the reception area of the Pentagon. Accompanying this spatial passage is (not surprisingly) a new spiritual passage as well. Mailer marks it by saying that he felt as if he were being confirmed (138). Mailer feels like a novice in this new world: "Like a visitor from Mars, or an adolescent entering polite society, [he] had no idea of what might be important next" (140).

When he is finally loaded into the prison bus, its barred gate separating the prisoners from the driver, this enforced separation fosters a stage that Mailer has not yet reached in his rite of passage, the stage which Turner calls "communitas." When separated from previous social structures and statuses and subjected to the status-leveling of ritual humiliation, a sense of communion and community tends to grow in all initiates, be they fraternity pledges, religious novices, pilgrims, or prisoners. Friday morning at the Church of the Reformation Mailer had observed that "a sense of communion was natural" to the students prepared to turn in their draft cards as they sat separated from the rest (62). On his arrest Saturday he discovers that the cage at the rear of the prison bus "did the work of making [those inside] an ensemble" (149). During his hours in prison Mailer will experience the invigorating power of communitas that, Turner claims, often provides the atmosphere for the development of creative alternatives to social structures.

Mailer's attitude toward his clothes is indicative of the equalizing power of communitas. At the beginning of his arrest, when he is forced to climb over the tailgate of an army truck, Mailer admits to finding this awkward, "for he did not wish to dirty his dark blue pinstripe suit" (141). Later, however, he tells us that "each hour in jail, [his] vest became more absurd" (177), and when he goes to breakfast Sunday morning it is sans vest, sans tie, in mere dirty white shirt and wrinkled jacket. He has become more like his fellows, and when it comes time to don his regimental tie and return for *re-incorporation* into society, Mailer complies, yet maintains his new appreciation of the absurdity of sartorial status. He confesses that he feels "like the people's choice between Victor McLaglen and Harpo Marx" (202). Noteworthy in respect to Mailer's continued depiction of himself as a comic hero is Turner's observation that the fool in ancient cultures was able "through jest and mockery to infuse communitas throughout the whole society" (TRP 202). This may be the goal of Mailer's entire rhetorical project.

The leveling power of communitas is apparent not only in Mailer's changed attitude toward dress, but also in his behavior regarding wealth.

He passes out the $200 he has in his wallet to help various prisoners pay their $25 fines, sharing with two prisoners he does not even like. "Some vague principle of man's equality before the law seemed here to apply," he explains (164).

While experiencing the openness and spiritual communion of communitas Mailer is simultaneously aware, however, of his liminal status. He knows he is in a stage of separation from society, and sexual continence (as well as his previous abstention from food and drink) is part of the way this is brought home. Turner has written that sexual continence is a feature of religious behavior in almost all societies, and that the resumption of sexual relations is usually a ceremonial mark of the return to society "as a structure of statuses" (TRP 104). This resumption, of course, will occur to Mailer after his release as part of his *reincorporation* into society, but here it is significant that Mailer thinks he must increase his sense of social separation while in prison in order to advance spiritually. "Slowly, patiently, the idea of going to a party tonight was severed from his expectations," he explains; "slowly the thought of seeing his wife and family this weekend was subdued" (165). In a passage suggestive of both the unifying and generative powers of communitas he explains that he

knew—looking at Teague—that if he were to hold on to the value of what had happened to him (and he knew by the unfamiliar variety of happiness he now felt that much indeed had happened to him . . .) he must take the next step and give up any quick idea of savoring, installing, banking the value of the experience by way of some enjoyable revery on the trip home tonight. (160)

And paradoxically (yet not paradoxical, for this is the raison d'etre for the liminal experience), just as Mailer's use of parody has the effect of increasing our awareness of the structures (literary and social) undergoing reinterpretation, Mailer's separation from his wife only makes him more aware of her: "Separations made them painfully aware of each other—they each traveled then in the psyche of the other . . . they rarely felt so close to each other as when they were separated. Then at last they understood each other" (170, 167).

Mailer later personifies America as a woman, and perhaps it is only through the enforced isolation of his arrest that Mailer comes to understand American society, for it is not in some quick "enjoyable revery," but in the "long revery" during his night at Occoquan prison that he comes to his understanding of the war in Vietnam, "the charges against it, the defenses for it," and the fact that "there was no one in America who had a position even remotely like his own" (180).

In his extended essay "Why Are We in Vietnam?" in *Armies* Mailer is not the first to suggest that America leave Vietnam to the Vietnamese and the Communists, but he *is* alone in his metaphoric characterization of the war. During his long night's revery (literally to Fitzgerald's three o'clock in the morning) Mailer comes to understand that the war in Vietnam placed Americans in a schizophrenic position, one of unendurable contradiction. On the one hand, the war was begun by those whom Mailer characterizes as medieval "Wasp knights" for the noble purpose of preserving Christian culture from communism. However, because Mailer believes that the center of Christianity is the "love of the Mystery of Christ" and that the center of technology (used to fight the war) was "the love of no Mystery whatsoever" (188), Americans were in the untenable position of using the negation of Mystery to preserve Mystery. How could Mystery survive? Or America's sanity? Thus Mailer can offer the metaphor in his Sunday morning sermon: "We are burning the body and blood [i.e., the Mystery] of Christ in Vietnam."

Mailer has only four hours' sleep before he must confront several Sunday morning challenges. The first is presented by Tuli Kupferberg's decision to take the five days in prison rather than promise to stay away from the Pentagon for six months. This stand impels Mailer to reintroduce the metaphor of the moral "ladder." To many readers, the moral ladder will recall not only Lowell's leaping chinook, but also the Genesis account of Jacob's ladder.[10] After this moral challenge the final stages of redressive action begin. Turner has written that societies seek to redress social crises by both legal procedures (secular ritual) and religious ritual. Through both types of rites "an interpretation . . . is constructed to give the appearance of sense and order to the events leading up to and constituting the crisis" (FRTT 75). As Sally Falk Moore has explained, "ritual is a declaration of form against indeterminancy" (FRTT 77). Significantly Mailer participates in both forms of ritual before his final *re-incorporation* into society.

Indeed, the above may explain as nothing else can the extensive space Mailer devotes to detailing the machinations of the U.S. legal system. It represents a secular rite. In fact, in keeping with the evocation of Jacob, Mailer depicts the Jewish lawyer Hirschkop as struggling with the Wasp judge, and eventually making a "breach" in the sepulchral legal line through which Mailer passes to freedom (210).

Ultimately, however, Mailer finds the redressive action of legal rites unsatisfactory. The "evil" he perceives in America can be healed only through the symbolic actions of religion and art, and specifically through the metaphor of sacrifice. Turner has noted that rites of passage frequently conclude with a ritual of sacrifice which represents the symbolic death of the old order and prepares for the rebirth of the new. Friday, on the steps of the Justice Department, Mailer came to the humbling recognition that his role could only be that of "victim," that the logic of the war "might compel sacrifice" (78, 79). What troubles him, then, about his potential jail sentence and fine in the legal rite is that it would make him a martyr "for so little" (206).

Such sacrifice or martyrdom would not be ultimately compelling. Thus, in his Sunday morning speech on his legal liberation, the newly modest Mailer substitutes for his own slight sacrifice the powerful sacrifice of Jesus: "You see, dear fellow Americans, it is Sunday, and we are burning the body and blood of Christ in Vietnam" (214). By thus metaphorically equating the war in Vietnam with the sacrificial death of Jesus, Mailer is able to (a) induce in the American public a sense of moral horror at the killing in Vietnam (now perceived as a repetition of the crucifixion); (b) hint that we are destroying the Mystery of Christianity (which Mailer calls the "foundation" of the American Republic) through the war in Vietnam; and (c) provide the ritual sacrifice necessary for new perceptual orders to begin.

This is impressive work for one metaphor, yet I think it succeeds. Mailer does not merely substitute Christianity's paradigm of martyrdom for his own small sacrifice. Chapter 10 is called "The Communication of Christ," and we should note that just as Mailer presented himself as possessed by the spirits of Lyndon Johnson and black power on Thursday evening, during his final Sunday morning ritual, he suddenly feels Christ within him, and thus his sacrifice *merges* with Christ's.

The ritual sacrifice now offered, the rite of passage is done and Mailer is *re-incorporated* into society. Those present to congratulate him on his release from prison are pleased with his "communication." In truth, the result of the four-day rite is growth for both Mailer and society. Mailer has discovered that

all effort was not the same, and to eject oneself from guilt might yet be worth it, for the nausea on return to guilt could conceivably prove less: standing on the grass, he felt one suspicion of a whole man closer to that freedom from dread which occupied the inner drama of his years, yes, one image closer than when he had come to Washington four days ago. (212–13)

And on the shuttle back to New York City, "the air between New York and Washington was orgiastic with the breath of release, some promise of peace and new war seemed riding the phosphorescent wake of this second and last day's siege of the Pentagon, as if the country were opening into more and more on the resonance of these two days" (214).

Book Two: The Collective Novel and
Collective Rite of Passage

If Book One of *The Armies of the Night,* "History As A Novel," recounts the personal rite of passage of Norman Mailer, Book Two, "The

Novel As History," portrays the rite on a massive social scale. Indeed, the shorter Book Two might be read as a casebook of Turner's social drama. Mailer begins his history by describing the many factions into which U.S. society had splintered in the months preceding the March. By April 1967, he notes, "the rifts were profound between the races and the generations" (222). Formal *breaches* of the social order, such as the October March on the Pentagon, are, therefore, planned to precipitate crisis and the redressive actions required to bring about social change.

Perhaps Mailer's greatest contribution as a historian in *The Armies of the Night* is his recognition that *redressive actions* (Turner's stage 3) actually get under way *before* the literal social *breach* (stage 1) and *crisis* (stage 2) occur. He astutely notes that the very negotiations between government and protest leaders over the times and locations of the March are redressive actions on the part of the government that have the effect of diminishing the symbolic power, the revolutionary aesthetic, of the March. Such counselling with the "enemy" makes the act of mass social *breach* more difficult.

This analysis of the social drama helps us to appreciate the obstacles to action confronting all Americans at the time. We are likely to believe Mailer's insistence on "the extraordinary demand for initiative on the side of the demonstrators if they were to do anything at all" once they arrived at the aesthetically dull north parking lot of the Pentagon (252). Yet triumphing over the dull aesthetic and their own unconscious respect for authority, the protestors do act; they (like Mailer) break through the wire and the military police line. The *breach* of social order is made.

Once the protestors make their *breach* and enter the liminal world of *transition* where all sorts of crises and redressive actions will occur, Mailer makes a parallel breach of his stipulated form of discourse (the history), for a freer, more speculative form:

It is on this particular confrontation [the protestors with the MPs] that the conceit one is writing a history must be relinquished. . . . an explanation of the mystery of the events at the Pentagon cannot be developed by the methods of history—only by the instincts of the novelist. . . . the novel must replace history at precisely that point where experience is sufficiently emotional, spiritual, psychical, moral, existential, or supernatural to expose the fact that the historian in pursuing the experience would be obliged to quit the clearly demarcated limits of historic inquiry. So these limits are now relinquished. The collective novel which follows, while still written in the cloak of an historic style, and, therefore, continuously attempting to be scrupulous to the welter of a hundred confusing and opposed facts, will now unashamedly enter the world of strange lights and intuitive speculation which is the novel. (254, 255)

Mailer, indeed, *must* relinquish the role of historian, for as he enters the *transitional* "world of strange lights" he next wants to say that "each side is coming face to face with its own conception of the devil!" (256). This is certainly coherent with his rite-of-passage metaphor, but not with the traditional discourse of a historian.

What follows is the first *crisis* confronting the protestors. Their first test, like Mailer's, is a staring contest with the soldiers, and they (like he) are elated to win. We should note the diction of animism Mailer employs to depict the event:

When this vanguard confronted soldiers now, and were able to stare them in the eye, they were, in effect, saying silently, "I will steal your elan, and your brawn, and the very animal of your charm because I am morally right and you are wrong and the balance of existence is such that the meat of your life is now attached to my spirit. . . . (258–59)

This initial successful test spurs other positive rites. As it begins to grow dark Saturday evening the young people begin a ritual of commitment, of draft card–burning, in what becomes, through Mailer's haunting language, a moving rite of fire: "wild revolutionary youth, conservative middle-class boy, keeper of draft cards—his schizophrenia is burning and the security of the future with it. He looks for a girl to kiss in reward" (270).

In this way, as the evening progresses, the state of communitas is created among the novice protestors, just as it is being fired for Mailer thirty miles away in Occoquan prison. After the ritual of fire a peace pipe (filled with hashish) is lit and passed about, "even to the soldiers here and there" (263). Sandwiches and beer arrive and, Mailer insists, "Saturnalia came in" (268). Filled with the communitas spirit the demonstrators talk with the soldiers through the early hours of the night.

Thus the first liminal tests are positive for the middle-class initiates. They stare down their enemy and then invite him to join their new order. But after midnight, when the first troops are replaced with Vietnam veterans, a new test for the demonstrators arises in "The Battle of the Wedge." The account Mailer chooses to cite (from the *Washington Free Press*) is one making the event seem to be one of ritual slaughter. The seated demonstrators have locked arms in a chain, and

as [the soldiers] clubbed the marked person, usually a girl, in the first row, and dragged her away, the ranks in back closed in tighter. The person in the row behind became the front, was subjected to blows and kicks, dragged away, and the troops went on to the third row. Then the fourth, the fifth, the sixth rank. . . . One hundred people were methodically beaten and carried away to the paddy wagons. (273)

One wonders, Mailer queries, "why no musicians were playing as the clubs came down" (277).

Mailer observes that from the government's view, the beatings were to "drive something into flesh"—perhaps the government's authority and power (276). This allusion to the crucifixion introduces (as in Book One) the concept of sacrifice after communitas that paves the way for a new order: "United in the community of the day . . . many of them felt that one could not leave the slaughter, but must passively remain to make a personal witness, a penance through suffering for the horrors committed to our Vietnamese brothers" (274).[11] And like Mailer in Book One, "they were shriven in the hours till dawn"; for indeed, "they were now engaged in that spiritual test so painful to all—the rite of passage" (278). Here Mailer explores at greatest length the metaphor that is central, as I hope I have illustrated, to the entire volume. The rite of passage for the demonstrators entails both piercing the cyst of the disease infecting America and then, having probed deeply inward, climbing the moral ladder. Mailer inquires:

How many of these demonstrators, certain at the beginning of the night by the firm conviction of their ego that they would not leave until morning, must have been obliged to pass through layers and dimensions and bursting cysts of cowardice they never knew to exist in themselves, as if each hour they remained extracted from them a new demand, a further extension of their moral resolve, another rung up the moral ladder which Mailer had glimpsed in Occoquan and had made to refuse. . . . So it became a rite of passage for these tender drug-vitiated jargon-mired children, they endured through a night, a black dark night which began in joy, near foundered in terror, and dragged on through empty apathetic hours while glints of light came to each alone. Yet the rite of passage was invoked, the moral ladder was climbed, they were forever different in the morning than they had been before the night, which is the meaning of a rite of passage, one has voyaged through a channel of shipwreck and temptation, and so some of the vices carried from another nether world into life itself (on the day of one's birth) may have departed, or fled, or quit; some part of the man has been born again. (279, 280–81)

It is enough to say that the action of the "collective novel" has been parallel to the ritual passage of Mailer in Book One—only perhaps with greater sacrifice. Individual action is authenticated as a model for social action, and the rite-of-passage metaphor provides the paradigm for both.

SEX AS A METAPHOR: *GENIUS AND LUST*, *THE PRISONER OF SEX*, AND *MARILYN*

If *The Armies of the Night* represents Mailer's rite of passage from youth to manhood, the middle period of his nonfiction career involves adult love affairs with women and literature. *Genius and Lust*, published in 1976, offers the key to the earlier volumes in this period, for in *The*

Prisoner of Sex (1971) and *Marilyn* (1973) the work of Henry Miller provides the inspiration. "Never has literature and sex lived in such symbiotic relation before," Mailer writes of Miller in *Genius and Lust* (90).

Mailer's anxiety before Miller's oeuvre is daringly confessed in a metaphor depicting Miller as a giant elm and Mailer in a state of desire—
even penis envy:

Miller, his work embraced, which is to say swallowed in four or five weeks, and
then re-read over another month or two, can sit in one's mind with all the
palpability of a huge elm lying uprooted in your backyard. The nobility of the
trunk and the relations of the branches are all on the ground for you to ex-
amine and try to compare. . . . Fibers of root-hair emerge from the soil like
ideas drawn into wires. One hallucinates: every scent comes off every crotch of
the roots—wholesale corruption may beckon here along with organic integrity.
(GAL x-xi)

Mailer speaks of "the irrigation Henry Miller gave to American prose"
(GAL 5), and the passage above even suggests a homosexual scenario
with Mailer embracing and swallowing Miller whole.

Later, in his section titled "Crazy Cock," Mailer will write: "To enter
Miller's mind is to write like him. Sometimes, his writing even has the
form of a fuck" (GAL 92). These sentences can be taken as a gloss for
The Prisoner of Sex, which is nothing less than rhetorical intercourse
with the women's movement in homage to and emulation of Miller's
Tropic of Cancer. The sexual scenario of *The Prisoner of Sex* introduces
readers to an impotent, unnaturally attacked male ego in Section I and
progresses to foreplay in Section II. In Section III Mailer trades rhetorical thrust for thrust, rhetorical orgasm for orgasm, in a *menage a
cinq* involving feminist critic Kate Millett, Henry Miller, D. H. Lawrence, Jean Genet, and himself, and the final section concludes with a
single, soulful rhetorical "fuck"—an entry into the womb's prison for
the prize. If *The Prisoner of Sex* is read, then, not as a profound exploration of the issues raised by the feminist movement, but as a rhetorical
"gang-bang" of feminists in general, and as an extended session of rhetorical intercourse with Kate Millett in particular, *ultimately for the pur-
poses of art,* a more accurate assessment of the book's achievement can
be made. In truth, the rhetoric of sex throughout the volume points to
this reading, and readers would be well advised that the most interesting action occurs at the level of sexual metaphor rather than that of
political and social ideas.

In "The Prizewinner," the book's opening section, Mailer confesses
that he would like to begin a discourse on women's liberation from the
elevated podium of a Nobel Prizewinner—but he cannot. "Failed Prizewinner" is more accurate, and Mailer's diction makes clear he is in a
state of ennui, indeed—let us face it—in a state of impotence:

It was simply that his ego *did not rise* very often these days to the emoluments of the Prizewinner. His mood was nearer to the dungeon. For his battered *not-so-firm ego* was obliged to be installed in Provincetown through a long winter to go through the double haul of writing a book about the first landing on the moon while remaking himself out of the loss of a fourth wife. (POS 9, emphases added)

Mailer finds that the women's movement will provide provocative enough stimulus for him to "rise" to the occasion and make himself anew. In fact, his animus rises when women take the initiative in the rhetorical intercourse:

While the Prizewinner was packing lunches this picknicking summer, the particular part of his ghost-phallus which remained in New York—his very reputation in residence—had not only been ambushed, but was apparently being chewed half to death by a squadron of enraged Amazons, an honor guard of revolutionary (if we could only see them) vaginas. (13)

The feminists are trying to emasculate him. Kate Millett is trying to "snip off" Henry Miller (and D. H. Lawrence) as well. Mailer projects himself as a weak and innocent hero under unnatural attack.[12] "On *came* the ladies with their fierce ideas," PW (the Prizewinner) cries at the end of the section (31, emphasis added). Yet Mailer promises to make his mark deep: "For the PW was now off on a search and knew that the longer he looked, the less we would see of him" (31).

The second section of *The Prisoner of Sex,* titled "The Acolyte," chronicles Mailer's approach to the womb. First he must penetrate "all that prior thicket of polemic and concept which revolved around Freud, penis envy, and the virtue or vice of the clitoral orgasm. Sexual theories undulated like belly dancers in every bend" (70). Feminists are shown here beckoning and arousing Mailer. He then initiates (reluctantly) his (rhetorical) descent: "the damnable descent of the PW into the arguments of liberated women was obliged to continue. The mysteries of the feminine orgasm, as revealed by their literature, continued to wash over him" (74). Mailer continues outraged at feminists' achieving "satisfaction" first. "What abuse a man had to take!" he exclaims (74) as he prepares to take the sexual offensive in the third, "Advocate," section.

Here Mailer "bangs" at Millett's rhetoric for a while and shows her banging at Henry Miller (115). Mailer defends Miller and then says, as if pausing for a cigarette, "Let us relax a moment on the moralisms of Millett" (118). Round two is not far away, however, for Mailer soon says: "Henry won't be allowed to rest for long. Squirt bomb at the ready [i.e., rhetorical orgasm], Millett is laying for him" (121). At the end of this subsection, Mailer depicts Millett as trying to emasculate *Miller's* ghost-phallus in her "confetti-making . . . ideological mincers" (124).

In the Lawrence section the orgy begins anew. In terms of Mailer's anxiety regarding Miller's influence this section is particularly important, for (as Mailer asserts twice in *Genius and Lust*) Miller was never able to finish his own work on Lawrence.[13] Mailer is thus able both to complete and surpass Miller's work. As the orgy continues Mailer first sees women "withdraw" respect from men (126); then Millett is pictured as "embolden[ed]" (128), trying to be "more manly than the men," wanting "to push past the argument" with her "social lust," her "cerebral passion" (129). Soon Millett and her cohorts are "*case-hardened guerilla[s]*," yet Mailer foolishly believes that a dose of D. H. Lawrence will render them impotent: "which stout partisan of the Liberation would read such words and not *go soft* for the memory of some bitter bridge of love they had burned behind" (135, emphases added).

Millet, however, proves perdurable, and Mailer describes her rhetoric as if it were toxic orgasm: her words "poisoned [Lawrence's prose] by the acids of inappropriate comment" (144). Mailer, however, will show her how it is properly done: "Take off your business suit, Comrade Millett. . . . it is hardly the time for a recess" (144). Mailer feels little need to bang at Millett over Genet, and so closes "The Advocate" section as he prepares to go alone toward that ultimate prize/prison of the womb.

The action of this final section, titled "The Prisoner," takes place predominantly within the uterus. The thought of unification of egg and sperm, man and woman, "rouse[s]" Mailer (210). And when he quotes from his own *An American Dream*, the hero does find "new life [beginning] again in me," through intercourse with a woman (225). It is, Mailer's narrator acknowledges, "like a gift I did not deserve" (225). Mailer's hero discovers that the meaning of love is that "we would have to be brave," revealing Mailer's own hope for new literary life in this bold rhetorical intercourse with the women's movement, hope for new life as a gift (prize) he does not deserve (225). He thus ends his "portentious piece" in parentheses (the typographical equivalent of the womb) with the suggestion that he is merely imitating God's own desire to "go all the way" (234).

Thirty-four episodes of explicit sexual intercourse are included in the Miller excerpts chosen by Mailer for *Genius and Lust*. Seven of these are from *Tropic of Cancer*, the volume that begins with "the prison of death," yet moves within paragraphs to woman, and intercourse, and Miller proclaiming: "I am still alive, kicking in your womb, a reality to write upon" (2). Mailer's close of *The Prisoner of Sex*—"he had been able to end a portentious piece in the soft sweet flesh of parentheses)"—is a subtle remodeling of this statement. Mailer describes the Miller of *Tropic of Cancer* as "the man with iron in his phallus, acid in his mind, and some kind of incomparable relentless freedom in his heart" (GAL 12), and this would be a good description of Mailer's unrelenting persona in *The Prisoner of Sex*. So fervid indeed is Mailer regarding his literary enterprise that he calls to mind Miller's words in *Tropic of Capricorn*: "It came over me, as I stood there, that I wasn't thinking of her anymore; I was thinking of this book which I am writing, and the book had become more important to me than her. . . . I realized that the book I was planning was nothing more than a tomb in which to bury her" (333, 334).

This last sentence might apply as well to *Marilyn*, which represents Mailer's homage to Miller's post-*Tropic of Cancer* fiction. Monroe represents for Mailer the June/Mona/Mara figure that would haunt, and ultimately elude, Miller throughout his life. Mailer writes in *Genius and Lust*:

The mysteries of his relation with Mona have so beguiled him that he has spent thirty-six obsessive years living with her and writing about her and never succeeds, never quite, in making her real to us. . . . She hovers in that space between actual and the fictional where everything is just out of focus. (181)

This last is true of Mailer's *Marilyn* as well; in fact Mailer's continuing obsession with Monroe, as shown in *Of Women and Their Elegance* and the play *Strawhead*, suggests the persistent influence of Miller (as well as Monroe) on his artistic imagination.

It is only by viewing Marilyn Monroe as Mailer's Mara/Mona that *Marilyn* comes into sharp focus.[14] Three times Mailer compares Monroe with Valentino, describing her as the female incarnation of love. This equation becomes more meaningful when we learn that Mona, in *Sexus*, changes Henry Miller's name to Val, another "diminutive of Valentine" (GAL 264).

In that same excerpt Miller teases Mona about her stomach, which was becoming "rather generous" (266). He is quick to add, however, that he is "not critical of her opulent flesh. . . . It carried a promise, I thought" (266). Twice in *Marilyn* Mailer reprises this observation with the same approbation. Monroe's stomach, he writes, "popped forward in a full woman's belly, inelegant as hell, an avowal of a womb fairly salivating in seed" (16); "she has a belly which protudes like no big movie star's belly in many a year, and yet she is the living bouncing embodiment of pulchritude" (123).

Mailer further follows Miller in seeing in his Marilyn an incarnation of America. In an excerpt from *Tropic of Capricorn* that Mailer reproduces twice in *Genius and Lust* Miller depicts himself as passive, and Mona in the dominant, phallic role. She is America of two oceans and buffaloes in between, America of opulence and poverty, America of Broadway and gangsters, an American "sword" cutting him through

(201). Mailer opens *Marilyn* with a similar, though shorter apostrophe. Marilyn "was every man's love affair with America," he writes (15), yet it seems to me he surpasses Miller in developing this metaphoric equation throughout his volume. In at least twenty-eight passages in *Marilyn* he presents Monroe as a "magnified mirror of ourselves" (17). For the emigre photographer André de Dienes, Marilyn is the Girl of the Golden West (54). In *The Seven-Year Itch* she is "an American girl . . . as simple and healthy as the whole middle of the country, and there to be plucked" (123). Indeed, she is ice cream (15), "the cleanliness of all the clean American backyards" (15). Shifting from geography to economic class, Mailer notes that Marilyn's visit to Korea becomes a "newsman's love affair: G. I. Joe meets America's most gorgeous doll" (121). Her marriages to Joe DiMaggio and Arthur Miller are workingmen's dreams, and in her final days Marilyn comes to resemble "the brothers and sisters of America's most well-known Irish family," the Kennedys (221). She remains the "First Lady of American ghosts" (242).

Yet Marilyn is also "the secret nude of America's dream life" (94) and America as "an insane swamp" with a void in its sense of identity (27). Here Mailer, following Miller, begins to suggest that it is the very multiplicity of Monroe's roles that makes her not only representative of America, but also ultimately ungraspable. Given this admission, it is finally Monroe as artist, assuming roles, that interests Mailer more than Monroe as ungraspable America, and this is also true of Miller and his Mona.

In *Marilyn* Mailer speaks only fleetingly of Monroe's narcissism; in *Genius and Lust* he will devote a whole section to the subject in respect to Mona and Miller. Once again this later volume casts light on the former; indeed, the following lines hint at part of the attraction of both Miller and Monroe for Mailer: "The narcissist is always playing roles, and if there is any character harder for an author to create than that writer greater than himself, it may be a great actor. We do not even begin to comprehend the psychology of actors" (GAL 187–88). Narcissism is "an affliction of the talented," Mailer writes (GAL 190), and in *Marilyn* and *Genius and Lust* he speaks of Monroe, Mona, and Miller as in the *prison* of narcissism in need of another person/role to break them free. Mailer attempts this liberation for both Marilyn and Miller; simultaneously he must hope (and believe) that they are big enough subjects to take him out of *himself*. As he writes in *Genius and Lust*: "If one can only break out of the penitentiary of self-absorption, there are artistic wonders, conceivably, to achieve" (190).

June/Mona/Mara, however, ultimately eludes Miller—and Mailer acknowledges the same of both Marilyn and Miller. Even on Marilyn's last day on earth Mailer speculates that "in some part of herself she has to be calculating a new life that will be grander than she has known"

(236). And he closes *Marilyn* with Monroe's mysterious "Guess where I am?"

DEATH AS A METAPHOR: *THE FIGHT*

"[Henry] Miller had a message which gave more life than Hemingway," Mailer wrote in *Genius and Lust* (17). An index of Mailer's daring as a writer, his need (like Didion) continually to refine his vision and provide himself with artistic challenges, is his movement in the penultimate of his ages of man from Miller to Hemingway, from eros to thanatos. *The Fight,* Mailer's 1975 account of the Ali-Foreman heavyweight championship fight in Zaire, Africa, represents Mailer's restyling of *Death in the Afternoon,* his demonstration that new life can be found even in Hemingway.[15]

Mailer's references to Hemingway throughout *The Fight* are transparent in their revelation of his anxiety before his predecessor. When he first arrives in Kinshasa, Mailer suffers from intestinal illness. "Was it part of Hemingway's genius that he could travel with healthy insides?" Mailer enviously queries (22). Later, walking alone at night after running with Ali, Mailer is frightened by a lion's roar. "To be eaten by a lion on the banks of the Congo—who could fail to notice that it was Hemingway's own lion waiting down these years for the flesh of Ernest until an appropriate substitute had at last arrived?" Mailer queries, revealing his faith in himself as an appropriate Hemingway substitute, but also his fear of being swallowed in the act of embodiment (92).[16] Mailer escapes this lion. In fact, his assertion that Hemingway's own lion's roar may have come from the zoo implants the notion of Hemingway caged, imprisoned, and in need of liberation.

This liberation (or rebirth—for Hemingway and Mailer) will come through the victory of Muhammad Ali over George Foreman. The entire enterprise described by Harold Bloom as the anxiety of influence is exhibited in Mailer's volume: here Mailer associates himself with another artist (Ernest Hemingway/Muhammad Ali), and the result of this intermingling is triumph and regeneration for all. The essential interplay of all three—Mailer, Hemingway, and Ali—is laid bare in the following passage from *The Fight*:

It was as if contradictions fell away with a victory for Ali. That would be a triumph for . . . audacity, inventiveness, even art. . . . It would certainly come off as a triumph for the powers of regeneration in an artist. What could be of more importance to Norman? He knew some part of him would have to hate Ali if the fighter lost without dignity or real effort, even as a part of him could not forgive Hemingway because of the ambiguity of his suicide—if only there had been a note. (162)

The fates of Ali, Hemingway, and Mailer are thus inextricably linked in *The Fight*. In Part One of this volume, titled ominously "The Dead Are Dying of Thirst," Hemingway is dead, and Mailer presents first Ali and then himself as ill. Across the nine chapters of Part One Mailer links himself repeatedly with Ali, posits George Foreman as the lion poised for attack, and emphasizes the doubt and gloom surrounding Ali's chances of survival.

The opening chapter of Part One calls to mind the beginning of *The Prisoner of Sex*. Muhammad Ali, once the "World's Greatest Athlete" and perhaps "our most beautiful man," is now lacking in *n'golo* or vital force (3). He appears to be "sour and congested" (10) as well as in "deep fatigue" (6). His sparring is "spiritless" (3); indeed, he lacks "stimulation" (11)—that crucial quality for Mailer, who compares training to prison and Ali to a prisoner (12, 43). In fact, Ali's training camp at Deer Lake possesses actual replicas of slave cabins.

In Chapter 2, called "The Bummer," Mailer associates his own green countenance (20) with Ali's "sickly green" flesh (3, 9), and both with the "greenish gloom" of death-in-life suffered by the slaves in Joseph Conrad's *Heart of Darkness* (23). Just as boredom in training appears to be "killing [Ali's] soul" in Chapter 1 (12), Mailer confesses in Chapter 2 that he is bored with himself and decries his own "slavishness" (31). Ali's (and Mailer/Hemingway's) plight is further endangered by the presence of George Foreman, who is depicted as a lion ready to kill. "Taken directly, Foreman was no small representative of vital force," Mailer begins his first presentation of the reigning champion. "He did not look like a man so much as a lion standing just as erectly as a man. He appeared sleepy but in the way of a lion digesting a carcass" (44). Thus, in Part One, Mailer fears a "nightmare of carnage" for Ali (46). The view of Foreman's camp is that Ali does not have the stamina to go fifteen rounds at top speed with Foreman. "Yes," writes Mailer, "it would be equal to avoiding a keyed-up lion in a cage—not for one minute but for forty-five minutes. . . . Foreman would eat up the best of Ali's condition, consume his stamina, use up his surprises" (97).

Despite this impending peril, from Chapter 3 through the end of Part One Mailer chronicles small efforts by Ali, Bundini (Ali's trainer), and himself to increase the *muntu*, or amount of life, in Ali. Ali stages a ritual in which he allows himself to be knocked out only to rise again from the floor. He performs magic tricks at a press conference, equating himself with the "free bird" he releases from his hand (94). When Mailer returns to Africa after the fight's first postponement he feels "delivered" from the "bummer" of Chapter 2 (34). Continuing to intertwine his *muntu* with Ali's, he notes in Chapter 3 that he is called the "literary champ" in Africa and that his million-dollar book contract parallels Ali's own boxing commissions:

To sign for a sum that Heavyweight champs had not been able to make until Muhammad Ali came along—why, the optimistic element of the Black community, looking now at every commercial horizon in America, began to gaze at writing. Hang around this man [Mailer] went the word. Something might rub off! (35)

Mailer shares the Bantu belief in vital forces; he believes that his actions will "rub off," that they can influence Ali's, just as Ali's can influence his own. In the final chapter of Part One Mailer dares his own body to confront death at four in the morning, precisely the hour named for Ali's fight. As he stands on his railless balcony seven stories up thoughts of Hemingway, not surprisingly, enter his mind. In fact, they help to establish the stakes of Mailer's action:

the chance to whirl around that wall over to the next balcony offered vertigo. How ridiculous a way to get yourself killed. What could be worse than accidental suicide? A reverberation of Hemingway's end shivered its echo. . . . He knew Muhammad's chances would be greater if he did it than if he didn't. And was furious at the vanity. Ali did not need his paltry magic—"Ali even motivates the dead." Of course, considering Foreman, Ali might need all the help he could get. (123, 124)

And Mailer succeeds.

Though hoping his act of bravery will add to the store of Ali's *n'golo*, Mailer feels uncertain of the outcome. "It was conceivable he had reversed the signs," he avers, yet "in the morning he did not have the remotest idea whether he had brought aid and comfort to the Muslims or the Foremans" (125).[17] Thus Mailer chooses to end Part One with another foreshadowing of victory: the triumph of Bundini, Ali's trainer, as "King of the Flunkies."

The color black is associated with death and vital force in *The Fight*. Tension is generated by Mailer concerning which of the two fighters is the blacker, and thus the true representative of the people and force of Africa. On the surface Foreman appears once again to hold the edge. His skin is much darker than pale Ali's, and his retinue is noticeably blacker than Ali's racially mixed entourage. Yet Ali will prove to be the true fighter of the African people, the fighter most in touch with the dark forces of the dead and the living. This is intuited by Bundini before the fight when he calls Foreman "that big white man" (136). Bundini, in contrast, learns his own "black name" (131). *"Something like dark* is what they say Bundini means," he tells Mailer (132), and in the final moments of Part One, when Ali loses his voice, Bundini speaks for him and becomes "champ of the kingdom of flunkies" (138). Earlier Mailer has imitated Ali in a verbal contest with Bundini and won thereby the title of "Honorary Black" (132). Thus the ambiguous final line of

Part One, "Long live Nommo, spirit of words," is as much Mailer's chant for himself as for Bundini.

Despite these important moments of success, the dominant mood of Part One is one of impending disaster for Muhammad Ali. "Defeat was in the air," Mailer writes (94). After running with Ali, Mailer worries about the slowness of Muhammad's pace, and indeed at the weigh-in Ali is heavier than he predicted. The site of the fight is a literal prison and death house, and at the weigh-in Ali is able to evoke little response from the African audience. But promoter Don King offers the words that identify Ali's importance for Mailer. Ali "stimulates—and this is the most significant part—Ali motivates even the dead" (117). To these words Mailer, perhaps remembering Hemingway, replies, "Yes, even the dead who were dying of thirst and waiting for beer at the altar."

Thus the suspense in Part Two, titled *"N'golo"* or vital force, is whether Ali can "stimulate," indeed resurrect, his vital force and regain his lost champion's title. Ali tries to animate his frightened and somber retinue in the dressing room before the fight by crying repeatedly, "Are we going to dance?" (169, 170). His choice of an African robe over one selected by Bundini, and his repeated, almost ritualistic, dismissal of Bundini's protests are signs of his intuition of the true sources of his power.

Once the fight begins Mailer's Part One equations of George Foreman with a lion quickly fade as he begins to pay homage to *Death in the Afternoon* in Part Two. In this impressive reprise Foreman becomes a brave and directly charging bull, and Ali, a superb matador totally dominating the animal. Mailer initiates this parallel with Ali's arrival at the stadium: "It was equal to arriving in the retinue of a matador" (163). Round One of the fight is analogous to what Hemingway calls the "first act" of a bullfight, the bull's battle with the spear-wielding mounted picadors. "We're going to stick him," Ali cries in the dressing room (165), and before Round One, Mailer asserts that Ali's body "had a shine like the flanks of a thoroughbred" (175). In the bullring the bull seeks to kill these horses, and the mounted picador tries to fend off this slaughter with his spear. In the first punch that connects in the fight Ali "drove a lightning-strong right *straight as a pole* into the stunned center of Foreman's head" (177, emphasis added). Foreman, who had looked "sheepish" in the ring before the bell (176), "charged in rage" (178), and Ali responds by pushing Foreman's head down, just as the picadors' spears and the banderillas are meant to lower the bull's head. Ali strikes again and Foreman "charges," and with the third blow Mailer evokes the bullring directly: "Foreman responded like a bull. He roared forward. A dangerous bull. His gloves were out like horns. No room for Ali to dance to the side, stick him and move, hit him and move" (178–79). From this moment on it is difficult not to picture Foreman as a bull and Ali as a torero. By the end of the first round Foreman is "maddened," is in "a murderous rage,"but his hands [horns] have lost no speed (180).

Rounds Two through Five of the fight are analogous to Hemingway's "second act" of the tragedy of the bull, the placing of the banderillas to tire the bull and correct any tendencies in the bull to hook dangerously to the left or right. Can Ali "dismantle Foreman's strength before he uses up his own wit?" Mailer inquires between Rounds Two and Three (189). Here is where Mailer achieves his *clinamen,* or creative swerve, from Hemingway in the fact that it is Ali, his matador, who seeks *querencia* (a place of refuge) rather than Foreman, the bull. It is almost as if by usurping the bull's role (*kuntu*) Ali assumes Foreman's power, for earlier Mailer has written that Foreman's strength appeared in his catatonic posture: " 'Provided I do not move,' this posture says, 'all power will come to me' " (46). Ali makes Foreman move, and Mailer stresses that Ali's decision to back himself into the ropes (and thus seek *querencia*) was "the most dangerous option he had" (185). Linking this risk with his own daring scaling of the balcony Mailer adds, "For as long as Foreman had strength, the ropes would prove about as safe as riding a unicycle on a parapet" (185).

But Ali succeeds, and Mailer's explanation of the impact of this action on the boxing world applies equally to his own anxiety of influence. Ali, Mailer writes, "is turning the pockets of the boxing world inside out. He is demonstrating that what for other fighters is a weakness can be for him a strength" (191).

In Round Three Foreman begins "gagging a bit, the inside of his lips showing a shocking frothy white" (193). In Round Four he "snorts" at Ali's taunts, and begins "a long pawing movement of his hands" (194, 193). Foreman appears to "sniff" victory in this round and so, in Round Five, tries to knock Ali out (194). In this climactic round of Act Two of the boxing faena, all the while Foreman is trying to "chop Ali down" (195) and "lift him" (196), Ali is controlling the battle with his body and eyes. Ali was

tantalizing him, maddening him, looking for all the world as cool as if he were sparring in his bathrobe, now banishing Foreman's head with the turn of a matador sending away a bull after five fine passes were made, and once when he seemed to hesitate just a little too long, teaching Foreman just a little too long, something stirred in George like the across-the-arena knowledge of a bull when it is ready at last to gore the matador rather than the cloth, and like a member of a cuadrilla, somebody in Ali's corner screamed, "Careful! Careful! Careful!" and Ali flew back and just in time for as he bounced on the ropes Foreman threw six of his most powerful left hooks in a row and then a right, it was the center of his fight and the heart of his best charge . . . and Ali blocked them all. (196–197)

With this, something of Foreman's *n'golo* begins to depart (197). Ali reaches over to "prod" Foreman, and finally, like a bandillero, he takes the offensive, drives in at least twenty punches, and "Foreman staggered and lurched and glared at Ali and got hit again" (197–98).

Round Six is titled "The Executioner's Song," and these final three rounds of the fight parallel the final act of the faena: the kill. Mailer in fact opens this chapter: "So began the third act of the fight" (199). In boxing a knockout is analogous to the kill in the bullring, and Mailer's diction makes clear that *Death in the Afternoon* is still his model: "Ali had to dispose of Foreman in the next few rounds and do it well, a formidable problem. He was like a torero after a great faena who must still face the drear potential of a protracted inept and disappointing kill" (200). In the sixth round Ali is "almost tender" with Foreman (201):

[He] was now taking in the reactions of Foreman's head the way a bullfighter lines up a bull before going in over the horns for the kill. He bent to his left and, still crouched, passed his body to the right under Foreman's fists, all the while studying George's head and neck and shoulders. Since Foreman charged the move, a fair conclusion was that the bull still had an access of strength too great for the kill. (202)

By Round Seven, however, Foreman has no speed and is "proving too sluggish to work with" (203). In contrast, like the greatest matadors, Ali is "still graceful in every move" (204). At the end of the seventh round Foreman hardly can stand. In the eighth and final round Ali has an opportunity to kill quickly and easily with a blow to the neck, but he refuses. In *Death in the Afternoon* Hemingway twice decries the shame of sword blows to the neck (81, 256), and in *The Fight* Mailer writes that Ali "cocked a punch but did not throw it, as though to demonstrate for an instant to the world that he did not want to flaw this fight with any blow reminiscent of the thuds Foreman had sent to the back of the head of Norton and Roman and Frazier" (206). When Ali finally goes in for the kill Mailer's language transforms glove into sword: "a big projectile exactly the size of a fist in a glove drove into the middle of Foreman's mind, the best punch of the startled night, the blow Ali saved for a career" (208).

Thus the kill is perfectly executed; George Foreman is knocked out. Muhammad Ali, in Mailer's depiction, combines the best of Joselito, who had stature and natural grace, and Belmonte, who broke all the rules of the ring to create great art. Joselito died in the ring and Belmonte lived and triumphed, and thus Ali truly encompasses "the fearful and magical zone between the living and the dead" (73). Earlier Mailer has averred that he, as well, "would take his balance, his quivering place, in a field of all the forces of the living and dead" (38), and this is the important psychic locale of *The Fight*.

Mailer's *tessura* in his anxious struggle with Hemingway's art is to posit his *n'golo* against Hemingway's *death,* implying that Hemingway does not go far enough in his understanding of death. Hemingway's movement in *Death in the Afternoon* is ever toward death; through this emphasis he creates respect in the reader for the dangerous sport his book celebrates. In *The Fight* Mailer dares to insist that death is not simply the end, but is itself a vital force (*n'golo*) partaking of life as well as death. He demonstrates this through the regeneration of Muhammad Ali and the regeneration of his own art—and Hemingway's art through his.

Although his literal seat in the Zaire ring is only *contra-barrera,* second row as compared with Hemingway's *barrera* or first-row seat in Spain, Mailer still makes his claim. Mailer indeed dares to declare himself father of black power (the forces of death and re-birth). In Part One of *The Fight* he admits that "the deepest ideas that ever entered his mind were there because Black existed" (41). He observes that the American black "was sociologically famous for the loss of his father" (42), and at the moment of victory of black power (*n'golo*) in Part Two Mailer speaks "in a tone of wonder like a dim parent who realizes suddenly his child is indeed and indubitably married, 'My God, he's Champion again!' " (209).

But Ali is more than merely new Heavyweight Champion of the World. Hemingway speaks of bullfighters as potential "new Messiahs"in *Death in the Afternoon,* and after *The Fight* Ali seems to become a genuine new prophet to his people. Chapter 17 of *The Fight* is titled "A New Arena," and here Mailer imagines Ali as the leader of African peoples, bringing peace to the Near East (233). Ali speaks of "freedom for my people" and after his victory Mailer speaks of the "air of liberation . . . the n'golo of the living and the thirst of the dead" (216).

"With what immensity of anxiety must Ali live at the size of his world role and his intimate knowledge of his own ignorance," Mailer writes near the end of *The Fight,* which is itself a casebook in the anxiety of influence (223). By assuming Foreman's role Ali makes himself champion. Indeed, after the fight he is now the lion of Africa "roaring" to the crowd "I can lick anybody you got" (225). Mailer, in turn, mixes his spirit not only with Ali's, but also with Hemingway's in *The Fight,* and achieves a parallel victory. Mailer in fact reprises the conclusion of *Death in the Afternoon* by imitating, at the beginning of his final chapter, Hemingway's banter with his "Old lady." "Would you like more of an ending?" Mailer politely inquires (239). The African Tale that follows, and that Mailer chooses as his conclusion to *The Fight,* is a parable of the struggle undertaken: one sheep (Foreman) devoured and three sheep returned (Ali, Hemingway, and Mailer). The subtitle of *The Fight* should be *Death and Re-birth in the Early Morning.*

THE UNKNOWN AS METAPHOR:
THE EXECUTIONER'S SONG

The Executioner's Song, Mailer's 1979 volume chronicling the macabre life, love, and death of Utah murderer Gary Gilmore, unveils a new facet of Mailer's artistry. Not only is Mailer conspicuously absent as a character in this volume, but he uses metaphor in a completely new manner. Indeed, he employs metaphor for rhetorical effects opposite those for which he has wielded metaphor in all his previous work.

Readers of this Pulitzer Prize-winning "true life novel" immediately become aware of the volume's short sentences and large white spaces. The remarkable, though somewhat unnerving, achievement of *The Executioner's Song* is that while Mailer has employed metaphor as means to knowledge (and action) in all his previous nonfiction, in *The Executioner's Song* he uses it to suggest "not knowing" or the failure to know, and in this way it suggests the end of the line for Mailer's "ages of man"—the stage beyond death and re-birth, that of the ultimate unknown.

Readers accustomed to the rich, original, and extended metaphors in Mailer's previous volumes are struck first by the relative sparsity of metaphor in this 1,050-page book. The majority of metaphors that *do* appear can be characterized as simple and often banal, for Mailer is employing substitutionary narration. He is imitating the accents and diction of his subjects. Banal language is that which has lost power through overuse, said Hemingway, and indeed the majority of the Western and Eastern voices in this work speak in the weakest metaphoric cliches. "Poor as a churchmouse" (Bessie), "drunk as a skunk" (Gibbs), "out on a limb," "stabbed in the back" (Brenda), "off the wall" (Gilmore), "up the wall" (Farrell), "climbing the walls" (Schiller), "clutching at straws" (Gilmore), "spinning his wheels" (Farrell) represent only a small sampling of such cliched speech. And it is not only the poor, uneducated, and disaffiliated whose voices are those of vacant cliche; the educated lawyers and journalists employ them as well.

Joining this metaphor-of-cliche is the banal metaphor-of-slang through which Mailer also authenticates his saga. Gary Gilmore is "cruising for a bruising" (175), Roger Eaton's "ass is grass" (247), and the whole tragedy to Dr. Woods is "the pits" (635). Such metaphors not only help to create the general air of unpleasantness in the world Mailer is depicting, but also disclose a lack of original perception on the part of its inhabitants. Humans fall into cliched speech because it is at hand, thus obviating the need for deep reflection on experience. The metaphor of slang and cliche in *The Executioner's Song,* therefore, reveals the lack of cerebration in the cast of characters and forms one of many impenetrable barriers for the reader seeking deeper knowledge of the events.

John Garvey has written that "if future readers want to know how America sounded in the 1970s they can come to this book," (135). If this is true, and in some respects it is, the volume brims with social criticism.

Mailer's art, of course, lies in his ability to capture this banal idiom.[18] Perhaps even more to his credit, however, are the series of simple, homespun metaphors that further enhance the Western atmosphere of the Utah setting. Bessie, Gilmore's mother, had been raised "root straight down" (323), and talking to Nicole was "like sitting on the back porch for all of a hot July afternoon" (541). However, even the thoughts of New York–born entrepreneur Larry Schiller are presented by Mailer in homespun terms. "Schiller needed more money the way a farmer without a tractor needs a tractor," Mailer writes, noting that Schiller figured there must be "tons of meat and potatoes" in Gilmore's letters (710, 709). Through use of these tropes Mailer forces readers to perceive his story through the consciousness of the Western inhabitants.

Discord in Gary Gilmore's ambiguous character is first sounded through these homespun metaphors. Gilmore is both of and not of his region. Born in Texas and raised in Utah and Oregon, he is undeniably a son of the West, yet he has been separated so long from society that he is not at home in the contemporary West. Schiller's first impression of Gilmore is that he "looked like he wouldn't be comfortable in a restaurant with a tablecloth" (658), and a certain irony and tension are created precisely through the ordinary metaphors Mailer fashions to depict Gilmore's inordinate emotions. "The more [Gilmore] spoke [of the police], the angrier he got. It came off him like an oven with the door open," Mailer writes (44–45). When Gilmore leaves Nicole Baker, the great love of his life, "he dropped her off . . . as easily as going down to the grocery for a six-pack" (183). Such metaphors make Gilmore's saga both familiar and frightening.

Anthropologist Victor Turner has written that when people's backs are to the wall, subconscious models (metaphoric paradigms) are what sustain them (DFM 71). A further index of the shallowness of the majority of Mailer's characters is that their models are derived primarily from popular culture rather than from any deeper historical or philosophical tradition. Gilmore tells his lawyer Dennis Boaz, "It's like I'm the Fonz and you're Richie" (528), and Boaz, in turn, thinks of Utah Attorney General Robert Hansen as "a Clark Kent character" (531). Police informant Gibbs's foremost desire is to appear on the Johnny Carson Show (757). Even when richer paradigms are suggested it is only to be undercut. Mailer begins his portraits of Gilmore's victims by saying that Colleen Jensen "had once been told she looked like a Botticelli. . . . Yet she hardly knew Botticelli's work" (207).

It should not be surprising, therefore, that one of the largest metaphoric systems in *The Executioner's Song* involves parallels to the great American myth, the "western." Near the beginning of the volume Mailer writes: "Overhead was the immense blue of the strong sky of the American West. That had not changed" (19). Indeed, the popular myth of the West seems to be the subconscious model by which the majority of characters in the volume operate. Bessie Gilmore is the granddaughter of pioneers on both sides of her family (314), and when Gary returns to Utah from the Maycomb, Illinois, prison Mailer reminds us that he retraced "practically the same route" his Mormon great-grandfather followed (10). Gilmore is named for cowboy movie star Gary Cooper (313), is described as a "loner" (55), occasionally speaks in a Texas accent (34), and thinks of himself as "a Texan forever" (465), despite the fact that he lived only the first six weeks of his life in Texas. Considerable evidence exists in Mailer's text to suggest that Gilmore conceives of himself as a Gary Cooperlike, taciturn, high-noon cowboy. Gilmore plays poker and goes to the Silver Dollar Bar, and we can feel Mailer's hand shaping the Western equation in the following richly metaphorical passage: "When [Gary's] stories got too boiled down, when it got like listening to some old cowboy cutting a piece of dried meat into small chunks and chewing on them, why then he would take a swallow of beer and speak of his Celestial Guitar. He could play music on it while he slept" (104).

A significant shift from guitar-strumming cowboy to hunted Western "critter" occurs, however, after Gilmore's crimes. At the moment of his capture Gilmore appears to Lieutenant Peacock to be "a wildcat in a bag" (269), and Brenda tells him, "I didn't know any other way to round you up" (281). Gilmore's whole strong-man struggle with the American legal system might be seen as an effort to reverse this metamorphosis from cowboy to hunted animal, to regain his humanity, yet despite his heroics, Mailer titles the chapter describing his execution "The Turkey Shoot."

The truth is that Gilmore is not the only one enacting an inner Western scenario. Mailer is careful to record that practically every character in the volume comes from a ranch background. Max Jensen, the first of Gilmore's victims, feeds and brands cattle in the weeks before he dies (214), and even the Mormon chaplain Cline Campbell grows up "thinking of himself as a second Butch Cassidy," as someone who could shoot "from the hip" (485). The "lair" of Judge Ritter, the non-hanging judge who stays Gilmore's execution, is a hotel with nineteenth-century decor, "real elegant Wild West" (918, 917), while Ritter's hanging counterpart, Judge Bullock, we are told, probably set the execution at sunrise "to put a little frontier flavor into the judgment" (946). At the execution Ernie Wright, director of the Board of Corrections, is "practically gallivanting with his big white cowboy hat" (981).

Furthermore, Mailer's narration implies that it is not only the Western voices of America that are struggling under the burden of America's Wild West mythology. The Eastern voices of Larry Schiller and his
fellow journalists sound similar refrains. Schiller, Mailer reminds us,
comes to Utah after twenty-five years of "galloping out of explosions"
into cover portraits (597). It is he, in fact, who created the still mon-
tages in *Butch Cassidy and the Sundance Kid* (597). Mailer portrays Schiller's fellow Eastern journalists as even more "low down" in the Western
scenario. Repeatedly they are presented as vultures waiting Gilmore's
demise (992, 1004). At the sight of him, moments before the execution,
they are like a "herd spooked into stampede" (975).

Operating as a substructure of this pervasive Western motif is a related series of metaphors and conflicts built around the myth of the
American strong man. In fact the words "strength" and "strong" appear an inordinate number of times across the volume. Both physical
strength and mental toughness seem to be Gary Gilmore's ruling passions. He tells Lieutenant Nelson that prison "demanded you be a man
every step of the way" (287), and he later asks of his brother: "Do you
know how strong you have to be, year after year, to keep yourself together in this place?" (847).

At the beginning of the volume, when Gilmore is released from prison,
displaying physical superiority seems excessively important to him. He
is dismayed when Brenda's brawny husband beats him in a casual contest of strength, as well as later when his Uncle Vern bests him in arm
wrestling. Some readers have viewed Gilmore's murder of Ben Bushnell in the motel next to Vern's home as his way of showing his soft-
spoken but powerful uncle how tough he can be. Indeed, this is an
interpretation Mailer stressed in his 1982 teleplay of *The Executioner's
Song*. Gilmore's last words to Vern at his execution seem to support
this interpretation. Having failed to impress Vern with his physical
strength, Gilmore settles for mental fortitude at his hour of death. "I
want to show you," he tells Vern. "I've already shown you how I live
. . . and I'd like to show you how I can die" (982).

Such a "strong man" obsession might also illuminate other Gilmore
actions. The Utah legal system is embodied in Attorney General Robert
Hansen, a man whom Mailer depicts (through lawyer Judy Wolback's
eyes) as being "a strong, righteous . . . good-looking man with a stiff,
numb face, dark horn-rimmed glasses" (951). When we recall that Gary's
early attorney, Dennis Boaz, has characterized Hansen as Clark Kent
(i.e., Superman), we see the foe Gilmore determines to engage for his
final (legal) wrestling match. In this final showdown Gilmore shares
traits with Judge Willis Ritter, the judge who stays his execution. Both
Ritter and Gilmore are loners; both are fighting the Mormon and legal
establishments, and both have shown remarkable ability to come back

from physical setbacks—Ritter from heart attacks and surgery; Gilmore from his battle with the prison drug Prolixin and from suicidal drug overdoses. Thus facing Superman Hansen are Gilmore and "the toughest Federal Judge in the State of Utah. Conceivably the toughest in the nation" (616).

Yet Ritter is not strong enough to beat Hansen and the Utah legal system, and though perhaps perversely victorious in achieving his wish to die, Gilmore obtains only Pyrrhic victory. His courage in death, however, should not be undervalued. In many ways Gilmore exhibits the bravery Mailer admires in his fictional heroes. Bravery does not come easily to Gary. He writes to Nicole about the need to be strong and overcome fear (474). In fact Nicole's own strength in defying the establishment is one of the qualities that draws Gilmore to her.[19]

In the final hours and minutes of his life Gilmore certainly exhibits admirable strength of will. We learn from Doug Hiblar that Gary may have persuaded his mother not to attend his execution because "it would take from [his] strength if he saw her" (885). Schiller notices that, though strapped into the execution chair, Gilmore "was still in control" (979), and despite his famous banal final words ("Let's do it"), Gary's bearing, according to Vern, reflects "the most pronounced amount of courage, he'd ever seen, no quaver, no throatiness, right down the line" (984). Cline Campbell, in fact, reports that "Gilmore was so strong in his desire to die right, that he didn't clench his fist as the count began" (985–86), and as the bullets sound we are given this "as if" metaphor, transforming Gilmore's last moments into a subtle salute to Mailer's beloved Hemingway: "When it happened, Gary never raised a finger. Didn't quiver at all. His left hand never moved, and then, after he was shot, his head went forward, but the strap held his head up, and then the right hand slowly rose in the air and slowly went down as if to say, 'That did it, gentlemen' " (986).[20]

Some will claim that the heart of *The Executioner's Song* is this laconic Western strong-man refrain. The metaphoric systems certainly are present for such a reading. This would make *The Executioner's Song* another Mailer exploration of American machismo. But what is new and remarkable in *The Executioner's Song* is Mailer's ultimate abandonment of these very models which have preoccupied him. In this volume Mailer presents the Western myth without endorsing it; indeed, he undercuts such glib interpretations by offering them through the unreliable voice of Dennis Boaz: "Now that they had agreed to work together, Boaz began to ponder the tougher side of Gary. Macho to a certain extent. Of course, he had had to use a gun to prove his power. . . . 'Gary's on a real macho trip, that's for sure,' Boaz said" (527, 537).

Mailer implies that the truth of Gary Gilmore is more than machismo—and maybe less. Through the more reliable voice of Barry

Farrell he even sounds the view that Gilmore was not tough at all, that he was fundamentally a punk. Such conflicting views only serve to increase the mystery that is Gary Gilmore, the mystery abetted by the short paragraphs and blank white space, by the empty metaphors of cliche and slang, and the deceptively simple homespun comparisons. In addition to the American Western reprise at least four other possible "motivations" for Gilmore's crimes are suggested in the text, none wholeheartedly embraced by Mailer. Schiller and Farrell relentlessly pursue the standard delinquency theory that Gilmore becomes a thief and murderer because of lack of parental love. A contradiction does seem to emerge between Gilmore's frequent talk of love for his mother and his actions. He expresses concern for her financial plight, yet has to be goaded by his Uncle Vern to give her even $1,000, one of his smallest gifts. (He wants to give $3,000 to a babysitter whom he has known fewer than six months.)

Equally tantalizing is Farrell's discovery that Gilmore had been beaten severely by nuns during his elementary-school days in Oregon. Behind every abusive adult is an abused child, we are tempted to affirm, but nothing more comes of this tantalizing road. Then there's Farrell's more intricate theory that Gilmore is not a genuine murderer at all, but at heart actually a child molester—the very bottom of the prison pecking order. According to this theory, Gilmore murders in order to keep himself from molesting children (882). Certainly some evidence is present to support this view—in Gilmore's request for art books depicting children, in his preference for young girls rather than women, in his terms of affection for Nicole (Baby and Elf) and his request that she shave her pubic hair. But this becomes one more blind alley, no more conclusive than any of the others. Perhaps the most straightforward explanation comes from Gilmore himself. When asked by Schiller "Why did you kill Jensen and Bushnell?" Gilmore replies: "I killed Jensen and Bushnell because I did not want to kill Nicole" (691). His elaboration, significantly in poetry, seems an illustration of Mailer's widely known theory, articulated in his famous 1957 essay "The White Negro," that repressed rage leads inexorably to murder. "And it grew into a calm rage," goes Gilmore's poem."And I opened the gate and let it out" (692).

However, just as Mailer disengages himself from the Western macho saga, he also refuses to champion this reading of Gilmore, so compatible with his own pet theories. Ultimately he seems to find greatest truth in humanity's failure to know, in our inability to penetrate the mask of any of God's creatures.

Alongside the banal and homespun metaphors, Mailer creates a series of what can only be called metaphors of imprecision—a use totally opposite his previous precise, probing, and expanding mode of metaphorizing. Mailer writes that on the night of the Jensen murder April

Baker, Nicole's sister, "walked around Craig [Taylor] like he was a barrel or something" (221). Grace McGinnis, a Portland spiritualist who might, we think, be able to offer some insights, offers only this after a three-hour conversation with Bessie: "They covered a lot of the universe" (457). In her moments of fearing Gilmore the closest even Nicole Baker can come is: "He's a bad package"—contents apparently unknown (179). More than 500 pages later Barry Farrell expresses his own frustration at Gilmore's bland responses to his most probing questions of a similar metaphorical context: "Resolute refusal, thought Farrell, to attach value to any detail. Life is a department store. Lift what you can" (798). Thus, despite the proliferation of vivid particulars across 1,050 pages, we are given few conclusive perceptions about *this* "universe," about life as a department store, and the bad package that is Gary Gilmore. This is not a flaw in the work, but deliberate design—a design persistently frustrating any precise understanding of Gary Gilmore.

The reader arrives at resignation in the face of the unknowable, however, only after a long pursuit and after assailing numerous blank walls. This process, as Mailer confessed to William Buckley, was his own:

This material made me begin to look at ten or twenty serious questions in an altogether new fashion, and it made me humble in that I just didn't know the answers. I mean, I've had the habit for years of feeling that I could dominate any question pretty quickly—it's been my vanity. And it was an exceptional experience to spend all these months and find that gently but inevitably, I was finding myself in more profound—not confusion—but doubt about my ability to answer, to give definitive answers to these questions. . . . I thought it might be very nice for once just to write a book which doesn't have answers, but poses delicate questions with a great deal of evidence and a great deal of material and let people argue over it. . . . I've always leaned on the side that literature, finally, is a guide—that it explains complex matters to us, it gives us a deeper understanding of our existence. And I felt that maybe the time had come—at least for me in my own work—to do a book where I don't explain it to the reader, and in part I can't explain all of it to the reader.[21]

Thus the largest linguistic system in *The Executioner's Song*—encompassing even the grand American Western metaphorical paradigm—is that affirming the inability to know.[22] *The Executioner's Song* is filled with people who cannot comprehend the world. Bessie Gilmore admits that "she never asked why" she and her husband lived the drifting life they lived (323), and when she receives Gary's letters from prison "he spoke of violence with a gusto she could not comprehend. It was altogether outside every conversation or understanding they had ever had of each other" (470). Debbie Bushnell, wife of the slain Ben, seems to possess a similar insubstantial comprehension of life. Debbie "lived in a world of two-year-olds and four-year-olds," Mailer writes (240), and in language that hints at the rhetorical function of his textual breaks he explains that after Ben's murder, Debbie "kept trying to get the new thing together, but there had been too many breaks. Seeing the strange man in the motel office was a break in her understanding. Then the instant when she saw Ben's head bleeding. That was an awfully large break" (273).

The breaks in understanding indeed are everywhere: in April Baker's drug-damaged psyche as much as in the failure of the magicians to reach the spirit of Harry Houdini, Gilmore's "kin," on Halloween. Gary Gilmore and Nicole Baker are children exhibiting this same cosmic bewilderment. At the beginning of their relationship, Mailer writes, "Nicole got the impression that [Gary] was just like her and could hardly comprehend what was happening" (84). When Lieutenant Nelson asks Gilmore why he committed the murders he first says, "I don't know," and then "I can't keep up with life" (292). And it isn't just these childlike Westerners who are confounded, although certainly Mailer offers some criticism of their lack of sophistication. Mailer also implies that some issues are beyond comprehension. He reports psychiatrist Woods's admission that "the best-kept secret in psychiatric circles was that nobody understood psychopaths, and few had any notion of psychotics" (397). Death, of course, is particularly incomprehensible. In his summation at Gilmore's mitigation hearing Gilmore's lawyer states: "I don't excuse what Mr. Gilmore did, I don't even pretend to try to explain it' (444), and when the death sentence is read in court Mailer offers one of his acutely imprecise "as if' metaphors: "It was as if there had been one kind of existence in the room, and now there was another: a man was going to be executed. It was real but it was not comprehensible" (447).

Nor is Gary Gilmore, the bringer of death, comprehensible finally to anyone in the volume. One by one the American institutions forced to deal with him prove helpless: the family, the police, the legal system, the psychiatric profession, the church—and most certainly the fourth estate. Gilmore is a man of many masks and contradictions. Before he is released from prison Brenda observes that he has "a different face in every photograph" (8). Barry Farrell makes the most thorough, though ultimately futile, analysis, locating twenty-seven Gilmore poses.

Gilmore even eludes the man most obsessed with securing his story, Larry Schiller; in fact *The Executioner's Song* differs profoundly from *The Armies of the Night* in Mailer's insistence that even literature cannot encompass Gilmore. *The Executioner's Song* thus takes Mailer to the final stage in his "ages of man": to the unfathomable unknown beyond death. This may explain why Mailer has attempted no major works of nonfic-

tion since 1979.[23] Having completed his ages he has nowhere else to
go.

Where, then, might his vision of re-generation conceivably take him
in the years to come? It seems to me that what remains is to begin the
cycle again. Intriguingly, this is precisely what Mailer appeared to be
doing in *Ancient Evenings,* his novel of reincarnation. Yet this is fiction
rather than nonfiction. To my mind what will be required for Mailer
to begin a new generation of nonfiction is the proper circumstance. He
needs either to participate in a major American event or to find another researcher like Larry Schiller who will bring whole bodies of material to him. Furthermore, he would seem to benefit from an inspiriting American predecessor. Given another major American author (like
Whitman, Miller, Hemingway, and Melville) to haunt him, he is capable
of giving birth to himself anew.

Notes

INTRODUCTION: THE REALTORS

1. In recent years *The New York Times Book Review* at least has separated "Advice, How-to and Miscellaneous" volumes (such as cartoon books) into a separate best-seller list from its general "Nonfiction" list.

2. Tom Wolfe lists four characteristics of the "New Journalism"—scene-by-scene construction, dialogue in full, third-person point of view, and symbolic details of status life—in *The New Journalism* (New York: Harper & Row, 1973). John Hollowell adds to this list interior monologue and composite characterization in *Fact & Fiction: The New Journalism and the Nonfiction Novel* (Chapel Hill: University of North Carolina Press, 1977). In *The Literary Journalists* (New York: Ballantine Books, 1984) Norman Sims discusses literary nonfiction under six headings: Immersion, Structure, Accuracy, Voice, Responsibility, and The Masks of Men. Mas'ud Zavarzadeh's *The Mythopoeic Reality: The Postwar American Nonfiction Novel* (Urbana: University of Illinois Press, 1976) offers new terminology and the most ambitious taxonomy of the genre to date, but his theories have been widely criticized. Other significant books on the subject include Ronald Weber's *The Reporter as Artist: A Look at the New Journalism Controversy* (New York: Hastings House, 1974) and *The Literature of Fact: Literary Nonfiction in American Writing* (Athens: Ohio University Press, 1980); John Hellmann's *Fables of Fact: The New Journalism as New Fiction* (Urbana: University of Illinois Press, 1981); and Chris Anderson's *Style as Argument: Contemporary American Nonfiction* (Carbondale: Southern Illinois University Press, 1987).

3. The sole scholarly treatment of McPhee's work occurs in Ronald Weber's *The Literature of Fact* (Athens: Ohio University Press, 1980): 111–12, 115–22. See also William L. Howarth's "Introduction" to *The John McPhee Reader* (New York: Random House, 1977).

4. Chapters on Wolfe appear in Hollowell's *Fact & Fiction,* Zavarzadeh's *The Mythopoeic Reality,* Weber's *The Literature of Fact,* Hellmann's *Fables of Fact,* and Anderson's *Style as Argument.*

5. See Lennard J. Davis's excellent discussions of the "evolutionary," "os-

motic," "convergence," and Foucaultian discourse theories of the origin of the novel in *Factual Fictions: The Origins of the English Novel* (New York: Columbia University Press, 1983).

6. The "Editor's Note" to the original *New Yorker* magazine serialization of *In Cold Blood* states: "All quotations in this article are taken either from official records or from conversations, transcribed verbatim, between the author and the principals." For book publication Capote modified this statement to: "All the material in this book not derived from my own observation is either taken from official records or is the result of interviews with the persons directly concerned, more often than not numerous interviews conducted over a considerable period of time."

7. See "Aftermath," *New York Herald Tribune* 25 Apr. 1965: 4, 20, 22; Joseph Alsop, "A Fruitful Mummy," *New York Herald Tribune* 16 Apr. 1965: 16; Joseph Alsop, "The Hollow Men," *New York Herald Tribune* 19 Apr. 1965: 26; Dwight Macdonald, "Parajournalism, or Tom Wolfe and His Magic Writing Machine," *The New York Review of Books* 26 Aug. 1965: 3–4, and "Parajournalism II: Wolfe and *The New Yorker*," *The New York Review of Books* 3 Feb. 1966: 18–24; "Is fact necessary?" *Columbia Journalism Review* (Winter 1966): 29–34.

8. See Phillip K. Tompkins, "In Cold Fact," *Esquire* 65 (June 1966): 125, 127, 166–68, 170–71, and John Hersey, "The Legend on the License," *The Yale Review* 70 (Fall 1980): 1–15. To cite just two examples from Tompkins's meticulously researched article, Capote appears to have invented both Perry Smith's final apology before his hanging and an earlier equally sympathetic scene in which Perry cries and tells the sheriff's wife, "I am embraced by shame."

9. Gay Talese, personal interview, 18 Aug. 1984.

CHAPTER 1. GAY TALASE'S FATHERS AND SONS

1. "Playboy Interview: Gay Talese," *Playboy* May 1980: 80.

2. "Patterson's Pride Still Feels Sting of Punch," *The New York Times* 5 July 1959: 3-S.

3. "They Told Everyone but Patterson," *The New York Times* 3 Aug. 1960: 21.

4. "Suspicious Man in the Champ's Corner," *The New York Times Magazine* 23 Sept. 1962: 50.

5. "Experts Seem to Favor Liston But Hope Patterson Will Win It," *The New York Times* 23 Sept. 1962: 2-S.

6. "Patterson, a Former Champion, Seeking Obscurity of Solitude," *The New York Times* 27 Sept. 1962: 51.

7. "Portrait of a Young Prize Fighter," *The New York Times* 12 Oct. 1958: 3-S.

8. "No Disguise for Patterson's Feelings," *The New York Times* 1 Apr. 1965: 43. The "one person who knows him quite well" is undoubtedly Talese.

9. "Iphigine Sulzberger: The Hidden Power Behind the 'Times,' " *New York* 17 Jan. 1977: 37.

10. At the February 22, 1989, public reading of *Satanic Verses* by members

of the New York chapter of Poets, Essayists, and Novelists, Talese read the Lord's Prayer as his prayer for Salman Rushdie, the author condemned to death by Iran's Ayatollah Ruhollah Khomeini.

11. Gay Talese, personal interview, 18 Aug. 1984.

12. Gay Talese, "Intimacy from Without," address, Iowa Student as Critic Conference, University of Northern Iowa, 12 Apr. 1985. Published in *Critical Thinking/Critical Writing: Prizewinning High School & College Essays '85* (Cedar Falls, Iowa: University of Northern Iowa, 1985): 4.

13. When Bill Bonanno returns to New York near the end of the book he discovers that the Astor Hotel, the scene of this wedding reception, has been demolished (301).

14. The details of Joseph Bonanno's kidnap are presented for the first time in Joseph Bonanno's 1983 autobiography, *A Man of Honor*. During the writing of *Honor Thy Father*, according to Talese, he did not know who had kidnapped the senior Bonanno or why he was absent for twenty months, nor does he think Bill Bonanno knew.

15. See "Times Square Anniversary," *The New York Times* 2 Nov. 1953: 24. This was Talese's first piece for *The Times*. As a copy boy he wrote the article as a memo. The editors ran it as an editorial.

16. "Intimacy from Without," 4.

17. 29 May 1980.

18. Gay Talese, personal interview, 28 Dec. 1983.

19. Gay Talese, personal interview, 28 Dec. 1983.

20. To tailors, "pants maker," is a pejorative term. Personal interview, 28 Dec. 1983.

21. Talese describes Playboy bunnies "anointing [Hefner] in an erotic ritual" (369).

22. Talese acknowledges that he wrote an article celebrating caddies ("The Caddie—A Non-Alger Story," *The New York Times Magazine* 12 June 1960: 38, 56) because of his admiration for Fitzgerald's short story "Winter Dreams." Personal interview, 19 Aug. 1984.

23. Talese admitted in his *Playboy* interview that he did not masturbate until he was twenty—and far away from home (May 1980: 99).

24. Personal interview, 18 Aug. 1984.

25. The book's most affirmative review was given by Virginia Johnson-Masters, "Scholarly and Erotic . . . ," *Vogue* June 1980: 199–200. Other balanced or even slightly positive reviews were those of Robert Coles, "Transforming American Sexuality," *The New York Times Book Review* 4 May 1980: 3, 38–39; Benjamin DeMott, "A Sexual Pilgrim's Progress," *The Atlantic Monthly* May 1980: 98–101; Paul Robinson, "The Talese Report," *Psychology Today* April 1980: 105–6; and Richard Woods, O.P., *The Critic* 11 June 1980: 2–4.

26. Robert Sherrill, "Selling Sex in America," *Book World* 27 Apr. 1980: 1–2; Eliot Fremont-Smith, "Thy Neighbor's Old Lady," *The Village Voice* 28 Apr. 1980: 39–41; Barbara Grizzuti Harrison, *The New Republic* 3 May 1980: 33–36: John Leonard, *Playboy* May 1980: 56–58; Gillian Wilce, "Market Values," *New Statesman* 8 Aug. 1980: 17–18; Susan Jacoby, *The New York Times* 14 Aug. 1980: C2; and "Peeping Toms," *The Economist* 28 June 1980: 106–8.

27. Ellen Goodman, "Hits Book on Sex Without Love," Boston Globe News-

paper Co., 29 May 1980; John Leonard, *Playboy* May 1980: 56–58; Michael Gartner, "Talese's nine-year joy ride," *Des Moines Sunday Register* 18 May 1980: 4C; and Oren A. Peterson, *Unitarian Universalist World* Fall 1980.

28. Goodman, "Hits Book on Sex."

29. Gay Talese, personal interview, 28 Dec. 1983.

30. Gay Talese, personal interview, 19 Aug. 1984.

31. Gay Talese, personal interview, 28 Dec. 1983.

32. Four excerpts from this volume have appeared to date in *Esquire*: "A Memoir: Winter Sand," Aug. 1986: 61–63, 66, 68; "The Spirits of Maida," Sept. 1986: 75–79; "White Widows," Oct. 1986: 185–88, 190, 192, 194; and "Wartime Sunday: A boy in the early hours of rebellion," May 1987: 95–98, 100, 102.

33. Dedication to Carlotta, 1941 manuscript.

CHAPTER 2. TOM WOLFE'S AMERICAN JEREMIAD

1. Chet Flippo, *"The Rolling Stone* Interview: Tom Wolfe," 21 Aug. 1980: 37.

2. Tom Wolfe, letter to Cecil Woolf and John Baggeley, 13 Sept. 1966, Berg Collection, New York Public Library.

3. Wolfe was raised in the Presbyterian Church. He writes of attending, at the age of eleven, a catechism drill at the Church of the Revelation Sunday School in North Carolina ("Those Improbable Pals, TV and Books," *New York Herald Tribune Books,* 19 Aug. 1962: 3).

4. Because of Wolfe's unconventional use of ellipsis, it is necessary to distinguish his writing from my editing. Therefore, bracketed ellipses represent editing; all others appear in the Wolfe text.

5. Wolfe invites this interpretation through his extended passage in the Mexican chapters in which the Pranksters read the Bible and all become biblical characters (317–18).

6. This phrase evokes the lines from the national anthem: "O say can you see, by the dawn's early light, . . . Or the rockets red glare."

CHAPTER 3. JOHN MCPHEE'S LEVELS OF THE EARTH

1. Theodore Taylor, phone interview, 1 Jan. 1988.

2. John McPhee, phone interview, 22 June 1987.

3. John McPhee, phone interview, 22 June 1987.

4. In *The Crofter And The Laird* McPhee reveals that his perception is usually framed: "At home, I spend most of my time looking out of windows, and nothing changes the habit here" (43).

5. McPhee's *The Pine Barrens* (1968) was instrumental in the preservation of this New Jersey natural forest.

6. John McPhee, phone interview, 22 June 1987.

7. McPhee attended Deerfield Academy in Massachusetts.

8. Ronald Weber offers a discussion of this volume in *The Literature of Fact: Literary Nonfiction in American Writing* (Athens: Ohio University Press, 1980): 115–21. I disagree, however, with his assertion that *Coming Into The Country*

"stand[s] apart from McPhee's earlier work as far more ambitious and artful" (116). Each of McPhee's books strikes me as highly ambitious—and artful.

9. In this sentence McPhee salutes Thoreau's technique of reclaiming clichés, made famous in *Walden* by phrases such as: "I have been anxious to improve the nick of time, and notch it on my stick too."

10. McPhee sat down at his typewriter and the title *Levels of the Game* instantly came to him. He knew nothing else, but he knew his title (phone interview, 22 June 1987).

11. McPhee's father was a physician, and after his death McPhee wrote *Heirs of General Practice*.

12. McPhee has stated that Shakespeare has exerted a strong influence on him ("Talk with John McPhee," *The New York Times Book Review* 27 Nov. 1977: 50).

CHAPTER 4. JOAN DIDION'S LAMBENT LIGHT

1. *The Golden Moment: The Novels of F. Scott Fitzgerald* (Urbana: University of Illinois Press, 1970).

2. Susan Braudy, "A Day in the Life of Joan Didion," *Ms.* Feb. 1977: 109. Braudy is quoting from the original speech at Berkeley—not from Didion's published version of the speech, "Why I Write," *New York Times Book Review* 5 Dec. 1976: 2, 98–99. Chris Anderson describes Didion's rhetoric of particularity, rhetoric of gaps, and rhetoric of process in "Joan Didion: The Cat in the Shimmer," *Style as Argument: Contemporary American Nonfiction* (Carbondale: Southern Illinois University Press, 1987).

3. Joan Didion, "The Edge of the Precipice," *National Review* 19 Nov. 1960: 316.

4. Didion, "Edge of the Precipice," 315; Joan Didion, "A Celebration of Life," *National Review* 22 Apr. 1961: 255.

5. Joan Didion, "Evelyn Waugh: Gentleman in Battle," *National Review* 27 Mar. 1962: 216; "Notes from a Helpless Reader," *National Review* 15 July 1961: 22.

6. Joan Didion, "Into the Underbrush," *National Review* 28 Jan. 1961: 55.

7. Joan Didion, "Notes from a Summer Reader," *National Review* 10 Sept. 1960: 152; "Inadequate Mirrors," *National Review* 2 July 1960: 430.

8. Didion, "Notes from a Helpless Reader," 21–22.

9. Joan Didion, "Movies," *Vogue* May 1965: 143.

10. Joan Didion, "Movies," *Vogue* 1 Nov. 1964: 64.

11. Joan Didion, "Movies," *Vogue* 15 Feb. 1966: 58.

12. Joan Didion, "I Can't Get That Monster Out of My Mind," *The American Scholar* Autumn 1964: 630; "Movies," *Vogue* July 1965: 37.

13. Joan Didion, "Movies," *Vogue* 1 Mar. 1965: 97.

14. I concur with most reviewers in judging Didion's 1987 volume *Miami* to be an unsuccessful work of literary nonfiction.

15. Braudy, "A Day in the Life of Joan Didion," 109.

16. Didion, "Into the Underbrush," 55.

17. Didion follows Fitzgerald in her equation of gold and white. See Stern, *The Golden Moment*, 265–80.

18. Cf. "Just Folks at a School for Non-Violence," *New York Times Magazine* 27 Feb. 1966: 24–25, 32, 34, 41–42.

19. "San Francisco Job Hunt," *Mademoiselle* Sept. 1960: 170.

20. "The World Was His Oyster," *National Review* 1 Dec. 1964: 1064. This "want" is also apparent in Bishop James Pike, whom Didion portrays in "The Late Great Bishop of California,' *Esquire* Nov. 1976: 60, 62; reprinted as "James Pike, American" in *TWA*.

21. Joan Didion, "A problem of making connections," *Life* 5 Dec. 1969: 34.

22. Tantalus was the son of Zeus who suffered the severe punishment in Hades of being continuously tantalized by mirage. One of the crimes for which Tantalus is being punished makes him a further apt choice for Didion: he stole a golden dog belonging to his father.

23. Didion in fact quotes these Nick Carraway lines in her article: "I began to like New York, the racy adventurous feel of it at night, and the satisfaction that the constant flicker of men and women and machines gives to the restless eye" (103).

24. Jay Gatsby's curtains are soaked in the ominous afternoon rainstorm attending his reunion with Daisy.

25. Few readers have noted how thoroughly "Goodbye to All That" is Didion's re-working of Fitzgerald's "Babylon Revisited." In this Fitzgerald story the children in Paris play in "the yellow oblongs that led to other rooms." Charlie Wales, Fitzgerald's surrogate, reflects that Paris "was nice while it lasted," but that his extravagant living "hadn't been given for nothing." He asserts that "his own rhythm was different now," and in the penultimate line Fitzgerald writes: "He wasn't young any more. . . . "

26. Braudy 109. Blue appears to represent an intermediate stage of the subconscious for Didion, as in the blue waterfall that leads Didion to John Wayne in "John Wayne: A Love Song," *Saturday Evening Post* 14 Aug. 1965: 77.

27. The irony, however, is the fact that in the next line Didion proceeds to describe her female ancestors as women with the penchant to start over—that is, with the characteristic Western tabula rasa mentality: "These women were pragmatic and in their deepest instincts clinically radical, given to breaking clean with everything and everyone they knew."

28. Joan Didion, "Questions About the New Fiction," *National Review* 30 Nov. 1965: 1102.

29. Joan Didion, "Letter from 'Manhattan,' " *The New York Review of Books* 16 Aug. 1979: 18–19.

30. In 1960 Didion wrote that Fitzgerald spoke for all American writers when he invited readers to "Draw your chair up close to the edge of the precipice and I'll tell you a story." ("The Edge of the Precipice," *National Review* 19 Nov. 1960: 315.)

31. We might also recall Didion's famous comment in her Preface to *Slouching Towards Bethlehem:* "*writers are always selling somebody out*" (XIV).

32. Joan Didion, "Black and White, Read All Over," *National Review* 5 Dec. 1959: 525.

33. Joan Didion, "Bosses Make Lousy Lovers," *Saturday Evening Post* 30 Jan. 1965: 34.

34. Didion, "A Celebration of Life," 254.

35. Note also Emily Dickinson's poem 1145:

In thy long Paradise of Light
No moment will there be
When I shall long for Earthly Play
And mortal Company—

36. See Maureen Daley, "Joan Didion," *Publishers Weekly* 9 Oct. 1972: 27, and Sara Davidson, "A Visit with Joan Didion," *The New York Times Book Review* 3 Apr. 1977: 1.

37. Joan Didion, *"Falconer,"* *The New York Times Book Review* 6 Mar. 1977: 22, 24.

38. "Joan Didion: Staking Out California," *Joan Didion: Essays and Conversations,* ed. Ellen G. Friedman (Princeton, N.J.: Ontario Review Press, 1984): 30.

CHAPTER 5. NORMAN MAILER'S AGES OF MAN

1. See Robert Scholes's and Robert Kellogg's discussion of the epic as an amalgamation of mythic, mimetic, and historical materials in *The Nature of Narrative* (New York: Oxford University Press, 1966). In an intuitive rather than naive manner Mailer draws his narratives from this early stage of the narrative tradition.

2. See Robert J. Begiebing, *Acts of Regeneration: Allegory and Archetype in the Works of Norman Mailer* (Columbia: University of Missouri Press, 1980); George Steiner, "Naked but not Dead," *Encounter* Dec. 1961: 67–70; rpted. in *Critical Essays on Norman Mailer,* ed. J. Michael Lennon (Boston: G. K. Hall, 1986): 49–54; Michael Cowan, "The Quest for Empowering Roots: Mailer and the American Literary Tradition," *Critical Essays,* 156–74.

3. Despite his early critical and popular success as a novelist with *The Naked and the Dead* (1947), Mailer has acknowledged that this work is derivative, reflecting the influence of James T. Farrell and John Dos Passos. The critical position I am taking is that Mailer really does not find his original voice as a writer until his nonfiction. Ihab Hassan also makes this assertion in *Contemporary American Literature 1945–1972* (New York: Frederick Ungar, 1973): 34.

4. Limitations of space have forced me to omit discussions of Mailer's ages of politics (*Miami and the Seige of Chicago* and *St. George and the Godfather*) and religion (*Of a Fire on the Moon*).

5. In his introduction to a 1968 edition of *The Naked and the Dead* (Holt, Rinehart & Winston), Chester E. Eisinger describes Mailer as a "legitimate descendant of Whitman" and notes that Mailer's jacket photograph for *Advertisements For Myself* is similar to the frontispiece of *Leaves of Grass,* showing a bearded Whitman in an open shirt (viii, ix-x). In *Three American Moralists: Mailer, Bellow, Trilling* (Ind.: University of Notre Dame Press, 1973) Nathan A. Scott, Jr., titles his chapter on Mailer "Norman Mailer—Our Whitman," but he does not explore the ties between *Advertisements* and *Leaves of Grass.*

6. My approach to metaphor in this chapter has been influenced by Max

Black, *Models and Metaphors* (Ithaca, N.Y.: Cornell University Press, 1962), and Paul Ricouer, *The Role of Metaphor: Multi-disciplinary Studies of the Creation of Meaning in Language* (Toronto: University of Toronto Press, 1978).

7. "The Real Me," *The New York Review of Books* 26 April 1984: 3.

8. English translation: *The Rites of Passage* (London: Routledge & Kegan Paul, 1960).

9. Turner notes that one function of the Ndembu twinship ritual in which the woman raises the frontal flap of her dress to expose to all the source of her excessive fecundity is "suspension of the rules of modesty, which are normally rigorously incumbent on Ndembu women" (TRP 45). Mailer's inclusion of this episode of micturition may be to achieve a related suspension.

10. Certainly Mailer's human creatures, ascending and descending the moral ladder, are not unlike the "angels of God" in Genesis moving up and down Jacob's ladder to heaven. In light of Mailer's immediately preceding reverie concerning the "Wasp knights' " war in Vietnam, it is worth noting that after Jacob dreams of his ladder, he wrestles successfully with a messenger of God, who takes away his old name (Jacob) and re-christens him *Israel,* which has the subsidiary meaning of "*God's* knight" (Trepp 229). Through his ladder metaphor Mailer may be subtly urging citizens to replace the Wasp knights' medieval quest with a more ancient quest, that of each man's struggle to become God's Knight.

11. This quotation is from the *Washington Free Press* account.

12. Cf. Judith Fetterley's "*An American Dream: 'Hula, Hula,' Said the Witches,*" *in The Resisting Reader: A Feminist Approach to American Fiction* (Bloomington: Indiana University Press, 1978): 154–89.

13. Miller's *The World of Lawrence: A Passionate Appreciation* (Santa Barbara, Calif.: Capra Press) was published posthumously in 1980.

14. In *Marilyn* Mailer plays on the similarity between "Marilyn" and "Mailer," but in truth "Mailer" converts to "Miller" with even fewer changes. The similarities between "Mara" and "Marilyn" and "Mona" and "Monroe" are also noteworthy.

15. See also Mailer's earlier "Homage to El Loco" published in *Existential Errands* (1972).

16. In *Shadow Box* (New York: G. P. Putnam's, 1977) George Plimpton writes that Mailer spoke of Zaire as "Hemingway's territory, which was going to require him to be on his mettle" (259). Plimpton states that Mailer couldn't make up his mind whether he'd prefer to be killed by Hemingway's lion or Melville's whale (277). At boxing matches Plimpton reports that Mailer "would begin to sway"; "the rhythm and motion of the fighter seemed to activate him like puppet strings" (323–24).

17. For a discussion of a parallel episode in *An American Dream,* see Tony Tanner's "On the Parapet,"in *City of Words: American Fiction 1950–1970* (New York: Harper & Row, 1971): 344–71.

18. The tape recordings at Mailer's disposal certainly would have facilitated this work.

19. Nicole's grandmother is named Mrs. Strong (588), and Schiller reflects that "Sissy," Nicole's nickname, is "quite a nickname for a girl who got into suicide pacts" (750).

20. The subtitle of Lillian Ross's famous "Portrait of Hemingway" is "How Do You Like It Now, Gentlemen?" and in this portrait the phrase comes to represent Hemingway's courage in the face of encroaching death.

21. *Firing Line,* 11 Oct. 1979.

22. Cf. Chris Anderson's perceptive analysis in *Style as Argument: Contemporary American Nonfiction* (Carbondale: Southern Illinois University Press, 1987): 118–32.

23. *Of Women and Their Elegance,* Mailer's 1980 return to his haunting love Marilyn Monroe, is far from a major work. To my mind it is the least of his works of nonfiction.

Works Cited

Aristotle, *The Complete Works of Aristotle.* Rev. Oxford trans. Ed. Jonathan Barnes. 2 vols. Princeton, N.J.: Princeton University Press, 1984. Vol. 2.

Bateson, F. W. "The Function of Criticism at the Present Time." *Literary Taste, Culture and Mass Communication: Volume 13 The Cultural Debate Part I.* Eds. Peter Davison, Rolfe Meyersohn, Edward Shils. Teaneck, N.J.: Chadwyck-Healey: 111–37.

Bercovitch, Sacvan. *The American Jeremiad.* Madison: University of Wisconsin Press, 1978.

Bloom, Harold. *The Anxiety of Influence: A Theory of Poetry.* New York: Oxford University Press, 1973. Abbreviated (TAOI).

Braudy, Susan. "A Day in the Life of Joan Didion." *Ms.* Feb. 1977: 65–68, 108–9.

Bree, Germaine. "The Ambiguous Voyage: Mode or Genre." *Genre* 1 (Apr. 1968): 87–96.

Cohen, Ted. "Metaphor and the Cultivation of Intimacy." *Critical Inquiry* 5 (Autumn 1978): 3–12.

Critchley, Macdonald. "Migraine: From Cappadocia to Queen Square." *Background To Migraine.* Ed. Robert Smith. London: Whitefriars Press, 1967: 28–38.

Davis, Lennard J. *Factual Fictions: The Origins of the English Novel.* New York: Columbia University Press, 1983.

Didion, Joan. "Bosses Make Lousy Lovers." *Saturday Evening Post* 30 Jan. 1965: 34, 36–38.

———. "The Edge of the Precipice." *National Review* 19 Nov. 1960: 315–16.

———. "N.Y.: The Great Reprieve." *Mademoiselle* Feb. 1961: 102–3, 147–48, 150.

———. *Salvador.* New York: Simon & Schuster, 1983. Abbreviated (S).

———. "San Francisco Job Hunt." *Mademoiselle* Sept. 1960: 128–129, 168–70.

———. *Slouching Towards Bethlehem.* New York: Farrar, Straus & Giroux, 1968. Abbreviated (STB).

————. "Thinking about Western thinking." *Esquire* Feb. 1976: 10, 14.

————. *The White Album*. New York: Simon & Schuster, 1979. Abbreviated (TWA).

Dillard, Annie. *Living By Fiction*. New York: Harper & Row, 1988.

Donahue, Deirdre. "A Wolfe at the door: Tom aims his pen at the rich and vain." *USA Today* 27 Oct. 1987: 1D, 2D.

Drabelle, Dennis. "A Conversation with John McPhee." *Sierra* Oct.-Nov.-Dec. 1978: 61–63.

Dundy, Elaine. "Tom Wolfe . . . But Exactly, Yes!" *Vogue* 15 Apr. 1966: 124, 152–55.

Dunkel, Tom. "Pieces of McPhee." *New Jersey Monthly* Aug. 1986: 37–39, 41–43, 45–51.

Dunlop, Sir Derrick. "The Therapeutics of Migraine." *Background To Migraine*. Ed. Robert Smith. Chichester, England: R. J. Acford, 1969. 72–85.

Emerson, Ralph Waldo. *Representative Men: Seven Lectures*. Boston: Houghton Mifflin, 1876.

Flippo, Chet. "*The Rolling Stone* Interview: Tom Wolfe." *Rolling Stone* 21 Aug. 1980: 31–37.

Garvey, John. "*The Executioner's Song*: Mailer's Best In Years." *Commonweal* 14 Mar. 1980: 134–35.

Gilder, Joshua. "Creators On Creating: Tom Wolfe," *Saturday Review* Apr. 1981: 40, 42–44.

Green, Michael. "Raymond Williams and Cultural Studies." *Literary Taste, Culture and Mass Communication: Volume 13 The Cultural Debate Part I*. Eds. Peter Davison, Rolfe Meyersohn, Edward Shils. Teaneck, N.J.: Chadwyck-Healey: 211–228.

Hellmann, John. *Fables Of Fact: The New Journalism as New Fiction*. Urbana: University of Illinois Press, 1981.

Hemingway, Ernest. *Death In The Afternoon*. New York: Charles Scribner's Sons, 1952.

Horwich, Richard. "Civilized Man." *The New Republic* 5 July 1975: 30.

Macdonald, Dwight. "Parajournalism, or Tom Wolfe & His Magic Writing Machine." *The New York Review of Books* 26 Aug. 1965: 3–5.

————. "Parajournalism II: Wolfe and *The New Yorker*." *The New York Review of Books* 3 Feb. 1966: 18–24.

McPhee, John. *A Roomful of Hovings and Other Profiles*. New York: Farrar, Straus & Giroux, 1968. Abbreviated (AROH).

————. *A Sense of Where You Are: A Profile of William Warren Bradley*. New York: Farrar, Straus & Giroux, 1965.

————. *Basin and Range*. New York: Farrar, Straus & Giroux, 1981.

————. *Coming Into The Country*. New York: Farrar, Straus & Giroux, 1977.

————. *The Crofter And The Laird*. New York: Farrar, Straus & Giroux, 1970.

————. *The Curve of Binding Energy*. New York: Farrar, Straus & Giroux, 1974. Abbreviated (TCOBE).

————. *The Deltoid Pumpkin Seed*. New York: Farrar, Straus & Giroux, 1973.

————. *Encounters with the Archdruid*. New York: Farrar, Straus & Giroux, 1971. Abbreviated (EWTA).

————. "Eucalyptus Trees." *The Reporter* 19 Oct. 1967: 36–39.

————. *In Suspect Terrain.* New York: Farrar, Straus & Giroux, 1983.

————. *La Place de la Concorde Suisse.* New York: Farrar, Straus & Giroux, 1984.

————. *Levels of the Game.* Newe York: Farrar, Straus & Giroux, 1969.

————. *Oranges.* New York: Farrar, Straus & Giroux, 1967.

————. *The Pine Barrens.* New York: Farrar, Straus & Giroux, 1968.

————. *Rising From The Plains.* New York: Farrar, Straus & Giroux, 1986.

Mailer, Norman. *Advertisements For Myself.* New York: G. P. Putnam's Sons, 1959.

————. *The Armies of the Night: History As A Novel/The Novel As History.* New York: New American Library. 1968. Abbreviated (TAOTN).

————. *The Fight.* Boston: Little, Brown, 1975.

————. *Genius and Lust: A Journey Through the Major Writings of Henry Miller.* New York: Grove Press, 1976. Abbreviated (GAL).

————. *Marilyn.* New York: Grosset & Dunlap. 1973.

————. *The Prisoner of Sex.* Boston: Little, Brown, 1971. Abbreviated (POS).

Mills, Hilary. *Mailer: A Biography.* New York: Empire Books, 1982.

Miller, Henry. *Tropic of Cancer.* New York: Grove Press, 1961.

————. *Tropic of Capricorn.* New York: Grove Press, 1961.

Miller, Perry. *Errand in the Wilderness.* Cambridge, Mass.: Harvard University Press, 1958.

Parsons, Talcott. Introduction. *The Sociology of Religion.* By Max Weber. Trans. Ephraim Fishoff. Boston: Beacon Press, 1963. xix–lxvii.

Phillips, Larry W., ed. *F. Scott Fitzgerald On Writing.* New York: Charles Scribner's Sons, 1985.

Sheed, Wilfrid. "A Fun-House Mirror." *The New York Times Book Review* 3 Dec. 1972: 2, 10.

Singular, Stephen. "Talk with John McPhee." *The New York Times Book Review* 27 Nov. 1977: 1, 50–51.

Stamberg, Susan. "Cautionary Tales." Interview, *All Things Considered,* Natl. Public Radio, 4 Apr. 1977; reprinted in *Joan Didion: Essays and Conversations.* Ed. Ellen G. Friedman. Princeton, N.J.: Ontario Review Press, 1984. 22–27.

Talese, Gay. *The Bridge.* Drawings Lili Rethi. Photos. Bruce Davidson. New York: Harper & Row, 1965. Abbreviated (TB).

————. *Fame and Obscurity.* New York: World Publishing, 1970. Abbreviated (FO).

————. *Honor Thy Father.* New York: World Publishing, 1971. Abbreviated (HTF).

————. *The Kingdom and the Power.* New York: World Publishing, 1969. Abbreviated (K&P).

————. *Thy Neighbor's Wife.* Garden City, N.Y.: Doubleday, 1980. Abbreviated (TNW).

Tuchman, Barbara. *Practicing History: Selected Essays.* New York: Alfred A. Knopf, 1981.

Turner, Victor. *Dramas, Fields, and Metaphors: Symbolic Action in Human Society.* Ithaca, N.Y.: Cornell University Press, 1974. Abbreviated (DFM).

————. *From Ritual to Theatre: The Human Seriousness of Play.* New York: Performing Arts Journal Publications, 1982. Abbreviated (FRTT).

————. *The Ritual Process: Structure and Anti-structure.* Chicago: Aldine, 1969. Abbreviated (TRP).

Wolfe, Tom. "The Courts Must Curb Culture." *Saturday Evening Post* 3 Dec. 1966: 10, 12.

———. "Down With Sin!" *Saturday Evening Post* 19 June 1965: 12, 14.

———. *The Electric Kool-Aid Acid Test.* New York: Farrar, Straus & Giroux, 1968. Abbreviated (EKAT).

———. "A Feast of Tempting Titles And That Supermarket Trance." *New York Herald Tribune Paperback Books* 7 Apr. 1963: 3.

———. *From Bauhaus To Our House.* New York: Farrar, Straus & Giroux, 1981.

———. *In Our Time.* New York: Farrar, Straus & Giroux, 1980.

———. *The Kandy-Kolored Tangerine-Flake Streamline Baby.* New York: Farrar, Straus & Giroux, 1965. Abbreviated (KK).

———. *Mauve Gloves & Madmen, Clutter & Vine.* New York: Farrar, Straus & Giroux, 1976. Abbreviated (MG).

———. *The New Journalism With An Anthology Edited By Tom Wolfe and E. W. Johnson.* New York: Harper & Row, 1973. Abbreviated (TNJ).

———. *The Painted Word.* New York: Farrar, Straus & Giroux, 1975.

———. *The Pump House Gang.* New York: Farrar, Straus & Giroux, 1968.

———. *The Right Stuff.* New York: Farrar, Straus & Giroux, 1979.

———. "Three Merry Obsessions: Salvation." *Esquire* Dec. 1973: 201, 308, 310.

———. "Those Improbable Pals, TV and Books." *New York Herald Tribune Books* 19 Aug. 1962: 3, 11.

———. "The Tinkerings of Robert Noyce: How the sun rose on the Silicon Valley." *Esquire* Dec. 1983: 346–48, 353–54, 356, 358–60, 362, 364, 367–68, 371–73.

Index

About the Author

BARBARA LOUNSBERRY is an associate professor of English at the
University of Northern Iowa and a member of the Iowa Humanities
Board. She is currently co-editing with Gay Talese an anthology of literary nonfiction for Harper & Row, as well as editing her own college
reader titled *The Writer in You: A Writing Process Reader/Rhetoric*. Her essays have appeared in the *Philological Quarterly, Georgia Review, Hemingway Review, Modern Drama, Black American Literature Forum*, and other
publications.